SCHOLASTIC

Grades 3–5

Getting Started With the Traits

Writing Lessons, Activities, Scoring Guides, and More for Successfully Launching Trait-Based Instruction in Your Classroom

Ruth Culham and Raymond Coutu

New York • Toronto • London • Auckland • Sydney
Mexico City • New Delhi • Hong Kong • Buenos Aires

Teaching Resources

To all those intermediate teachers who have been there for us from the start and every day thereafter, particularly Mike Freborg, Pat McCarty, and Debbie Stewart. Our deepest thanks for your considerable contributions to our work.

Editor: Raymond Coutu
Production Editor: Sarah Glasscock
Cover design by Brian LaRossa
Interior design by Holly Grundon
Copy editor: Eileen Judge
ISBN-13: 978-0-545-11190-4
ISBN-10: 0-545-11190-0

Contents

Chapter 3: Trait-Based Lessons for the Whole Class

Chapter 4: Trait-Based Activities for Independent and Small-Group Work

Introduction

For years, we have been researching, writing about, and speaking about the traits of writing and their application at the intermediate level. In that time, we have learned that student writers benefit greatly from understanding how strong pieces of writing are created and how to apply that knowledge to their own work. Their growth soars, and watching that growth is quite remarkable. From coast to coast, the traits have found their rightful place in the writing classroom. We are always on the lookout for new ways to make the traits visible and help students use them as they learn to write. The work is evolving, becoming more nuanced and precise, as it should.

One of the most significant areas of development has been using the language of the traits as a basis for communicating with students about how their writing is progressing. Rather than opting for generic comments, such as "Good work!" and "Awkward," teachers are using the scoring guides on pages 24–29 as sources of specific comments to help students see where their writing is strong and where it could use revision and editing.

This book contains all the nuts-and-bolts information and materials you need to get started with the traits and begin achieving the success that so many teachers are already experiencing.

- ❊ Chapter 1 spells out what the traits are and are not, and their benefits. Each trait is clearly defined, with special considerations for weaving it into the intermediate classroom.

- ❊ Chapter 2 shows you how to assess papers for each trait and provide constructive feedback. You'll find reproducible scoring guides, step-by-step instructions for using those guides, scored sample student papers, and sample conference comments to help you hit the ground running.

- ❊ Chapter 3 contains 24 lessons organized around the key qualities of each trait so that you can get students to apply those qualities right from the start of the year. We also offer handy tips for teaching about the trait and annotated lists of picture books to use as mentor texts.

- ❊ Chapter 4 offers trait-based writing activities that students can do in small groups, in pairs, or on their own. These are teacher-tested activities, guaranteed to fire up students and get them to produce their best work possible.

- ❊ Chapter 5 provides answers to the questions teachers ask us most, such as "Are the traits a writing curriculum?" "In what order should I cover the traits?" and "How often should I use prompts to help students get started?"

We round out the book with an appendix that contains reproducible student-friendly scoring guides, a revision checklist, and an editor's marks chart to help you boost students' writing skills.

As you'll see in the appendix, the student-friendly scoring guides range from "Just Starting" at the lowest point to "I've Got It!" at the highest. Most likely, you're just starting your work in the traits. That's an exciting place to be. Let's go!

Chapter 1

What Are the Traits and What Makes Them So Great?

In this age of standardized tests, educational accountability, and "no fail" programs coming your way all the time, teaching writing in today's upper-elementary school is more difficult than ever. But it can also be invigorating, if you know exactly how to help students become the best writers they can be. That requires a focused approach. And that's the concept behind the traits of writing model—an effective, research-based tool for assessing and teaching writing.

You might be tempted to think the trait model is the magic box with all the answers inside. But no box is big enough for all the answers. And you know what? You don't need one. What you do need is a model for assessing and teaching writing that honors your wisdom and strengths as a professional.

That said, the trait model is more than an approach to assessing and teaching writing. It's a vocabulary teachers use with each other and with their students to describe what good writing looks like. Whether it's a story about a dancing cat, an essay on recycling, or a persuasive piece on the benefits of school uniforms, six characteristics make the writing work:

* **Ideas:** The content of the piece; its central message and the details that support it.

* **Organization:** The internal structure of the piece—the thread of logic, the pattern of meaning.

* **Voice:** The tone of the piece—the personal stamp of the writer, which is achieved through a strong understanding of purpose and audience.

* **Word Choice:** The specific vocabulary the writer uses to convey meaning and enlighten the reader.

* **Sentence Fluency:** The way words and phrases flow through the piece. It is the auditory trait and is, therefore, "read" with the ear as much as the eye.

* **Conventions:** The mechanical correctness of the piece. Correct use of conventions guides the reader through the text easily.

Once you know these traits and begin teaching with them, you will see them stand out in the work of your students. Your students will embrace the traits and become self-assessors with the skills to revise and edit their own work.

The trait scoring guides on pages 24–29 allow you to assess student writing and provide feedback that students can use to make their current and future work stronger. Scores range from 1 to 6 in each of the traits. For example, if a student writes the roughest of drafts, showing little control and skill in the trait for which you are assessing, he or she would receive a score of 1, "rudimentary." But if his or her piece shows strong control and skill in the trait, he or she would receive a score of 6, "exceptional."

Once you've assessed the papers, you can use the scores to determine the most appropriate targets for instruction. For example, if many of the students in the class score a 1 or 2 in organization, you would plan to teach and reinforce key qualities of this trait in lessons and activities over the next few weeks. Teaching to areas of greatest need: that's how we use assessment data as the focus for instruction.

This book brings the writing traits model to life by providing all the assessment tools, focus lessons, and extension activities you need to get started. The model is exciting, and it really works. And in today's world, effective models like the traits have never been more important.

The Traits and the Intermediate Writer

When students take the giant leap from learning to read to reading to learn, it's cause for celebration because they're using their skills to comprehend text and gain knowledge. The same is true for writing. When students move from learning to write to writing to learn, they're using their skills to *create* text and *share* knowledge. This leap typically happens during third grade, but we've found that it can happen as early as second grade and as late as fifth, depending on where a child falls on the developmental spectrum. As an intermediate teacher, you know that even though your students are approximately the same age, they don't possess the same skills—in writing or in any other subject. At the start of each year, you expect students who can write full-blown essays, students who can barely muster a paragraph, and students who can do everything in between.

Take a look at the two samples on page 11 written by third graders. The first writer is ready for the materials and ideas in this book, and the second for those in its companion book, *Getting Started With the Traits: K–2* (2009).

Do you like your house? I do, my house is my favorite place. Now your'e probably thinking this person is weird. You are wrong, if you thought about it a while you would think so to. Let me tell you about it. If you where alone how would you feel, sad, lonlely, something of the type. You see, the house contains the family, the food you eat and a shelter to sleep in. Can you live without these things? You can, for a while. But if you didn't have a family, you'd be lonely, if you had no food you'd be weak and hungry. If you had no shelter you would get colder and colder. A house contains things that make life better. I hope you keep these things in mind. For if you don't you will have to learn agian. This is one reason my house is my favorite place. Another reason my house is my favorite place, is makes me think of love. Love is very powerful, love is what connects everybody together. You are full of love. To live you have to love. to love you have to have a family and a family lives in a house. A house is a very important thing, remember this for ever. Remember that a house is very, very important. Just please remember that.

this is abut my dog Tippy. evey monning I go to her and Say I love her. win I wasa baby Tippy wuade lay by me and I love her very much.

For students to grow as writers, it's important to take them from where they are and move them forward one step at a time. After all, true differentiation means supporting students using methods that match their specific abilities and needs. You can determine the level of your students by assessing their writing using the scoring guides on pages 24–29. If a student's writing score is low, it's important to check it against the primary scoring guides (which you'll find in *Getting Started With the Traits: K–2*) to pinpoint what the student requires to get on track. All students have a right to know how to improve their work, regardless of how much they know about writing when they enter your classroom. Selecting the appropriate scoring guide is essential to making the traits work for you and your students. And fear not: the students you worry about most will make great strides in writing, as proven by students in writing-traits classrooms across the country and throughout the world.

Chapter 1: What Are the Traits and What Makes Them So Great?

11

Just look at these samples from a fifth grader. The first piece was written at the beginning of the year. The second piece was written after he had learned and applied the writing traits. What a difference time and the traits can make!

My Special Day!

On Summer I went to the beach I went with my family and I saw my friends I went with them in the water and we went to the sand an then we walked to rocks an we went fishing and I almost got a fish but it slipped of an then the fish went back to the water and then I went to the water to get a crab and the crab almost bit me sow I let it go back to the water an then I went to eat food an that was the best day ever.

Shopping with mom

Long ago when I was five or younger, while my mom was shopping, I would tag along. I always start dying of bordome. I could literally feel my body shutting down, my arms feel like noodles, my eyes drop down and my mouth refuses to swallow. But just then I would start thinking the entire store is a science fiction alien base. The employees would be armed, hostile aliens. Remember those little red coupon despensers. Well those would be auto-fire lazer cannons. And worst of all, the Forklift of DOOM! It was practically the mother alien all you had to do was run, and every time it makes a little beep noise that would mean it saw you and is going to hunt you, and you could not be seen by the employees, coupon despensers, and most of all, the forklift! Annnnd if I got bored of that, I would just keep on nagging my mom, "When are gonna get out of here!?"

Once you assess your students' writing, examine the results to determine which trait or traits require the most attention. Share results with students in conferences and conversations so they understand what they are doing well and what they aren't. Their interest will increase when they understand that the skills you are teaching are the same ones they need to become better writers. There's no point in keeping the secret to good writing a secret! (For more on assessing student work, see Chapter 2.)

In our experience, most intermediate students want to write. They take pride in their work. It's not unusual for us to be greeted in the morning by a student waving a paper and asking, "I wrote this last night. Will you read it?" Of course, we want to honor the request, and we usually do when writing time rolls around. We capitalize on the student's energy by reading the paper quickly, picking one trait or more, and conferring with him or her. Later, we might assess the paper more closely using the scoring guides to provide richer feedback, if we feel it will be useful to the writer.

Furthermore, we've found that most intermediate students not only want to write, they want to write long, complex pieces in a variety of genres and formats. As they hone their skills in those genres and formats that may be new to them, they learn that the writing world is a big place. So we must respond clearly, deeply, and precisely to their work, using the language of the traits to help them find their way. For example, we must teach them that writing well means more than choosing the first word that comes to mind; it means choosing the best words to make their message clear and compelling. And, we must teach them that real writers create more than stories or simple explanations; they create a wide variety of texts for specific purposes. In short, we must teach students the writing skills they need to write well, skills they will use the rest of their lives every time they write.

Intermediate students are eager, enthusiastic, and energetic. They've mastered the basics, and that feels good. It's important to keep in mind, however, that it hasn't been long since they knew very little about writing. Just a year ago, your students may have been struggling to get a simple sentence down on paper. Although their writing skills are gelling, they are not fully set. So be gentle. Demanding too much too fast will deflate them as surely as a pinhole will deflate a beach ball. Criticizing them will not motivate them. It will only discourage them. However, offering honest feedback, based on key qualities of the traits, deepens students' understanding of writing and lifts their confidence.

When you use assessment to guide instruction, you can plan and carry out your teaching more effectively and, as a result, see huge growth in your intermediate students' writing performance.

QUESTIONS TO CONSIDER WHEN GETTING STARTED

Consider these three questions as you begin working with your intermediate writers:

* Am I using the developmentally appropriate scoring guide to assess my students' writing?

* Do the results show what students know as well as what they don't know?

* Do the results help me provide targeted instruction so each student continues to improve in measurable ways?

Chapter 1: What Are the Traits and What Makes Them So Great?

13

A Word on the Writing Process

The writing process is just that, a process. Its beginning, middle, and end flow like a river, always going somewhere but often taking its own sweet time to get there. The writing process enables us to show intermediate students what it's like to be a writer. It allows us to open the door to possibilities in writing, giving students topic choices, teaching them skills, showing them how to work through problems, and allowing them time to arrive at solutions. With it, we can demonstrate how to think aloud on paper and follow the steps that successful writers follow so students can do the same in their own work—and to remind them that these steps are flexible and recursive, not rigid and linear. In its most general form, the writing process looks like this:

Prewriting:	The writer comes up with ideas for the work. **Predominant trait:** ideas
Drafting:	The writer gets the ideas down in rough form. **Predominant traits:** ideas, organization
Sharing:	The writer gets feedback on the draft from a reader or listener. **Predominant traits:** ideas, organization, voice, word choice, sentence fluency
Revising:	The writer reflects on the draft and makes changes based on the first five traits. **Predominant traits:** ideas, organization, voice, word choice, and sentence fluency
Editing:	The writer "cleans up" the piece, checking for correct capitalization, punctuation, spelling, paragraphing, grammar, and usage. **Predominant trait:** conventions
Publishing:	The writer goes public with the finished piece.

Intermediate classrooms should be places where there are writing demonstrations and discussions every day about what comes next and why. They should be places where there's a strong connection between reading and writing, as students look to mentor texts as models. They should be places where teachers and students interact using trait-specific language to question if the work is clear and focused, if it is organized so the reader can see where the idea is going, if the voice is truly the writer's, if the words are accurate and precise, if the sentences flow smoothly, and, of course, if conventions are used correctly.

Is Your Classroom Process-Centered or Product-Centered?

In a process-centered classroom:

- Students work on different tasks at different rates.
- Teachers encourage many short, interesting pieces of writing, any of which may lead to one or two longer pieces over time.
- Students work alone, in pairs, small groups, and as a class.
- Writing is shared as it is being created.
- One piece may lead to another on a new topic that is discovered during the writing.
- Mistakes provide opportunities to stretch and grow.
- Questions like these are typical: *Does this work? What else could I try? Will you help me find a better way to say this? What would happen if I changed it to show . . . ?*

In a product-centered classroom:

- Students do the same tasks at the same rate.
- All students complete the same predetermined writing assignments.
- Students usually work alone.
- Writing is shared only when it's finished.
- When a piece is finished, students ask for or are given the next task.
- Mistakes are to be avoided. Emphasis is placed on getting it right the first time.
- Questions like these are typical: *Is this long enough? Is this what you want? Is this going to be graded?*

Every time our intermediate writers put pencil to paper, they should realize that they have choices—that the writing process is a series of flexible steps for them to use to help them write well. In the next section, we present a lesson to help you build that understanding.

| Lesson | UNDERSTANDING THE WRITING PROCESS |

I n this lesson, students learn, from the author's perspective, how ideas germinate into full-blown stories. *What Do Authors Do?* (1995), the book upon which the lesson is based, shows clearly where ideas come from, how they are drafted and revised, and how they wind up as books. It's a charming book, intended to teach and entertain at the same time.

MATERIALS:

❊ a copy of *What Do Authors Do?* by Eileen Christelow

❊ cut-apart list described in step #1 below

❊ pencils, pens, markers, crayons

❊ drawing paper

WHAT TO DO:

1. Make an overhead transparency of the following list, cut apart the items, and mix them up.

    ❊ Think of an idea using a favorite book or a memorable experience as inspiration. Talk about it with another writer before you write.

    ❊ Write your idea down and add details.

    ❊ Read your draft to another writer. Does he or she have suggestions to make it better?

    ❊ Keep writing. Add pictures.

    ❊ Check the writing for mistakes. Compose a final copy.

    ❊ Share your finished piece with family members and friends.

    ❊ Start planning your next piece.

2. Read *What Do Authors Do?* showing the pictures as you go.

3. Tell students they are going to capture the steps of the writing process that Christelow describes in her book.

4. Pick up a transparency strip, read it aloud, and ask students to help you decide where this step goes in the writing process. Move each strip to make room for the new one, changing the order as necessary.

5. When you have all the strips in order, read them aloud with the students. Ask if there are other steps in the writing process that they recall from the book and, if so, where these steps fit into the list.

6. Make a bulletin board showing each item in the list. Group students in pairs and ask them to illustrate one of the steps. Place their creations next to the appropriate items on the bulletin board to help students remember the steps.

FOLLOW-UP ACTIVITIES:

❋ Ask students which step of the writing process they feel will be the easiest for them and which will be the most challenging. Discuss ways that writers overcome difficulties.

❋ Read and discuss *Ish* (2004) by Peter H. Reynolds. Talk to students about how every writer feels "ishy" about what they write, but over time, with lots of help, this feeling turns to confidence.

GREAT PICTURE BOOKS FOR TEACHING ABOUT THE WRITING PROCESS

Aunt Isabel Tells a Good One
Kate Duke, Author and Illustrator
Dutton, 1992

This adorable book explains how writers work with character, plot, and setting to tell stories. Penelope, a young mouse, and her Aunt Isabel work out all the elements of a clever story, including the use of details to capture the reader's interest. For example, Aunt Isabel adds villains as she explains to Penelope that stories must have problems to be resolved. This text is a terrific place to begin discussions of what makes a good story as students plan their own pieces.

Chapter 1: What Are the Traits and What Makes Them So Great?

17

You Have to Write

Janet S. Wong, Author

Teresa Flavin, Illustrator

Margaret K. McElderry, 2002

Stepping into the shoes of the student writer who is told to write but really doesn't want to, Wong shares valuable ideas about how to get going: the smallest everyday events or observations can make fascinating reading. An appreciation of the difficulty of learning to write winds through this book. Wong anticipates what will challenge students most and provides the inspiration to find the ideas that will excite those students as writers and, in turn, engage us as readers.

Author: A True Story

Helen Lester, Author and Illustrator

Houghton Mifflin, 1997

Lester's autobiography of her writing life is a treasure. She documents her first writing effort—a grocery shopping list only she could read—to her attempts at writing a picture book and getting it published. Throughout, the reader is reminded that writing is hard, that ideas come from everywhere, and that many runs at the text are necessary to get it just right. Lester's personal journey as a writer is a celebration. Though she is honest about the struggle, she is joyous about the outcome. Students who read this text will get a balanced view of the writing process.

Show, Don't Tell! Secrets of Writing

Josephine Nobisso, Author

Eva Montanari, Illustrator

Gingerbread House, 2004

One of the secrets to good fiction and nonfiction writing is to be descriptive and help the reader fall deeply into the idea. In this visually appealing and interactive book, Nobisso puts the just-right adjective with a noun to make the writing come to life. (Yes, you get to feel textures and push buttons for sounds.) She explores the use of metaphors and similes, too, helping the reader see how images can be created by using all the senses.

A Word on Writing Conferences

Whether they're completing an assignment that you give them, such as one of the activities in Chapter 4, or a self-initiated writing task, students benefit from conferences, in which they feel safe to air their accomplishments and struggles—and receive substantive, constructive, individualized feedback from you.

TALKING TO STUDENTS ABOUT REVISION

Always begin with something you notice the student can do, something that is working well, and then move on to what is yet to be learned. Don't start with criticism. For instance, you might notice that the piece contains very precise, sophisticated words. Compliment the writer; this is a huge deal. After that, you can point out something that needs attention, such as sentences that begin the same way, but again, don't start with criticism. In this all-important battle to help students see themselves as writers, we must take time to recognize the knowledge and skills they bring to the writing table. It's always easier to work on problems if you have already established that there are strengths.

In students' work, no matter how rough, look for early indicators of success. For example, the writer may be experimenting with time by alternating verb tenses or using the words *now* and *later*. Perhaps he or she has played with new words and sound patterns, or reinvented old ideas in new, quirky ways. These are entry points to support the revision process. Notice what students are trying to do and praise it. Celebrate small victories. Stretch their thinking; encourage them to be patient and keep at it. If you have questions, begin them with "I wonder." Tread carefully because the message we send to our younger writers can determine how willing they are to move their work forward and take ownership.

Also, when talking to students about their work, use *and*, not *but*, to connect the comments. *And* implies that writing is a continuous process and supports your positive statement; *but* negates it. For example, "I'm really into your description of the spaceship, Charles. Your details make your idea clear to me. And now, let's work on organizing those details for better flow."

See below for some simple questions students should ask themselves as they revise their work for ideas, organization, voice, word choice, and sentence fluency. Feel free to give students individual questions or clusters of questions, depending on their levels and needs, and revise the questions to be developmentally appropriate.

Ideas

* Does my writing make sense?

* Does my writing show that I understand my topic?

* Is my writing interesting?

Chapter 1: What Are the Traits and What Makes Them So Great?

19

Organization

❋ Do I start off strong?

❋ Are all my details in the best possible order?

❋ Are similar thoughts grouped together?

Voice

❋ Can the reader hear me in the writing?

❋ Can the reader tell I care about this idea?

❋ Is the voice I've chosen right for my audience?

Word Choice

❋ Do the words I've chosen sound and feel just right?

❋ Have I used words that I've never used before?

❋ Have I painted a picture with words?

Sentence Fluency

❋ Does my writing sound good when I read it aloud?

❋ Do my words and phrases flow together?

❋ Have I included sentences of varying lengths and with different beginnings?

TALKING TO STUDENTS ABOUT EDITING

Unlike revision, editing is about cleaning up the text to make it readable. When we assess intermediate writing for conventions, we look for skill in punctuation, capitalization, spelling, paragraphing, and grammar and usage. In other words, we look at whether the piece meets the conventions of writing.

The first step in teaching editing skills to intermediate students is to identify which skills they already have and which ones they don't by using the scoring guide on page 29. Otherwise you run the risk of giving students editing activities they don't need or that are too challenging for them. On page 21 are some questions to share with students to help them understand conventions. Post these under the heading "Editing Questions," clearly separating them from the revision questions listed in the last section.

Conventions

❖ Is the punctuation correct and does it guide the reader through the text?

❖ Did I capitalize all the right words?

❖ Is my spelling accurate—especially for words I read and write a lot?

❖ Did I follow grammar rules to make my writing clear and readable?

❖ Did I indent paragraphs in all the right places?

Concluding Thought

Plain and simple, the traits help students become better writers. The model empowers students to think like writers, talk like writers, and write like writers because it gives them the language to do so. The stunning simplicity of the traits, the shared vocabulary that they generate, will add energy—an "I can do it" spirit—to your writing program. It's a privilege for us to share the ideas in this book with you.

Chapter 1: What Are the Traits and What Makes Them So Great?

21

Chapter
2

Assessing Student Work

When students are presenting their ideas clearly on paper—when they choose a great topic and support it with important details, when they compose a strong sentence made up of carefully chosen words, when they try a new genre using the appropriate voice for that genre—they deserve to hear from us, their teachers, about what is working and why, and how proud we are of their accomplishment. Conversely, when students are struggling, they depend on us for clear, focused direction. Targeted, trait-specific feedback is what student writers need to progress.

That's why the kind of assessment we're about to describe is so important. It gives you the background knowledge you need to provide that targeted feedback, by asking you to delve deeply into the text to communicate what you discover to the writer. It's far more useful than traditional assessment based on rubrics that lead to a single score. You get precise, concrete information about your students as writers, and your students get truly constructive responses to their work. This chapter gives you both parts of that essential equation: what to look for and what to say.

Guidelines for Assessing Student Work

We won't lie. Assessing your first few papers may be challenging and time-consuming. It's important, though, to give it your best effort. If you invest energy in understanding the different performance levels for each trait now, it will pay off later. In fact, it will make your job easier, more effective, and more enjoyable. To get started, simply follow these guidelines.

1. Choose a paper that, upon a quick reading, shows strengths and/or weaknesses in particular traits that you wish the student to work on further.

2. Assess the paper using the scoring guides that appear on pages 24–29. Read the scoring guides' descriptors for each of the six levels, from top—6: *Exceptional*—to bottom—1: *Rudimentary*. Assign a score of 1, 2, 3, 4, 5, or 6 to each of the traits and write it on the paper or in your grade book.

3. Pinpoint specific items from the scoring guide on which you want to focus. Don't overwhelm the student by choosing too many items at once. Pick one or two items that capture the student's strengths and one or two that capture weaknesses, and leave the rest for another paper or another day. For example, maybe you want to focus on the child's stellar lead and the less-than-stellar spelling. Or maybe his or her use of vivid details or sophisticated words. Or maybe the voice—how natural it sounds . . . or doesn't.

4. As the student becomes more skilled, progressing past the *Rudimentary* and *Emerging* stages, think about making one comment about revision (ideas, organization, voice, word choice, or sentence fluency) and one about editing (conventions).

5. In your discussions with the student, begin with something he or she is doing well. Then gently move on to something the student should do next. For more advice on working with individual students, see pages 19–21.

Remember, your goal should be to collect data that captures what students do well so they can do it again, and what they're not doing well so you can help them do it better. It's not about the numbers or scores; it's about clear communication on writing performance. The better you know the scoring guides, the more skilled you'll be at assessing papers.

Scoring Guides and Scored Sample Papers

The nine sample papers on pages 30–38 capture the wide range of writing skills typically found in grades 3 to 5. Review the scoring guides on pages 24–29, read each paper closely, assess the paper, and then read our scores and comments to see how they compare to yours. Do the sample papers reflect the writing of students in your classroom? Try out the scoring guides on your students' work after you've practiced on these.

Keep in mind that, since intermediate writers benefit as much from oral communication as written, it's important to hone your skills at finding just-right words for use in conferences, small groups, and even whole-class lessons. So we've provided comments on each paper to serve as examples of what you might say.

Scoring Guide: Ideas

The content of the piece, its central message and the details that support it.

score 6 — HIGH

Exceptional

A. **Finding a Topic:** The writer offers a clear, central theme or a simple, original storyline that is memorable.

B. **Focusing the Topic:** The writer narrows the theme or storyline to create a piece that is clear, tight, and manageable.

C. **Developing the Topic:** The writer provides enough critical evidence to support the theme and shows insight on the topic. Or he or she tells the story in a fresh way through an original, unpredictable plot.

D. **Using Details:** The writer offers credible, accurate details that create pictures in the reader's mind, from the beginning of the piece to the end. These details provide the reader with evidence of the writer's knowledge about and/or experience with the topic.

score 5 — Strong

score 4 — MIDDLE

Refining

A. **Finding a Topic**: The writer offers a recognizable but broad theme or storyline. He or she stays on topic, but in a predictable way.

B. **Focusing the Topic:** The writer needs to crystallize his or her topic around the central theme or storyline. He or she does not focus on a specific aspect of the topic.

C. **Developing the Topic:** The writer draws on personal knowledge and experience, but does not offer a unique perspective on the topic. He or she does not probe the topic deeply. Instead, the writer only gives the reader a glimpse at aspects of the topic.

D. **Using Details:** The writer offers details, but they do not always hit the mark because they are inaccurate or irrelevant. He or she does not create a picture in the reader's mind because key questions about the central theme or storyline have not been addressed.

score 3 — Developing

score 2 — LOW

Emerging

A. **Finding a Topic:** The writer has not settled on a topic and, therefore, may offer only a series of unfocused, repetitious, and/or random thoughts.

B. **Narrowing the Topic:** The writer has not narrowed his or her topic in a meaningful way. It's hard to tell what the writer thinks is important since he or she devotes equal importance to each piece of information.

C. **Developing the Topic:** The writer has created a piece that is so short the reader cannot fully understand or appreciate what the author wants to say. The writer may have simply restated an assigned topic or responded to a prompt, without devoting much thought or effort to it.

D. **Using Details:** The writer has clearly devoted little attention to details. The writing contains limited or completely inaccurate information. After reading the piece, the reader is left with many unanswered questions.

score 1 — Rudimentary

Scoring Guide: Organization
The internal structure of the piece—the thread of logic, the pattern of meaning.

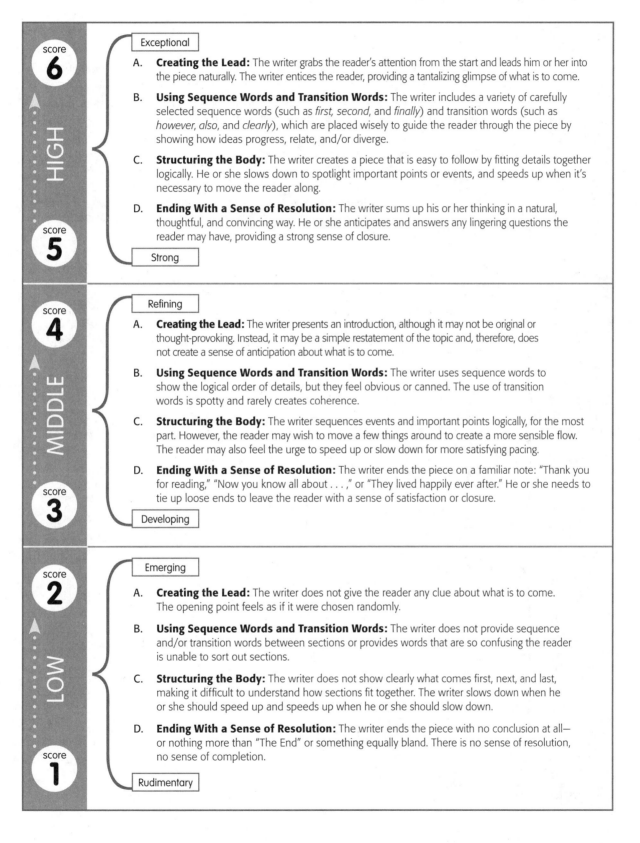

score 6

HIGH

Exceptional

A. **Creating the Lead:** The writer grabs the reader's attention from the start and leads him or her into the piece naturally. The writer entices the reader, providing a tantalizing glimpse of what is to come.

B. **Using Sequence Words and Transition Words:** The writer includes a variety of carefully selected sequence words (such as *first, second,* and *finally*) and transition words (such as *however, also,* and *clearly*), which are placed wisely to guide the reader through the piece by showing how ideas progress, relate, and/or diverge.

C. **Structuring the Body:** The writer creates a piece that is easy to follow by fitting details together logically. He or she slows down to spotlight important points or events, and speeds up when it's necessary to move the reader along.

D. **Ending With a Sense of Resolution:** The writer sums up his or her thinking in a natural, thoughtful, and convincing way. He or she anticipates and answers any lingering questions the reader may have, providing a strong sense of closure.

score 5

Strong

score 4

MIDDLE

Refining

A. **Creating the Lead:** The writer presents an introduction, although it may not be original or thought-provoking. Instead, it may be a simple restatement of the topic and, therefore, does not create a sense of anticipation about what is to come.

B. **Using Sequence Words and Transition Words:** The writer uses sequence words to show the logical order of details, but they feel obvious or canned. The use of transition words is spotty and rarely creates coherence.

C. **Structuring the Body:** The writer sequences events and important points logically, for the most part. However, the reader may wish to move a few things around to create a more sensible flow. The reader may also feel the urge to speed up or slow down for more satisfying pacing.

D. **Ending With a Sense of Resolution:** The writer ends the piece on a familiar note: "Thank you for reading," "Now you know all about . . . ," or "They lived happily ever after." He or she needs to tie up loose ends to leave the reader with a sense of satisfaction or closure.

score 3

Developing

score 2

LOW

Emerging

A. **Creating the Lead:** The writer does not give the reader any clue about what is to come. The opening point feels as if it were chosen randomly.

B. **Using Sequence Words and Transition Words:** The writer does not provide sequence and/or transition words between sections or provides words that are so confusing the reader is unable to sort out sections.

C. **Structuring the Body:** The writer does not show clearly what comes first, next, and last, making it difficult to understand how sections fit together. The writer slows down when he or she should speed up and speeds up when he or she should slow down.

D. **Ending With a Sense of Resolution:** The writer ends the piece with no conclusion at all— or nothing more than "The End" or something equally bland. There is no sense of resolution, no sense of completion.

score 1

Rudimentary

Scoring Guide: **Voice**

The tone of the piece—the personal stamp of the writer, which is achieved through a strong understanding of purpose and audience.

score 6

HIGH

Exceptional

A. **Establishing a Tone:** The writer cares about the topic, and it shows. The writing is expressive and compelling. The reader feels the writer's conviction, authority, and integrity.

B. **Conveying the Purpose:** The writer makes clear his or her reason for creating the piece. He or she offers a point of view that is appropriate for the mode (narrative, expository, or persuasive), which compels the reader to read on.

C. **Creating a Connection to the Audience:** The writer speaks in a way that makes the reader want to listen. He or she has considered what the reader needs to know and the best way to convey it by sharing his or her fascination, feelings, and opinions about the topic.

D. **Taking Risks to Create Voice:** The writer expresses ideas in new ways, which makes the piece interesting and original. The writing sounds like the writer because of his or her use of distinctive, just-right words and phrases.

score 5

Strong

score 4

MIDDLE

Refining

A. **Establishing a Tone:** The writer has established a tone that can be described as "pleasing" or "sincere," but not "passionate" or "compelling." He or she attempts to create a tone that hits the mark, but the overall result feels generic.

B. **Conveying the Purpose:** The writer has chosen a voice for the piece that is not completely clear. There are only a few moments when the reader understands where the writer is coming from and why he or she wrote the piece.

C. **Creating a Connection to the Audience:** The writer keeps the reader at a distance. The connection between reader and writer is tenuous because the writer reveals little about what is important or meaningful about the topic.

D. **Taking Risks to Create Voice:** The writer creates a few moments that catch the reader's attention, but only a few. The piece sounds like anyone could have written it. It lacks the energy, commitment, and conviction that would distinguish it from other pieces on the same topic.

score 3

Developing

score 2

LOW

Emerging

A. **Establishing a Tone:** The writer has produced a lifeless piece—one that is monotonous, mechanical, or repetitious, and off-putting to the reader.

B. **Conveying the Purpose:** The writer chose the topic for mysterious reasons. The piece may be filled with random thoughts, technical jargon, or inappropriate vocabulary, making it impossible to discern how the writer feels about the topic.

C. **Creating a Connection to the Audience:** The writer provides no evidence that he or she has considered what the reader might need to know to connect with the topic. Or there is an obvious mismatch between the tone and the intended audience.

D. **Taking Risks to Create Voice:** The writer creates no highs or lows. The piece is flat and lifeless, causing the reader to wonder why the author wrote it in the first place. The writer's voice does not pop out, even for a moment.

score 1

Rudimentary

Scoring Guide: Word Choice
The specific vocabulary the writer uses to convey meaning and enlighten the reader.

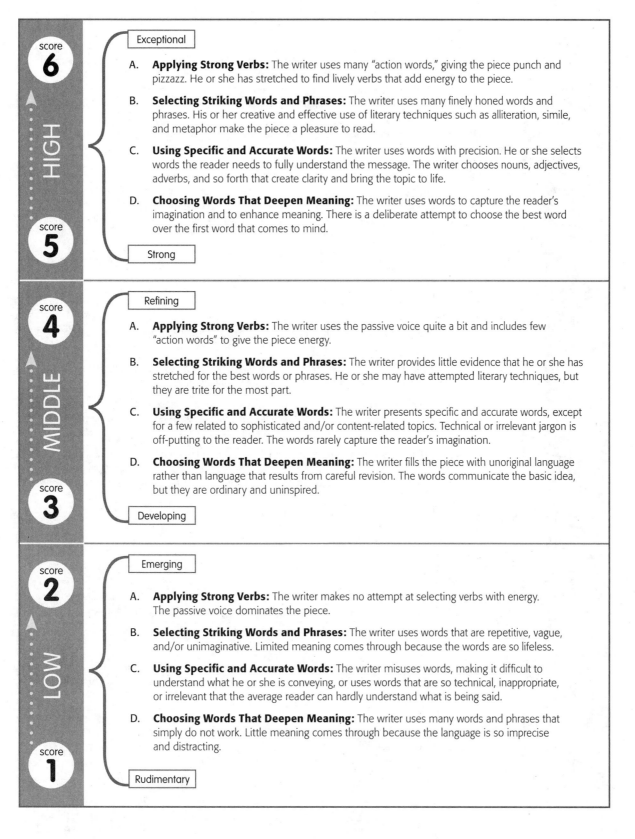

score 6 · HIGH · score 5

Exceptional

A. **Applying Strong Verbs:** The writer uses many "action words," giving the piece punch and pizzazz. He or she has stretched to find lively verbs that add energy to the piece.

B. **Selecting Striking Words and Phrases:** The writer uses many finely honed words and phrases. His or her creative and effective use of literary techniques such as alliteration, simile, and metaphor make the piece a pleasure to read.

C. **Using Specific and Accurate Words:** The writer uses words with precision. He or she selects words the reader needs to fully understand the message. The writer chooses nouns, adjectives, adverbs, and so forth that create clarity and bring the topic to life.

D. **Choosing Words That Deepen Meaning:** The writer uses words to capture the reader's imagination and to enhance meaning. There is a deliberate attempt to choose the best word over the first word that comes to mind.

Strong

score 4 · MIDDLE · score 3

Refining

A. **Applying Strong Verbs:** The writer uses the passive voice quite a bit and includes few "action words" to give the piece energy.

B. **Selecting Striking Words and Phrases:** The writer provides little evidence that he or she has stretched for the best words or phrases. He or she may have attempted literary techniques, but they are trite for the most part.

C. **Using Specific and Accurate Words:** The writer presents specific and accurate words, except for a few related to sophisticated and/or content-related topics. Technical or irrelevant jargon is off-putting to the reader. The words rarely capture the reader's imagination.

D. **Choosing Words That Deepen Meaning:** The writer fills the piece with unoriginal language rather than language that results from careful revision. The words communicate the basic idea, but they are ordinary and uninspired.

Developing

score 2 · LOW · score 1

Emerging

A. **Applying Strong Verbs:** The writer makes no attempt at selecting verbs with energy. The passive voice dominates the piece.

B. **Selecting Striking Words and Phrases:** The writer uses words that are repetitive, vague, and/or unimaginative. Limited meaning comes through because the words are so lifeless.

C. **Using Specific and Accurate Words:** The writer misuses words, making it difficult to understand what he or she is conveying, or uses words that are so technical, inappropriate, or irrelevant that the average reader can hardly understand what is being said.

D. **Choosing Words That Deepen Meaning:** The writer uses many words and phrases that simply do not work. Little meaning comes through because the language is so imprecise and distracting.

Rudimentary

Scoring Guide: **Sentence Fluency**

The way words and phrases flow through the piece. It is the auditory trait and is, therefore, "read" with the ear as much as the eye.

score 6

HIGH

score 5

Exceptional

A. **Capturing Smooth and Rhythmic Flow:** The writer thinks about how the sentences sound. He or she uses phrasing that is almost musical. If the piece were read aloud, it would be easy on the ear.

B. **Crafting Well-Built Sentences:** The writer carefully and creatively constructs sentences for maximum impact. Transition words such as *but*, *and*, and *so* are used successfully to join sentences and sentence parts.

C. **Varying Sentence Patterns:** The writer uses various types of sentences (simple, compound, and/or complex) to enhance the central theme or storyline. The piece is made up of an effective mix of long, complex sentences and short, simple ones.

D. **Breaking the "Rules" to Create Fluency:** The writer diverges from standard English to create interest and impact. For example, he or she may use a sentence fragment, such as "All alone in the forest" or a single word, such as "Bam!" to accent a particular moment or action. The writer might begin with informal words such as *well, and,* or *but* to create a conversational tone, or he or she might break rules intentionally to make dialogue sound authentic.

Strong

score 4

MIDDLE

score 3

Refining

A. **Capturing Smooth and Rhythmic Flow:** The writer has produced a text that is uneven. Many sentences read smoothly, while others are choppy or awkward.

B. **Crafting Well-Built Sentences:** The writer offers simple sentences that are sound but no long, complex sentences. He or she attempts to vary the beginnings and lengths of sentences.

C. **Varying Sentence Patterns:** The writer exhibits basic sentence sense and offers some sentence variety. He or she attempts to use different types of sentences, but in doing so creates an uneven flow rather than a smooth, seamless one.

D. **Breaking the "Rules" to Create Fluency:** The writer includes fragments, but they seem more accidental than intentional. He or she uses informal words, such as *well, and,* and *but*, inappropriately to start sentences, and pays little attention to making dialogue sound authentic.

Developing

score 2

LOW

score 1

Emerging

A. **Capturing Smooth and Rhythmic Flow:** The writer has created a text that is a challenge to read aloud since the sentences are incomplete, choppy, stilted, rambling, and/or awkward.

B. **Crafting Well-Built Sentences:** The writer offers sentences, even simple ones, that are often flawed. Sentence beginnings are repetitive and uninspired.

C. **Varying Sentence Patterns:** The writer uses single, repetitive sentence pattern throughout or connects sentence parts with an endless string of transition words such as *and, but, or, because,* and so on, which distracts the reader.

D. **Breaking the "Rules" to Create Fluency:** The writer offers few or no simple, well-built sentences, making it impossible to determine if he or she has done anything out of the ordinary. Global revision is necessary before sentences can be revised for stylistic and creative purposes.

Rudimentary

Getting Started With the Traits: Grades 3–5

Scoring Guide: Conventions

The mechanical correctness of the piece. Correct use of conventions (spelling, capitalization, punctuation, paragraphing, and grammar and usage) guides the reader through text easily.

Scoring Guides

Sample Papers

Lessons

Activities

FAQs

score 6

HIGH

score 5

Exceptional

A. **Checking Spelling:** The writer spells sight words, high-frequency words, and less familiar words correctly. When he or she spells less familiar words incorrectly, those words are phonetically correct. Overall, the piece reveals control in spelling.

B. **Punctuating Effectively:** The writer handles basic punctuation skillfully. He or she understands how to use periods, commas, question marks, and exclamation points to enhance clarity and meaning. Paragraphs are indented in the right places. The piece is ready for a general audience.

C. **Capitalizing Correctly:** The writer uses capital letters consistently and accurately. A deep understanding of how to capitalize dialogue, abbreviations, proper names, and titles is evident.

D. **Applying Grammar and Usage:** The writer forms grammatically correct phrases and sentences. He or she shows care in applying the rules of standard English. The writer may break from those rules for stylistic reasons, but otherwise abides by them.

Strong

score 4

MIDDLE

score 3

Refining

A. **Checking Spelling:** The writer incorrectly spells a few high-frequency words and many unfamiliar words and/or sophisticated words.

B. **Punctuating Effectively:** The writer handles basic punctuation marks (such as end marks on sentences and commas in a series) well. However, he or she might have trouble with more complex punctuation marks (such as quotation marks, parentheses, dashes) and with paragraphing, especially on longer pieces.

C. **Capitalizing Correctly:** The writer capitalizes the first word in sentences and most common proper names. However, his or her use of more complex capitalization is spotty within dialogue, abbreviations, and proper names ("Aunt Maria" versus "my aunt," for instance).

D. **Applying Grammar and Usage:** The writer has made grammar and usage mistakes throughout the piece, but they do not interfere with the reader's ability to understand the message. Issues related to agreement, tense, and word usage appear here and there, but can be easily corrected.

Developing

score 2

LOW

score 1

Emerging

A. **Checking Spelling:** The writer has misspelled many words, even simple ones, which causes the reader to focus on conventions rather than on the central theme or storyline.

B. **Punctuating Effectively:** The writer has neglected to use punctuation, used punctuation incorrectly, and/or forgotten to indent paragraphs, making it difficult for the reader to find meaning.

C. **Capitalizing Correctly:** The writer uses capitals inconsistently even in common places such as the first word in a sentence. He or she uses capitals correctly in some places, but has no consistent control over them.

D. **Applying Grammar and Usage:** The writer makes frequent mistakes in grammar and usage, making it difficult to read and understand the piece. Issues related to agreement, tense, and word usage abound.

Rudimentary

PAPER #1:
GRADE 3

What we think of the piece, based on points in the scoring guides:

Without question, this writer is writing from experience. Her topic is focused, and her details are accurate and relevant. Her low opinion of bees comes through not only in her words, but also in her tone. To top things off, the piece is well edited. The writer's spelling and use of capital letters and punctuation are strong. Therefore, she deserves kudos for ideas, voice, and conventions. Her organization, however, could be better. She makes it clear from the start that she does not like bees because they sting— and she ends the piece with the same message, along with the all-too-common line, "And that is why . . ." There is no momentum—no real thrust to the idea. We also wish she had chosen her words more carefully and courageously. The piece is a bare-bones explanation.

> Bees
> I do not like bees because it hurts when they sting. I hate their buzzing sound If you accidently hit theire nest, they will chase you. And if you try to shoe them a way they sting you. The main part I don't like about bees is theire stingers. And that why I don't like bees.

How we score this piece:

* Ideas: 5	Word Choice: 2
* Organization: 2	Sentence Fluency: 3
Voice: 4	* Conventions: 5

* Traits we choose to focus on in a conference.

Comments to the writer:

"Your piece tells me that you know a lot about what angers bees. It also suggests you've had a bad run-in or two with bees. Am I right? [Let the student answer.] Your experience has provided you with a great idea. How about folding in some of that experience to illustrate *why* you don't like bees? Rather than starting and ending with pretty much the same statement, start with something that will grab the reader—and end with something that will make sure he or she never forgets your piece. Your organization will shine! Your use of conventions is excellent. Be sure to continue applying them so well."

Getting Started With the Traits: Grades 3–5

PAPER #2: GRADE 3

<u>football</u>

Football is a very fun Sport. I just love to hit the snot out of people when I am mad at them. But it is not fun geting cloked by somone else on the other team. When they make me mad. I get **steamy** mad!

What we think of the piece, based on points in the scoring guides:

Can you imagine this kid on the football field? Heaven help the other team! To us, his passion comes through mainly in his word choice. Though quite unappetizing, phrases like "hitting the snot out of people" and "getting clocked by someone" capture the rough-and-tumble nature of the game perfectly. The piece flows well, too, largely because the writer begins and structures each sentence in a different way. It's weak, however, in ideas, not because it isn't focused—it most definitely is—but because it lacks details. Why does the writer enjoy football? What, specifically, makes him angry? How does his anger impact his game? Answering questions like these would add dimension to the piece.

How we score this piece:

* Ideas: 3
  Organization: 3
  Voice: 4

* Word Choice: 5
* Sentence Fluency: 4
  Conventions: 3

* Traits we choose to focus on in a conference.

Comments to the writer:

"It's so important for writers to write about their passions—and that's just what you've done here. You're passionate about football. I can tell by your word choice. [Point to phrases like "hitting the snot out of people" and "getting clocked by someone."] Your words are so colorful and natural. They put me in the game. Your sentence fluency is strong, too. I admire the way you start and structure each sentence differently. The piece flows. That said, I have questions about your idea: Why do you enjoy football? What makes you mad? How does your anger make you a better player? [Let the student answer.] Great! Why don't you weave in some of those details? As a reader, I'd really like to know them."

PAPER #3: GRADE 3

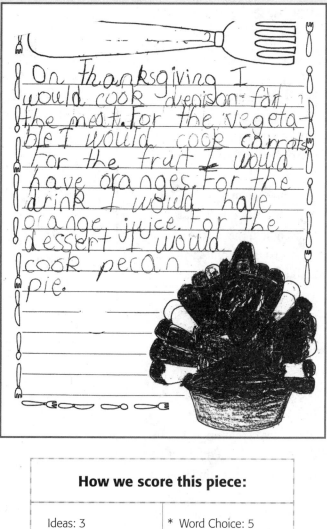

What we think of the piece, based on points in the scoring guides:

This piece has "prompt" written all over it: "If you were planning Thanksgiving dinner, what would you serve?" And the writer completed the assignment. But that's all she did. She shows no connection whatsoever to the topic—and gives no indication that she cares about it. As a result, the piece lacks voice. The repetitive sentences (for the most part, all beginning with "I would cook . . .") provides further evidence of the writer's indifference to the topic. Her word choice is good, though. "Venison," "carrots," "oranges," and "pecan pie" give the reader a clear picture of the menu because those words are precise.

Comments to the writer:

"This piece is making me so hungry! Do you know why? Because your words are so precise. Instead of just saying "meat," you say "venison." Instead of just saying "dessert," you say "pecan pie." By choosing your words so carefully, you enable me, the reader, to see clearly each delicious menu item. It's not clear to me, though, why you picked these items. I suspect it's because they are your favorites, but that's not coming through in the writing. Is there a way to add your personal stamp? In other words, add more voice? You may want to try writing like you speak. Imagine telling your best friend what you're serving for Thanksgiving. What would that sound like? Write it down. By doing this, you'll not only add voice, but you'll bring more flow, or sentence fluency, to the piece. I can't wait to see your next draft."

How we score this piece:

Ideas: 3	* Word Choice: 5
Organization: 2	* Sentence Fluency: 2
* Voice: 1	Conventions: 4

* Traits we choose to focus on in a conference.

PAPER #4: GRADE 4

What we think of the piece, based on points in the scoring guides:

This writer has certainly done his homework about the similarities and differences between penguins and pelicans. His idea is strong—and he includes so many rich, relevant details, which he organizes in a straightforward, sensible way. The reader walks away with a lot of good information about these birds. However, the piece lacks voice and sentence fluency. Like the writer of paper #3, this writer was most likely given a standard assignment—to write a comparison/contrast paper (for English class, as the title suggests), based on facts he collected in a Venn diagram. And he rose to the challenge.

Comments to the writer:

"You have done your research on penguins and pelicans, that's for sure. I'm so impressed by all the facts you give and the way you've organized them by discussing the birds' similarities in the first paragraph and their differences in the second. The piece is very easy to read because of your organization and excellent use of conventions. Now let's work on bringing your idea to life. You can do that in a couple of ways: In addition to facts about penguins and pelicans, include your thoughts and feelings about them. That will bring out your voice. And try to construct a few of your sentences in different ways so that they all don't feel so similar. [Show examples of similar sentences.] That will enhance your piece's fluency."

English

Penguins and Pelicans are alike in some ways. One way they are alike is they both are birds. Another way the birds are similar is they live near the water. Also they both have feathers. Some more ways they are alike are they both eat fish, lay eggs, and they both live in colonies (not like the 13 colonies).

Penguins and Pelicans also differ in ways also. A way that they are different is Pelicans can fly, but Penguins can not; they can only walk and swim. Also Pelicans have a huge pouch on their bills, and Penguins have small beaks. Another way the birds differ is Penguins are black and white, but Pelicans are white with brown, gray, or black. Some other ways they are different is Penguins swim veary fast under water, but Pelicans

swim on top of water, and Penguins live in cold climates, wh Pelicans live in warmer areas. Tha is how Penguins and Pelicans ar alike and different in many wa

---

How we score this piece:

* Ideas: 5	Word Choice: 4
Organization: 3	* Sentence Fluency: 2
* Voice: 2	Conventions: 4

* Traits we choose to focus on in a conference.

PAPER #5: GRADE 4

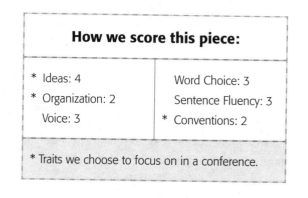

Reading
IS
Power

Reading is fun
And gives you power if
you read. you Can learn about
stuff like animals. Today we
went to a play. this boy
could not read his homwork
but he trid and tiid but
at the end he could read.
If you could read
you could not read rode sings
are you would get lost
you have to read to get throw.
school if you did'int you would
fell.
reading is power becous
if you read a lot about
somthing you will no a lot
about it.
If you cant read
you beeter learn to.

What we think of the piece, based on points in the scoring guides:

We respect what this student is trying to do: Persuade her classmates to read by writing about the value of reading in everyday life. The fact that she touches on the full range of texts available to us, from road signs to research materials, suggests that she truly understands the important role reading plays in school and beyond. So we give her high marks for ideas. However, the writing lacks a logical sense of direction. The details are strung together loosely at best. Further, the writer's mediocre use of conventions interferes with our ability to follow her argument and, in the end, buy it.

How we score this piece:

* Ideas: 4
* Organization: 2
  Voice: 3

  Word Choice: 3
  Sentence Fluency: 3
* Conventions: 2

* Traits we choose to focus on in a conference.

Comments to the writer:

"Something tells me you love to read. That's terrific! As you point out so clearly in your piece, reading serves many purposes—from preventing us from getting lost to helping us learn about things in our world (like animals). So your idea works. Do you feel it's also important to read for pleasure? [Let the student answer.] You may want to weave in that detail. From there, think about putting *all* your details in an order that makes sense to the reader. For example, combine your point about animals in the first paragraph with your point about knowing a lot about things in the third paragraph. Improving your organization that way will make the piece easier to read and even more persuasive. And, you clearly know how to use most conventions, so when you spot words that don't look right as you're revising, try to correct them. If you think your piece needs some heavy editing, save that for later. I'll help you."

PAPER #6: GRADE 4

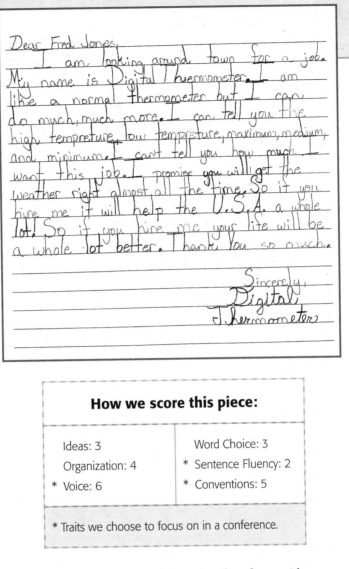

Dear Fred Jones,

I am looking around town for a job. My name is Digital Thermometer. I am like a normal thermometer but I can do much, much more. I can tell you the high tempreture, low tempreture, maximum, medium, and minimum. I can't tell you how much I want this job. I promise you will get the weather right almost all the time. So if you hire me it will help the U.S.A. a whole lot! So if you hire me your life will be a whole lot better. Thank you so much.

Sincerely,
Digital
Thermometer

What we think of the piece, based on points in the scoring guides:

This student chose to become a digital thermometer (from a list of weather-forecasting tools) and write a letter of application to a meteorologist, explaining why he'd be the perfect hire. Although the assignment is a bit farfetched, we sense the student enjoyed carrying it out because his voice is strong. (Voice is usually a reliable indicator of the student's interest in an assignment.) Pride in his unique skills and qualities as a thermometer rings out. He makes a compelling argument, which is easy to follow because of his excellent use of conventions. Although the sentences are mechanically correct, though, they lack variety. Notice that all but the last two are nearly identical in length and begin with the word *I*. Therefore, we'd encourage work on sentence fluency.

How we score this piece:

Ideas: 3	Word Choice: 3
Organization: 4	* Sentence Fluency: 2
* Voice: 6	* Conventions: 5

* Traits we choose to focus on in a conference.

Comments to the writer:

"Your piece has all the elements of a strong letter of application: you explain why you are writing, why you would be perfect for the job, and how you would improve the quality of life for your employer. Your message is persuasive, in other words—and that comes through in your voice. I sense you really want the job *because* of your voice. You deserve high marks for conventions, too. Your grammar and mechanics are, for the most part, perfect, which makes reading your writing a pleasure. One way you could improve your piece is to bring more sentence variety to it. Notice how almost every one of your sentences is about the same length and begins with the word *I*. How about changing a couple to add interest and create rhythm?"

PAPER #7: GRADE 5

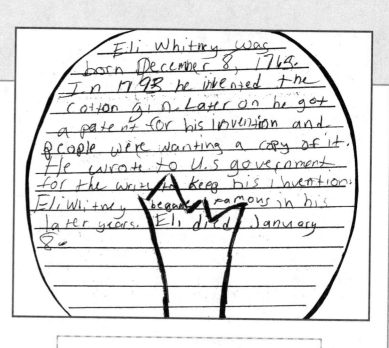

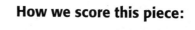

What we think of the piece, based on points in the scoring guides:

Although the beginning of this piece is far from bold and its ending far from excellent, its middle provides good, reliable, well-organized information about Eli Whitney. In fact, organizing biographies chronologically is a tried-and-true technique. Professional writers have been doing it for generations. So the main idea and organization are working— but the piece severely lacks details. The writer provides only bare-bones information about Eli Whitney. We want more. Although the writer begins and ends sentences clearly and uses some nice prepositional and transitional phrases, he doesn't vary them at all, making the piece easy to read, but lifeless.

How we score this piece:

* Ideas: 2	Word Choice: 3
* Organization: 4	Sentence Fluency: 2
* Voice: 2	Conventions: 4

* Traits we choose to focus on in a conference.

Comments to the writer:

"Eli Whitney is an important figure in history. Without a doubt, you got all your facts straight—and have organized them in a way that makes sense: chronologically. Good for you! At the same time, the piece leaves me with more questions than answers. Where was Eli born? In what year did he die? What is a cotton gin, and *why* did he invent it? Did it solve a problem for him and his community? If so, what was the problem? You say he became famous in his lifetime. Was he happy about that? Or was fame a burden? I'm asking a lot of questions, I know. But that's because you, as a writer, have piqued my curiosity. Answering questions like these will help you add details. It also might help you add variety to your sentences so that the subject of each one isn't *he* or *Eli Whitney*."

PAPER #8: GRADE 5

What we think of the piece, based on points in the scoring guides:

It's interesting to compare this paper to the last one. Both were written by fifth graders. Both are about people in history. Both focus on significant events in the lives of those people. But the similarities end there. Unlike the last piece, this one contains some nice details such as "When I came through Ellis Island, my name was changed . . ." "I caught a glimpse of her and waved . . ." "I had to live in a boarding house . . ." There are also some nice moments of sentence fluency: "I remember when I first came to America. The year was 1890." Finally, the writer's superb use of conventions makes reading a pleasure. However, the organization needs work. The piece lacks a clear sense of direction. The details, as good as they may be, are strung together randomly. There is only a hint of internal structure.

Hi my name is Meyer Yezierska. When I came through Ellis Island my name was changed to Max Mayer. I am Hattie's older brother. I have five family members that also came to America.

I remember when I first came to America. The year was 1890. I had to meet my family at Ellis Island. I was trying to see my sister Anzia. I caught a glimpse of her and waved. She didn't know that my name had been changed because they couldn't pronounce it. I led my family across the streets of New York City. I had to live in a boarding house and sweatshops just like Anzia. My mother died and my father gave lessons to boys in Plotsk.

I turned out to be very rich because of my job. I had traveled back to Plotsk with Anzia. Finally, I got married and had three children.

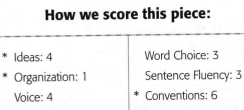

How we score this piece:

* Ideas: 4	Word Choice: 3
* Organization: 1	Sentence Fluency: 3
Voice: 4	* Conventions: 6

* Traits we choose to focus on in a conference.

Comments to the writer:

"Through your writing, you have become Max Mayer. Your ideas and voice particularly make me a believer. And your excellent use of conventions allowed me to read the piece with ease. Thank you. That said, I feel you've given snapshots of Max's life, rather than a full-blown movie. Think about organizing your fine details in a way that makes more sense. Maybe begin with why you came to America in the first place and from where, how you got here, how you felt when you arrived, and so forth. From there, explain what it was like meeting your family on Ellis Island, where you lived, where you worked, and your general impressions of America. You've already given the reader many of these details; now it's just a matter of structuring them more logically and adding more details as necessary to fill in any missing information in Max's amazing story."

PAPER #9: GRACE 5

"If I Could Choose"

If I could choose to be an astronaut or and oceanographer, I would be an astronaut. Being an astronaut would be so much fun. And since I am only eleven years old, I would gather information about the benifits from space I have learned, that I can apply on Earth.

Just seeing Earth from space would make me want to float around for hours because there is no gravity. I would even explore the affects of pollution outside Earth. I would also try to look for other life, maybe aliens. I would try to find and explore a new planet that has never been seen before.

Being an astronaut would be cool. Except for having to be in collage from 4-8 years. ☹ I would deffinatly be too tired of school then.

What we think of the piece, based on points in the scoring guides:

Could this paper be any clearer or more focused? The writer knows what she wants to say—and says it, without wasting a word. She doesn't just state that she aspires to be an astronaut over an oceanographer, she explains why by providing compelling, convincing details. The words she has chosen, such as *gravity, explore, pollution, aliens,* and *planet*, bring details to life and are appropriate for the topic and audience. The piece stumbles a bit, though, when it comes to sentence fluency. It hums along steadily, but in a predictable, almost businesslike fashion. The writer could do more to make it sound more fluid and natural.

How we score this piece:

* Ideas: 6	* Word Choice: 5
Organization: 4	* Sentence Fluency: 3
Voice: 4	Conventions: 4

* Traits we choose to focus on in a conference.

Comments to the writer:

"You are an excellent writer, and this piece proves it. After reading it, I had a clear sense of *why* you want to be an astronaut—to have fun, to apply all you've learned about outer space, to explore the effects of pollution, to look for other life forms and planets. Wow! There is real power in those details. There is also power in the words you chose because they tell me, the reader, that you know what you're talking about—words such as *gravity, explore, pollution, aliens,* and *planet.* Your sentences are composed correctly and support your details and words well. If you used more variety in your sentences, your work would be even stronger and more interesting to the reader. Try making some longer or shorter. Check to make sure they don't all start the same way. Then read your revision aloud to make sure it sounds more fluent."

Concluding Thought

We can't stress this point enough: We must explain to writers, or help them to discover for themselves, the reasons a piece is or isn't working and what to do about it, regardless of where they fall on the developmental continuum. The traits enable us to do that. When we use the scoring guides to communicate clearly with students, they learn, right along with us, how writing works. We also come to know, specifically, what we need to teach. The next two chapters contain lessons and activities for you to use once you've taken that step—once you've assessed your students' work using the scoring guides and have determined where they need help the most.

Trait-Based Lessons for the Whole Class

There is no better way to introduce the traits than by gathering students together and exploring them as a group. This chapter contains whole-class lessons for each trait, organized by key quality, with clear directions for carrying them out. The lessons on ideas, organization, voice, word choice, and sentence fluency center on developing critical revision skills, while the lessons on conventions center on developing critical editing skills—spelling, punctuation, capitalization, and grammar and usage. We round out the chapter with tips for publishing to ensure that students' work looks as good as it reads.

We've provided enough lessons to use on a regular basis—24 total. But that doesn't mean you need to follow them sequentially. You should use them in whatever order you wish, in a way that makes sense for you and your students. The important thing is to carry all of them out by the year's end. You may first want to assess your students' writing using the trait scoring guides on pages 24–29. Doing so will reveal traits that your students struggle with most and help you choose appropriate lessons.

Guidelines for Conducting Lessons

Every teacher has his or her own way of planning and giving lessons, but here are some tips that have proven effective in our work:

1. Read the lesson beforehand to familiarize yourself with it, anticipate children's questions, and collect the necessary materials.

2. Gather the children around you, making sure that each one can see you and any materials you will be using.

3. Introduce the lesson by telling children the trait and key quality you're exploring and why they're essential to becoming a good writer. Use the high points on the scoring guides on pages 24–29 if you need ideas for what to say.

4. Work through each step of the lesson, taking your cue from the students to determine how much time to spend on it. If they "get it," move on. If they don't, stick with it, repeating procedures, asking questions, encouraging answers, and so forth.

5. Allow students to share their responses and discuss issues raised in the lesson. Don't be afraid to diverge a bit.

6. If time allows, encourage students to practice by giving them one of the activities on pages 86–103 or by choosing pieces from their writing folders to revise or edit.

Regardless of how you conduct the lessons, students should take what they learn and apply it to the extended pieces that they're working on during independent writing. Since students are revising and editing these pieces over time, they can apply what they learn as they learn it, which leads to thoughtful, polished final pieces. When students revise and edit their own work using the language of the traits, they come to understand how and when to revise and edit, regardless of the purpose for their writing. The sooner they begin using the tools that successful, independent writers use to improve their work, the sooner they'll become successful, independent writers themselves.

Ideas Lessons

The goal of assessment is to improve instruction so that students perform better each time they attempt a task. So let's build a bridge from assessment to instruction for the trait of ideas. There are four key qualities of the ideas trait that every student can learn:

❧ Finding a Topic

❧ Focusing the Topic

❧ Developing the Topic

❧ Using Details

In the pages that follow, we offer lessons for teaching these qualities. As you carry out the lessons, keep your focus on the trait, while linking lesson goals to your school and district's curriculum. And, of course, feel free to adapt the lessons by weaving in your own good thinking.

| Lesson #1 | **FINDING A TOPIC** |

I deas for writing pop up when we least expect them and, therefore, can be lost all too easily unless we have a place to capture them. In this lesson, students learn to use a writer's notebook, or "seed idea notebook," to think about and jot down possible topics for writing.

WHAT TO DO:

1. Show students a filled-in sample page of a writer's notebook. If you wish, you can use an overhead of the reproducible on page 44, filling in the four sections using words, phrases, questions, pictures, and lists to capture ideas for writing. Emphasize that taking the time to enter even the quickest notation can help us remember a good idea.

2. Hand out a copy of the Seed Idea Notebook to each student. Tell students that this is what they will use as their own writer's notebook. Discuss why it is called Seed Idea Notebook and that you hope they will use it to let writing ideas grow. Students can personalize the cover by coloring in the picture and adding their own words and art.

3. Tell students to capture three ideas in their notebooks, reminding them that they can use words, phrases, questions, pictures, and/or lists. They need to write down only enough to retain the idea for consideration later.

4. Ask students to choose one of the three ideas as the topic for a piece of writing. They may wish to discuss their choice with a neighbor. Give them paper and pencils, and let them start to work.

FOLLOW-UP ACTIVITIES:

❉   After students have used their notebooks over a period of time, have them review the contents and talk with a partner about possible writing topics. Ask members of the class to share their notebook entries and resulting pieces of writing. Emphasize how the seed idea in the notebook leads to a longer piece of writing. Every two weeks, or as time allows, ask students to share why ideas in their notebooks are special. As one student shares, another may get a new idea to include in his or her notebook.

❉   Read *Amelia's Notebook* (2006) by Marissa Moss, a clever picture book that shows students the range of items and entries that might find its way into a writer's notebook. It provides a concrete example of how a notebook helps a writer find good ideas.

MATERIALS:

❉   an overhead transparency of the Seed Idea Notebook Pages reproducible (page 44)

❉   photocopies of the Seed Idea Notebook Cover reproducible (page 43) and the Seed Idea Notebook Pages reproducible (page 44): To create a notebook, cut apart covers and pages and staple together a cover, the 4 labeled notebook pages, and 2 blank pages behind each labeled page.

❉   writing paper

❉   pens or pencils

Seed Idea Notebook Cover

Seed Idea Notebook

_____
writer's name

Seed Idea Notebook

_____
writer's name

Seed Idea Notebook

_____
writer's name

Seed Idea Notebook

_____
writer's name

Seed Idea Notebook Pages

Things I notice:

Things I wonder about:

Things that make me laugh:

Things that worry me:

Lesson #2	**FOCUSING THE TOPIC**

This lesson gives students the opportunity to practice taking a big topic and focusing it to create a narrower, more manageable one. Specifically, students listen to Jon J. Muth's extraordinary book, *The Three Questions* (2002), use writing to find answers to the following questions, and, in the process, arrive at a "big idea" behind each one:

❋ When is the best time to do things?

❋ Who is the most important one?

❋ What is the right thing to do?

> **MATERIALS:**
>
> ❋ a copy of *The Three Questions* by Jon J. Muth
>
> ❋ small index cards, three per student
>
> ❋ writing paper
>
> ❋ pens or pencils

WHAT TO DO:

1. Give each student three index cards and ask them to label each at the top with one of these three questions: *When is the best time to do things? Who is the most important one? What is the right thing to do?*

2. Allow time for students to write a one- or two-sentence answer to each question on the cards. Have them draw a line under their answer. For example, for "When is the best time to do things?" a student might write, "In the morning when you are fresh." Or, "Right away when you are thinking about it so you don't forget." Have the class share responses and discuss.

3. Read *The Three Questions* and stop after page 6, which reads, "'Fighting,' barked Pushkin right away."

4. Ask students to write more about each question underneath the line on the front of their index card. This time when they write, expect to see more thoughtful answers focused on a big idea. As they think about the ideas in the story, students get a chance to write at a deeper level, getting right to the heart of the main idea.

5. Finish reading *The Three Questions*. Direct students to use the back of their index cards to write reactions to Muth's answer for each question. Ask students to write about any surprises they experienced in Muth's answers—and/or have them compare Muth's answers to each of their own answers and discuss their pieces as a class.

FOLLOW-UP ACTIVITIES:

❋ Have students create skits based on the pieces they write, demonstrating the importance of the three questions in everyday life at school.

❋ Read Tolstoy's original short story "The Three Questions" and explore the way Muth changed the characters and details, yet maintained the original theme.

| Lesson #3 | **DEVELOPING THE TOPIC** |

In *The Secret Knowledge of Grown-Ups* (1998), David Wisniewski explains all the "secret" rules that grown-ups follow but conceal from children. The result is a book that overflows with humor, energy, and imagination. In this lesson, students write their own secret rules—a wonderful way to learn how to develop a topic.

WHAT TO DO:

1. Read *The Secret Knowledge of Grown-Ups* to the class and discuss the key ideas that the author uses to intrigue the reader.

2. Review the trait of ideas with students, showing why the author would score high in developing his topic.

3. Lead the class in a discussion about "secret rules" that most kids have to follow, such as eating their vegetables and combing their hair. Write students' ideas on a transparency. Then choose one or two ideas that small groups or pairs can write about on their own.

4. Discuss the voice that they think will work the best. Explore the differences between a kid's voice in writing and an adult's voice.

5. Look at the patterns of organization in *The Secret Knowledge of Grown-Ups* to help students decide on an organization to fit their "secret rule" idea.

6. Allow plenty of time for students to write their piece and illustrate it with markers, paints, magazine cut-outs, and so on. Be sure to plan time to share their final work.

FOLLOW-UP ACTIVITIES:

❖ Create collections of "secret rules" books and share them with other classes.

❖ Have students use their writer's notebooks to keep a running list of possible new rules for future writing topics.

MATERIALS:

❖ a copy of *The Secret Knowledge of Grown-Ups* by David Wisniewski

❖ overhead transparencies and markers

❖ writing paper

❖ pens or pencils

❖ markers, paints

❖ magazines to cut up

Lesson #4 USING DETAILS

I n *Nothing Ever Happens on 90th Street* (1997), Roni Schotter addresses the age-old complaint: "I have nothing to write about." Young Eva wanders through her neighborhood, soliciting advice on topics for a class assignment. Everyone from the fish salesman to the limousine driver offers delightful words of wisdom:

❊ Write about what you know.

❊ Find the poetry: a new way with old words.

❊ Use your imagination.

❊ Ask, "What if?"

❊ Add a little action.

❊ And, yes, observe carefully and don't forget the details.

The result is a picture book that could be the focus of an entire course on writing.

> **MATERIALS:**
>
> ❊ a copy of *Nothing Ever Happens on 90th Street* by Roni Schotter
>
> ❊ a checklist of tasks (below)
>
> ❊ book-making supplies: large sheets of white paper, magazines to cut up, markers, pens, pencils, glue, tape, scissors

WHAT TO DO:

1. Read aloud and discuss *Nothing Ever Happens on 90th Street*.

2. Give students a checklist of at least ten tasks to do around the school and tell them to check off each one as they accomplish it. They should spend no more than two minutes on each activity. Here is what your checklist might look like:

❊ Take a seat inside the media center.

❊ Hang out in the music room.

❊ Sit at a table in the cafeteria.

❊ Check out the action in the back foyer.

❊ Watch a gym class.

❊ See what is happening in the art room.

❊ Visit a classroom you've never seen before.

❊ Follow the secretary or the custodian for two minutes.

❊ Observe a class at recess.

❊ Count the number of cars that pull in and out of the parking lot.

3. Stagger where students start and request that they follow the sequence of tasks on the checklist to avoid overcrowding at individual locations. Ask them to record information about each place—the sights, the sounds, the feel, the people—on their own.

4. Encourage students to gather two or three interesting details about their observations at each station and record them on their checklist. Invite them to illustrate their details, just like Eva does in the story. Remind them to be "invisible" and courteous during their visits and to follow the advice of Eva's 90th Street neighbors.

5. Have students share their details when they return to the classroom. From there, ask them to write, illustrate, and bind "Nothing Ever Happens at [the name of your school]" stories of their own to display in the library or media center for schoolmates to enjoy. Be sure to put a copy of Schotter's book next to the student-written books so readers see how picture books inspire good writing.

FOLLOW-UP ACTIVITY:

❉ Ask students to repeat this exercise at home, noting all the little things about everyday life on their street.

Organization Lessons

Now let's explore strategies for building skills in organization—or the internal structure of the piece. We're specifically concerned with these key qualities:

❉ Creating the Lead

❉ Using Sequence Words

❉ Structuring the Body

❉ Ending With a Sense of Resolution

Part of being able to organize well is knowing how to lay out the details that guide the reader through the text. If the writer doesn't do that, it is enormously frustrating to the reader. The writer can't just let the details loose to head down an unpredictable trail. Who knows where the reader will end up?! Writing needs to be more of a highway that gets the readers to where they want to go, as they take in some interesting scenery, explore new terrain, and discover new things along the way.

| Lesson #1 | **CREATING THE LEAD** |

When a paper begins, "I'm going to tell you about . . ." readers hit the snooze button. But when it begins, "Bang! I woke up and wondered what on earth was going on," readers pay attention. They want to know where the writer is going. What follows is a lesson for helping students kick off their writing with a bang.

WHAT TO DO:

1. Write the following techniques for creating bold beginnings on the front of individual index cards, then write or draw the examples on the back.

Lights, Camera, Action—The writer makes something happen.
Example: "For the last time," my dad said. "Put your gum here."

Single Word—The writer sets off an important word by itself and follows it up with more information.
Example: Gum. Gum was everywhere. It was in my hair. It was in the carpet. It was on my pillow.

Fascinating Fact—The writer presents an intriguing piece of information.
Example: I blew a bubble bigger than my brother's head.

Imagine This—The writer captures a moment in words or pictures.
Example: The gum made my bangs stick straight out from my head.

It's Just My Opinion—The writer states a belief.
Example: Kids should be able to chew gum any time they want.

Listen Up—The writer describes a sound.
Example: Smack, snap, slurp.

I Wonder—The writer asks a question or a series of questions.
Example: Have you ever wondered how many pieces of gum will fit into the human mouth? Five? Ten? More?

2. Arrange students in groups of three or four. Give each group a card.

3. Have a member of each group read the techniques and the examples. Then tell groups to come up with another example.

4. Ask groups to write the new examples on the cards. Encourage students to add pictures if they think it will clarify the message.

5. Prepare an overhead transparency of the original list of techniques and examples. Read them one at a time and ask each group to share its new lead and the technique on which it's based. Be sure all groups have a chance to share.

6. Collect the cards and punch a hole in the top left corner of each for binding with the loose-leaf ring. Put this ring of leads in the writing center as a resource for students when they can't think of a way to begin future work.

7. Encourage students to add techniques and examples to the ring as they think of them.

| Lesson #2 | **USING SEQUENCE WORDS** |

In *The Secret Shortcut* (1996), Wendell and Floyd are prone to telling some pretty tall tales about why they are late to school. Aliens, pirates, and a plague of frogs are excuses tried but discarded because their teacher doesn't believe them. So the boys commit to getting to school on time by taking a shortcut, which turns out to be more of a problem than a solution. In this two-session lesson, students create their own "shortcut stories," using sequence words and phrases to guide the reader.

MATERIALS:

❊ a copy of *The Secret Shortcut* by Mark Teague

❊ chart paper

❊ writing paper

❊ pens or pencils

❊ markers and drawing/ construction paper

WHAT TO DO ON DAY 1:

1. Read *The Secret Shortcut* aloud.

2. Discuss and list on chart paper all the things that happen to Wendell and Floyd on the way to school. Hang the list in a prominent place so all students can see and refer to it.

3. Give groups of two or three students a large piece of drawing/construction paper and have them draw a map containing a brand-new shortcut to school for Wendell and Floyd. Encourage students to expand on the text by including things the characters might encounter along the way, such as volcanoes, quicksand, and bottomless pits.

WHAT TO DO ON DAY 2:

1. Discuss the student-created maps as a prewriting activity.

2. Ask the small groups to create new "Secret Shortcut" stories based on their maps, using a sentence starter such as, "Wendell and Floyd took a new shortcut to school," if you wish.

3. Discuss sequence words and phrases that can help organize the events in the story, such as:

before	*first*	*first of all*	*in turn*
after	*second*	*to begin with*	*later on*
then	*third*	*in the first place*	*meanwhile*
next	*earlier*	*at the same time*	*soon*
during	*later*	*for now*	*in the meantime*
finally	*now*	*for the time being*	*while*
sometimes	*last*	*the next step*	*simultaneously*
often	*at first*	*in time*	*afterward*

4. Have groups write at least three detailed sentences to describe each event on the map.

5. Tell students to describe each event in a paragraph that begins with a sequence word or phrase. For example, if the map shows a bottomless pit, they might begin the paragraph this way: "After reaching the bottomless pit, Wendell and Floyd tiptoed around the edges, trying frantically not to fall in. The pit was dark, shadowy, and seemed as though it was reaching out to grab them as they tried to sneak by."

FOLLOW-UP ACTIVITY:

❖ Have groups find examples of sequence words and phrases in other texts and talk about how they help link details and events. Ask students to make a chart with the words and phrases, with examples of how to use them. Hang the chart in the classroom. Then have students look through other picture books to find strong and obvious organizational patterns that really work.

Lesson #3 **STRUCTURING THE BODY**

Franklin D. Roosevelt's statement "The only thing we have to fear is fear itself" may have soothed a nation, but it didn't do a thing for the title character in *Scaredy Squirrel* (2006), because he is afraid of everything— particularly germs, sharks, tarantulas, poison ivy, killer bees, and green Martians. So he never strays from his nut tree. That is, until the day he is visited by an unwelcome guest and, while diving for his emergency kit, makes a surprising discovery about himself. Mélanie Watt's interplay of text and visuals is fascinating. She combines elements of fiction (plot, characters, and so on) with elements of nonfiction (lists, charts, schedules, plans, and so on), proving that good organization is not only achieved through words, sentences, and paragraphs. In this lesson, students create their own lists, schedules, plans, and charts, using Watts's sweet, lively book as a model.

> **MATERIALS:**
>
> ❋ a copy of *Scaredy Squirrel* (2006) by Mélanie Watt
>
> ❋ slips of paper
>
> ❋ a box or hat
>
> ❋ chart paper and markers

WHAT TO DO:

1. Read *Scaredy Squirrel* to the class.

2. Brainstorm with the class a list of things Scaredy Squirrel writes about that shows his personality: (a) greatest fears, (b) benefits and drawbacks of change (leaving nut tree), (c) daily routine, (d) emergency kit contents, and (e) emergency exit plan.

3. Discuss the ways each type of writing in the book is organized:

   ❋ a list of items on a common topic

   ❋ a chart comparing two items to show differences or similarities

   ❋ a schedule or timeline

   ❋ a step-by-step plan to solve a problem

4. Write each type of organization on a slip of paper and place it into a box or hat.

5. Arrange the students into small groups and have one person from each group draw a slip and read it to the group. This will be the organization for the upcoming group writing. Replace the slips of paper in the box before the next group draws so all groups have the same options.

6. Ask each group to come up with a new list, chart, schedule, or plan, depending on what its slip says: (a) things they do well in school, or (b) things they like and don't like about going to school, or (c) a schedule of their school day, or (d) a step-by-step plan to get out of the classroom in case of an emergency. Give students time to record their writing on a large sheet of chart paper and ask them to draw pictures to illustrate their ideas.

7. Share what each group wrote and how members organized their ideas. Compare the differences and similarities of how each piece is organized.

FOLLOW-UP ACTIVITIES:

❊ Discuss with students what makes the organization of writing such as that found in *Scaredy Squirrel* different from a story or good information book. Emphasize the different ways of organizing for different purposes to make the ideas stand out.

❊ Share Mélanie Watt's sequel to *Scaredy Squirrel*, *Scaredy Squirrel Makes a Friend* (2006), and discuss how it is organized.

| Lesson #4 | ENDING WITH A SENSE OF RESOLUTION |

Wrapping up a piece of writing is a challenge. Ask any writer. That's probably why a lot of young students cap theirs off with something like, "Now you know three reasons why hippopotamuses are ferocious," "I hope you liked my story," or the perennial favorite, "The end." What's reassuring, though, is that writers have choices.

> **MATERIALS:**
>
> ❊ a copy of *Charlie Anderson* by Barbara Abercrombie
>
> ❊ an overhead transparency and markers

In Barbara Abercrombie's *Charlie Anderson* (1995), the reader gets not one, not two, but three choices of ending. Charlie Anderson, a very fat, gray-striped cat, has it made. He gets to live in two houses with two families who love him. During the day, he eats and sleeps at one house. During the night, he does the same at the other house. But neither family knows it is sharing the cat. Both families think "their" cat is out hunting when he's not home, and it's only through a creative surprise ending, which works on several levels, that the truth is revealed.

WHAT TO DO:

1. Ask students, "What are some of the things authors do to signal to readers that they are wrapping things up?" Write students' ideas on the overhead. Their list may include "The End," "Thank you for reading my story," or "And then I woke up, and it was only a dream." They may also come up with more original ideas such as, "Since that day, I've never eaten green food." Discuss how effective each of these endings is and how important it is to conclude writing with a powerful thought, an image, or an idea that makes the reader think.

2. Show students *Charlie Anderson* and tell them it has three endings and one of them is a surprise.

3. Read the book aloud, pausing to show the pictures. When you come to the end, read the last three pages—the three endings—and let the last one sink in. Then ask, "Did this ending surprise anyone? Where in the story did the writer give us a little hint that set up this ending?"

4. Discuss how there's usually a clue to surprise endings earlier in the text so that the ending, while a surprise, makes sense. For example, early on, Abercrombie explains that Elizabeth and Sarah often visit their dad and stepmother in the city. So, when the story ends with the conclusion that the cat and the girls are lucky to have two families who love them, the reader thinks, "Oh, yeah!" This ending reveals the theme: There are other ways to love and be loved outside of a traditional family. Although intermediate writers most likely couldn't create endings as powerful as Abercrombie's, it's never too early to point them in the right direction.

5. Revisit the book's two other possible endings. In the first, the problem of who owns the cat is diplomatically resolved by renaming him Charlie Anderson, a combination of the names he was called by each family who thought he was exclusively theirs. The second ending deepens the reader's experience of the story. It becomes personal when one of the girls asks Charlie Anderson to declare which family he loves best.

6. Read the story again, focusing on the three endings. Pause after each, letting the artistry of the writer sink in.

7. Encourage students to look at the endings in other high-quality books. Do the authors wrap up the story convincingly, dig deep, or work with a big idea?

Voice Lessons

Can you teach voice? Our short answer: Yes! Although you can't focus on something as concrete as beginnings, middles, and endings as you can with organization, you can do many things to build awareness of the critical role voice plays in writing. You can engage students in activities that build skills in recognizing voice in the writing of others and in applying it to their own. Stories, essays, poems, lyrics, brochures, advertisements, posters, memos—all forms of writing contain voice and, therefore, are worth examining. And once students see the powerful influence voice has on those forms of writing, they'll be more inclined to use it in their own writing. This section shows you how to help them do just that by focusing on these key qualities:

❊ Establishing a Tone

❊ Conveying the Purpose

❊ Creating a Connection to the Audience

❊ Taking Risks to Create Voice

Lesson #1 | **ESTABLISHING A TONE**

Voice jumps out when the point of view from which a story is being told changes. Famous fairy tales are excellent models for demonstrating this because they typically contain very familiar characters with very divergent personalities and perspectives. Becky Bloom's *Wolf!* (1999), a take-off on "The Three Little Pigs," is one example of many picture books in which the author creates a new story from an old one by shifting the point of view from the victims to the villain.

> **MATERIALS:**
>
> ❊ a copy of *Wolf!* by Becky Bloom
>
> ❊ a copy of "The Three Little Pigs" (any traditional version)
>
> ❊ overhead transparencies and markers
>
> ❊ writing paper
>
> ❊ pens or pencils

WHAT TO DO:

1. Discuss the genre of fairy tales with the class. Ask students to name their favorites and talk about the familiar characters in them, such as the mean wolf and the frightened little girl in "Little Red Riding Hood."

2. Read "The Three Little Pigs" aloud and then ask students to identify the voices they noticed. Are they warm and friendly? Distant and menacing? Somber? Humorous? See if students can pinpoint the most prominent voice.

3. Read *Wolf!* aloud and then discuss the similarities and differences between it and "The Three Little Pigs." Were the characters the same in both stories? Did both tales contain the same plotline, including the beginning and ending? What about the setting?

4. Ask students to identify the voice in *Wolf!* Is it the same as or different from the one used in "The Three Little Pigs"? If students feel it's different, ask them *how* it is different.

5. Create a chart on the overhead that compares the voices in the two books. Here's what it might look like:

Voices From *Wolf!*	Voices From "The Three Little Pigs"
patronizing	honest
aloof	scared
confident	nervous
positive	determined

6. Arrange students in small groups. Ask each group to select a traditional fairy tale and write a new version from the perspective of a different character, just as Bloom did. Remind students to pay close attention to the voice in which they write.

FOLLOW-UP ACTIVITIES:

✤ Encourage students to illustrate their stories and share them with younger students at school.

✤ Turn the stories into scripts and have students perform them. Be sure to allow plenty of time for rehearsal beforehand to build confidence and reading fluency.

Lesson #2   **CONVEYING THE PURPOSE**

Students need to understand that knowing their purpose for writing is a key to choosing the right voice. For example, when a student writes a thank-you note to a grandparent, he or she typically uses a voice that expresses gratitude, appreciation, and love. However, if the same student writes to a toy company about a robot that broke the first time he or she played with it, that student would most likely use a voice that expresses frustration, disappointment, and even anger. In this lesson, students redesign a home's floor plan to get an important message about writing: choosing the right voice requires understanding one's purpose for writing.

MATERIALS:

✤ a simple floor plan of a house, apartment, or other residential building (Contact a local architectural firm or contractor to obtain copies at no cost.)

✤ paper, markers, pencils, crayons

WHAT TO DO:

1. Arrange students in groups of three or four. Give each group a copy of a floor plan. Ask each group to find the kitchen, bathroom, bedrooms, living room, laundry room, dining area, and family room.

2. Have each group select a room for an "extreme voice makeover." Tell them to radically change the room's size, shape, window locations, door locations, and so on, to make it more functional. In order to do this, it will be important for students to think about how the room was used—and could be used, given their changes. Have groups draw a picture of what the room looked like before the makeover and after it. Encourage students to emphasize how much the room has changed.

3. Attach their pictures to the floor plans.

4. Ask students to describe the room before and after the makeover. They may say, "The kitchen had no counter space, so we put an island in the middle of it . . . with a built-in cotton candy maker!"

5. Have students write a description of the person they think would use the new room, matching their design decisions to the person's personality.

6. Ask students how redesigning a room to meet a specific purpose is like writing to meet a specific purpose. And how does writing to meet a specific purpose relate to the trait of voice? Record their ideas on a chart and discuss them.

| Lesson #3 | **CREATING A CONNECTION TO THE AUDIENCE** |

To a large extent, writing with voice means writing with emotion. A young mother's memoir about having a baby may be joyful. A commuter's editorial about rising gas prices may be angry. A soldier's letter from the front lines may be cheerful, but tinged with sadness and even fear. *Yesterday I Had the Blues* (2003) is full of emotion, as described by a young boy who starts out with the blues, but winds up with the "greens" (hopeful). His daddy has the "grays" (tense), his mama has the "reds" (annoyed), his sister has the "pinks" (cheerful), and so forth. By the end, we realize what the boy truly has is a real family with real feelings. In this lesson, students talk about a time they had the blues, as well as the greens, grays, reds, pinks, and so forth. From there, they put their ideas on paper. You'll be amazed at how colorful their voices can be.

> **MATERIALS:**
>
> ❋ a copy of *Yesterday I Had the Blues* by Jeron Ashford Frame
>
> ❋ writing paper
>
> ❋ pencils, crayons, markers
>
> ❋ magazines to cut up

WHAT TO DO:

1. Ask students to think about the mood they were in when they woke up. Were they in a good mood, looking forward to going to school? Or, were they in a bad mood, wishing they could roll over and go back to sleep? Perhaps they were feeling yet another way?

2. Have them talk to a partner about their mood and select a color that matches it. If they were happy, for instance, they might pick bright green or yellow. If they were sad, they might choose gray, brown, or black. Encourage them to match their mood to a color as closely as they can.

3. Read *Yesterday I Had the Blues* to the class, showing the pictures as you go.

4. Ask students to name the mood of each character and how they identified it. Their answers should include the color that the author used as well as his description of the character.

5. Instruct students to talk to their partner again about the mood they were in when they got ready for school and refine their thoughts, based on *Yesterday I Had the Blues*.

6. Ask students to write about and illustrate on paper their mood, explaining the color they think best reflects that mood and why they chose it.

7. Share the mood pieces with the class and discuss them. Explain to students that writing should capture mood, or voice, to help the reader feel what the writer is feeling.

FOLLOW-UP ACTIVITIES:

❉ Help students create a book of colors and moods. Print lists of colors from the Internet and ask students to attach a mood to each one. Then bind the lists as a book for student to consult when they write.

❉ Share *The Sound of Colors: A Journey of the Imagination* (2006) by Jimmy Liao and discuss how the author describes colors. Ask students to discuss the book's voice and how color helped them to identify that voice.

| Lesson #4 | **TAKING RISKS TO CREATE VOICE** |

To create writing with voice—writing that speaks directly to the reader—students must take risks. In other words, they must express ideas in interesting, original ways. They must try things that few writers have tried before. They must experiment. By doing so, they arrive at a voice that is appropriate for their audience. In this lesson, students take risks by writing about one idea from various points of view.

> **MATERIALS:**
>
> ❈ chart paper or overhead transparencies and markers
> ❈ writing paper
> ❈ pens or pencils

WHAT TO DO:

1. Write the following voiceless piece on chart paper or an overhead transparency and read it aloud to the class:

> "Rip in the Pants" by a fourth grader
>
> Just about a week ago my teacher had a rip in his pants. It was really funny. I didn't see it right away but someone told me then I saw it and wanted to laugh but I held it in. Then someone told him and everyone started to laugh. Then he went home to change.
>
> The End.

Discuss students' reaction to the piece.

2. Divide the class into small groups and, on chart paper or a transparency, jot down possible points of view for the writing:

   ❈   the student

   ❈   the principal

   ❈   the teacher

   ❈   another teacher

   ❈   a student who likes the teacher

   ❈   a student who dislikes the teacher

   ❈   the pants

3. Assign a point of view to each group of students and ask members to brainstorm ideas about how the voice would be different if the piece had been written from that point of view. For instance, what would the voice sound like if a student wrote about a teacher's pants ripping instead of the teacher himself writing about it?

4. Ask groups to rewrite the piece in the voice they feel is most appropriate. Three examples to share follow.

From the point of view of a student in the class:

Last week, my teacher Mr. Carroll had a colossal tear in the back of his pants. It happened when his pants got caught on the chalkboard edge. At first, I didn't notice it, but then my friend told me. We wanted to laugh at his bright pink boxers. We giggled, and he asked us what was so funny. We told him, and his face turned brighter than his boxers. He ran to the office to get Mrs. Holladay to sub for a while as he ran home to get changed. The whole class burst into laughter, and people had tears falling down their cheeks. We talked about it for the rest of the class. The next day, Mr. Carroll was very quiet and stayed as far away as possible from the chalkboard. He told us not to tell anyone. He would be the laughing stock of the school, the punch line in the teachers' lounge! Too late.

From the point of view of the teacher:

Rip! I didn't think much of it. Kids are always ripping something. I continued to teach. Giggle, snicker, snicker. I didn't think much of it. Students get off task. I addressed the giggling, and continued to teach. I felt a draft. I didn't think much of it, until I realized there shouldn't be a draft, especially there. I continued to teach. Then, a slow tingling, horrifying realization. The rip was from me and my pants—in a place it shouldn't be. The laughs were at me and my new drafty trousers. The red burned slowly from my neck to my forehead. My eyes met theirs. "Well," I said, "just get over it."

From the point of view of the pants:

This is not right. I wasn't made to be worn by a guy this big. Oww! Every time he does anything but stand still, I hurt. I'm packed, pulled, and stretched so tight I can hardly breathe. I need relief. What I really want is revenge. I know . . . I'll rip! Ha! That'll show him. But wait, what happens next? Maybe he'll just throw me out, and I'll never see the light of day again. Man, oh, man, why couldn't I be a tie? That way, I could choke him!

5. When students have finished, have a volunteer from each group read their piece aloud. Then ask the rest of the class to identify the voice and discuss whether it's appropriate for the person or thing speaking.

FOLLOW-UP ACTIVITIES:

❖ Read a picture book and have students think of how the voice might change if the story were told from various characters' points of view.

❖ Encourage students to explore all the possible voices for pieces they're working on. Once they've pinpointed an appropriate voice, have them add details that bring it out.

Word Choice Lessons

English is a complicated language, and it is easy for students to get lost in it. Intermediate students need help using familiar words in their writing and trying new ones. Reading to them, asking them questions about language, and piquing their curiosity about words will help students understand why it's important to find "just right" words as we write. The next section will help you do that. It contains lessons organized according to the following key qualities:

* ❊ Applying Strong Verbs

* ❊ Selecting Striking Words and Phrases

* ❊ Using Specific and Accurate Words

* ❊ Choosing Words That Deepen Meaning

| Lesson #1 | **APPLYING STRONG VERBS** |

Word choice is about using rich, colorful, precise language that communicates not just in a functional way, but also in a moving and enlightening way. In this lesson, students explore the role of verbs in *Into the A, B, Sea* (2001), a delightful, rhyming book about sea animals, and then create their own books about land animals. In the process, they see just how powerful applying strong verbs can be.

MATERIALS:

* ❊ a copy of *Into the A, B, Sea* by Deborah Lee Rose

* ❊ drawing paper

* ❊ markers, crayons, paints

* ❊ animal pictures cut from magazines or printed out from Web sites

WHAT TO DO:

1. Read *Into the A, B, Sea* to students, showing the pictures as you go.

2. Ask students to tell you which animals' actions were the most interesting to them and explain why. Point out the verb Rose used for each of those animals. Remind students that choosing the right verbs—verbs that capture the action perfectly—can make a piece of writing enticing, interesting, and memorable.

3. Ask students to recall for you any of the animals whose actions surprised them or stuck in their minds. Point out the precision of the verb in each case and why such precision is characteristic of memorable writing.

4. Tell students you're going to reread the book, but this time you want them to write down six of their favorite animals and their actions—for example, *anemones sting, barnacles cling; octopuses hide, penguins glide; sea stars grab, tiger sharks nab.*

5. When you've finished reading, ask students to share their animals and verbs. Then tell them they are going to use powerful verbs to write about land animals, the way Rose does about sea animals in her book.

6. Assign students individual letters of the alphabet and ask them to use print and electronic resources to find an animal that begins with that letter—one that lives in the forest, in the jungle, or on the plains.

7. Pair up students and have them brainstorm verbs that describe their animals' actions. For example, "Aardvarks burrow, amble, forage, and lick." If a student isn't sure of typical actions for an animal, demonstrate how to find that information in books or on the Internet.

8. From their lists of possibilities, tell students to select their favorite verb—the one that sounds good and captures the animal's action precisely, such as "aardvarks amble," and consider synonyms for that verb, such as *shuffle, meander,* and *stroll.*

9. Ask students to write the name of their animal and its action on a sheet of drawing paper, along with a sentence that contains those two words—for example, "Aardvarks amble across the plains, looking for a tasty meal of grubs." Then, ask them to include a list of synonyms they considered: *shuffle, meander, stroll.* And, finally, have them illustrate their animal in action, using markers, crayons, paints, and pictures cut from magazines or printed out from Web sites.

10. Bind the pictures together to make a class book entitled *ABC Land Animals*—or hang the pictures alphabetically in a prominent place in the classroom or hallway.

11. Discuss with students what this lesson taught them about applying strong verbs. Give students time to talk to a partner and then ask for volunteers to share key qualities of the word choice trait. Record these qualities on the board or on a chart for students to consider when working on future writing projects.

Lesson #2	**SELECTING STRIKING WORDS AND PHRASES**

The main character in *Fancy Nancy* (2006) is fancy. She likes to wear fancy clothes, eat fancy food, and, most of all, use fancy words like *chauffeur, plume,* and *merci.* However, her family is not fancy. Her mom, dad, and sister are perfectly content wearing T-shirts, eating ice-cream cones, and using ordinary words like *driver, feather,* and *thanks.* So Nancy takes it upon herself to educate them about the finer things in life by giving them a formal lesson, which ends in a wild game of dress-up. Then, to her delight, her dad suggests dinner out at the finest pizza joint in town. All heads turn when Nancy and her family enter the restaurant still wearing their flamboyant getups. "They probably think we're movie stars," Nancy muses. But then an embarrassing incident occurs, forcing her to rethink her priorities. In the lesson, students get a chance to look closely at Nancy's word choices and then try their hand at using fancy words of their own.

> **MATERIALS:**
>
> ❋ a copy of *Fancy Nancy* by Jane O'Connor
>
> ❋ chart paper and markers
>
> ❋ photocopies of the "Plain" Words List (page 64)
>
> ❋ photocopies of the "Fancy" Words List (page 64)

WHAT TO DO:

1. Read *Fancy Nancy* to students, pausing to point out some of the more interesting words as you read.

2. On the chart paper, make a list of the "fancy" words from the text: *fuchsia, plume, stupendous, accessories, posh, chauffeur, parfaits,* and *dressing gown.*

3. Ask students to tell you what the fancy words mean in plain English. Then write their responses next to each word. Encourage students to use the story context to guess the meaning of the fancy words if they are unfamiliar.

4. Discuss why authors are careful about choosing just-right words and how those words make the ideas more interesting.

5. Make photocopies of the "Fancy" Words List and "Plain" Words List. Cut them apart so that single words are on individual strips.

6. Divide the class in half. Give one "fancy" word to each student in one group. Give a "plain" word to each student in the other group.

7. Tell students that they have two minutes to find their word's partner. They should move around the room, calling out their word until they find a match. If students with "fancy" words ask for help, consult the master list at the top of the next page and give synonyms to help them figure out the meaning of their word.

Master List

bad: ghastly	big: enormous
good: delightful	cool: marvelous
happy: blissful	fast: swift
blue: turquoise	lazy: sluggish
sad: gloomy	hard: challenging
run: gallop	nice: pleasing
pretty: glamorous	walk: stroll

8. When students have found their matching word, ask them to sit down so that they don't distract others who are continuing to look.

9. Once all the students have found their matching word, ask them to come up in pairs to record their words on the chart paper under the headings "fancy" and "plain."

10. Ask students if they have any favorite "fancy" words and, if so, encourage students to write them in their writer's notebooks to use in their own writing later.

"Plain" Words List

bad	happy
sad	blue
run	pretty
big	good
cool	fast
lazy	hard
nice	walk

"Fancy" Words List

ghastly	blissful
gloomy	turquoise
gallop	glamorous
enormous	delightful
marvelous	swift
sluggish	challenging
pleasing	stroll

Lesson #3 | Using Specific and Accurate Words

Choosing the right words is essential to writing well, but learning how to do that takes time and practice. In this lesson, students examine a fascinating and fun nonfiction book, *Blood & Gore Like You've Never Seen!* (1997), for its specific and accurate use of scientific words. As you read the book aloud, students listen for unfamiliar words and use context clues to arrive at their meanings. From there, they create a poster using some of the specific and accurate words they learned from the book.

Materials:

- a copy of *Blood & Gore Like You've Never Seen!* by Vicki Cobb
- overhead transparencies and marker
- a photocopy of each of the following passages from the book: Blood, Skin, Bone , Muscle, Nerves, Digestion, Respiration
- poster board
- markers

What to Do:

1. Explain to students that you are going to read to them part of *Blood & Gore Like You've Never Seen!*, which contains lots of scientific facts about the human body—in particular about blood, skin, bone, muscle, nerves, and the digestive and respiratory systems. Read the table of contents aloud and ask students to vote on which section you will read.

2. Once a winner has been declared, ask students to call out any scientific words or phrases they anticipate will be included in the section. Record those words on a transparency entitled "Words and Phrases From *Blood & Gore*."

3. Show students the pictures that go with the passage they selected. Explain that an electron microscope was used to capture these photographs, sometimes magnifying parts of the human body millions of times.

4. Read the section aloud. When you have finished, ask students to recall some of the words or phrases that stuck in their minds and record them on the transparency.

5. Ask students to go back to the list of words and phrases and identify any that are scientific. Put a star next to those words and phrases.

6. Tell students to look at the list again and identify words or phrases that are not scientific but are memorable or interesting. Put two stars next to those words and phrases.

7. Discuss students' word choices and emphasize how Cobb not only uses accurate and specific words, but also lively and engaging words to explore scientific information.

8. Arrange students into small groups and give each group a photocopied passage from *Blood & Gore* dealing with one of the following topics: Blood, Skin, Bone, Muscle, Nerves, Digestion, and Respiration.

9. Tell students to read their passage and think about how Cobb uses words to convey information about the human body.

10. Ask each group to make a poster advertising the importance of their assigned body part or function. Tell them their posters must include the following:

   ❋ a slogan that captures the importance of the body part or function

   ❋ text written in first person; they should write from the point of view of this body part or function

   ❋ information about what happens if their part or function is not working properly

   ❋ at least three fascinating facts about their part or function

   ❋ a picture (either drawn or photocopied) illustrating their part or function—where it fits into the body and how it works

11. If you wish, have students read and research more about their topics in books, magazines, or science-related Web sites.

12. Ask students to highlight words or phrases that specifically and accurately explain their topics so they stand out on their posters.

13. When the posters are finished, invite another class to your classroom and ask your students to share their posters. Invite the visiting students to vote for the poster that has the most specific and accurate use of scientific language.

| Lesson #4 | **CHOOSING WORDS THAT DEEPEN MEANING** |

New words are added to the English language regularly. Browse the latest edition of an unabridged dictionary in your school library. Chances are, you'll find words and phrases you never would have dreamed of finding just ten years ago, such as *9/11* and *blog*. In this lesson, students explore the dictionary and then come up with their own words and phrases to add to it and use in their writing.

MATERIALS:

   ❋ writing paper
   ❋ pens or pencils
   ❋ dictionaries
   ❋ drawing paper and markers

WHAT TO DO:

1. Encourage students to explore the dictionary and make lists on the board of words they find interesting.

2. Brainstorm a list of words students can't find in the dictionary but think should be added. These words might include slang or references to popular TV shows, commercials, movies, favorite foods, or music they enjoy, such as *Big Mac* or *fantabulous*.

3. Ask each student to select one word from the list and write it down.

4. Tell students to illustrate the word, putting it in an appropriate context to help a reader understand its meaning. For example, if the word is *Spider-Man*, the student might draw a picture of the superhero scaling the Empire State Building and casting a web.

5. Ask students to write one interesting thing about the word on the same page. They may write, for example, "Spider-Man is a brave hero who saves people."

6. Post the work in a place for everyone to read and enjoy. Encourage students to use the words in their writing.

Sentence Fluency Lessons

Read the final lines of E. B. White's *Charlotte's Web* (1952):

> Wilbur never forgot Charlotte. Although he loved her children and grandchildren dearly, none of the new spiders ever quite took her place in his heart. She was in a class by herself. It's not often that someone comes along who is a true friend and a good writer. Charlotte was both.

The first time we read this passage, we wondered, "Is this as well written as we think it is?" The second time confirmed it—"Yes!" The syntax, or the sentence structure, is masterful. Using short sentences followed by longer ones, and ending on the shortest one of all, creates a lovely cadence and nails the book's central message about the importance of communication and companionship.

The lessons that follow address the range of sentence fluency skills at play in every intermediate classroom, from crafting simple sentences to full-blown essays and stories. We've organized them into four key qualities:

* Capturing Smooth and Rhythmic Flow

* Crafting Well-Built Sentences

* Varying Sentence Patterns

* Breaking the "Rules" to Create Fluency

| Lesson #1 | **CAPTURING SMOOTH AND RHYTHMIC FLOW** |

In this lesson, we encourage you to read aloud "What Is Green?," one of many stunning poems in Mary O'Neill's *Hailstones and Halibut Bones* (1961). "What Is Green?" contains carefully chosen words in just the right places, producing smooth and rhythmic flow. Then discuss with students the importance of sentence fluency in both poetry and prose. From there, students try changing sentence beginnings and lengths in their own writing to create the same kind of flow they discovered in O'Neill's writing.

> **MATERIALS:**
> ❋ a copy of *Hailstones and Halibut Bones* by Mary O'Neill
> ❋ chart paper with O'Neill's poem "What Is Green?" written on it

WHAT TO DO:

1. Discuss sentence fluency with students, emphasizing that it is the auditory trait. So when writers apply the trait, they think about the lengths of their sentences, the beginnings and endings of their sentences, how the words and phrases within their sentences sound, and how their sentences sound when they're strung together. Tell students that you will be reading aloud a poem and ask them to listen closely for fluency.

2. Read "What Is Green?" Take your time reading, emphasizing O'Neill's beautiful phrasing.

3. Enjoy yourself. When you're finished, ask students:

   ❋ "Did you think this piece was fluent?"

   ❋ "What did the writer do to make it sound good?"

   ❋ "What image or phrase stood out for you?"

   ❋ Show students the poem on the chart paper and ask:
   "Where is your favorite image or phrase? The beginning of a line? At the end? In the middle?"

4. Remind students that being fluent means writing sentences that do not all sound alike. Give them an example of a piece of writing with sentences that begin the same way and are the same length:

   ❋ My dog is big.   ❋ My dog is funny.

   ❋ My dog is red.   ❋ My dog smells.

5. Ask students to help you make one or more of these sentences more fluent. They might combine two or three sentences into one or they might try a new sentence beginning: "My big, red dog smells funny." "My dog is funny, and he smells." "It's funny to watch my big, red dog."

Getting Started With the Traits: Grades 3–5

6. Write their revisions on the board or on a chart to illustrate how to make bland, boring sentences sound more interesting.

FOLLOW-UP ACTIVITY:

❖ Tell students that you are going to create a piece of writing together. Write the first sentence on the board or overhead, such as: "When I wake up in the morning, I'm excited to come to school," and then ask one of them to give you the next sentence. And here's the fun part: their new sentence must begin with the last word of the first sentence. For example; "School is a fun place to play and learn." (You can use a form of the word if it makes it easier for students, and for you!)

Lesson #2 | CRAFTING WELL-BUILT SENTENCES

Most intermediate students struggle with sentence variety. They either write one long sentence or a series of short sentences, without understanding that the key to writing fluent pieces is *combining* sentences of differing lengths. What better way to build that understanding than by having children act out sentences? In this engaging lesson, students make sentences in a variety of lengths, using word cards, their bodies, and their imaginations.

MATERIALS:

❖ 8½-by-11-inch cards

❖ markers

WHAT TO DO:

1. Come up with a basic sentence, such as "My dog is brown," and write each word on a separate card. Give the cards to four students and ask them to create the sentence by lining up in the right order with their cards facing out. Ask the students to read their sentence aloud one card at a time.

2. Create more cards with words for expanding the basic sentence. You could write "fuzzy" or "snuggly" to modify "dog." Give the cards to other students and ask them to figure out how to weave them into the basic sentence in a way that makes sense, then to stand where they think their word would go.

3. Add as many words as you like and allow students time to make the best sentence they can. Each time students incorporate a new word, have them read the sentence aloud in its entirety one card at a time.

4. Repeat this lesson often, using new, interesting words to help students learn how to write sentences of different lengths.

| **VARYING SENTENCE PATTERNS**

*C*ome On, Rain! (1999) is an elegantly written book about a young girl and her mother who long for the rain on a hot summer's day. Because of its beautiful blend of dialogue and description, it invites expressive oral reading. Karen Hesse's words are pure poetry. This lesson uses *Come On, Rain!* as a model for showing students how to vary sentence length and type effectively in writing.

WHAT TO DO:

1. Tell students that you will be reading *Come On, Rain!* to them. But first, you want to review the different types of sentences that Karen Hesse uses in the book:

   Declarative: a statement
   Example: It was raining outside all day.

   Imperative: a command
   Example: Go get your boots and put them on.

   Interrogative: a question
   Example: Why aren't you wearing your rain boots?

   Exclamatory: an exclamation
   Example: Yikes!

2. Write these definitions and examples on a transparency and offer other examples from *Come On, Rain!*

   ❊ Come on, rain! (exclamatory)

   ❊ I am sizzling like a hot potato. (declarative)

   ❊ Put on your suit and come straight over. (imperative)

   ❊ Is that thunder, Tessie? (interrogative)

   ❊ Slick with sweat, I run back home and slip up the steps past Mamma. (declarative)

   ❊ Stay where I can find you. (imperative)

   ❊ I hug Mamma hard, and she hugs me back. (declarative)

   ❊ May I put on my bathing suit? (interrogative)

3. Read *Come On, Rain!* slowly and carefully, emphasizing the finely crafted sentences throughout. Ask students to listen to how the sentences flow from beginning to end.

MATERIALS:

❊ a copy of *Come On, Rain!* by Karen Hesse

❊ photocopies of the Sentence Fluency Script (page 72)

❊ photocopies of the Sentence Fluency Cards (page 73)

❊ poster board

❊ markers

4. Ask for four volunteers to come to the front of the class. Give each one a copy of the Sentence Fluency Script (page 72), and assign parts. Tell the volunteers they will be reading the script aloud to the class and allow time for them to practice their lines.

5. While the volunteers are practicing, hand out photocopies of the Sentence Fluency Cards (page 73) to the rest of the class and have students cut them apart.

6. Ask the volunteers to read the script in its entirety, using expression to help the class begin to identify each type of sentence.

7. Have the volunteers read the script again, pausing after each line. Let the rest of the class determine which type of sentence was read and hold up the appropriate card. (Answers: 1. Declarative 2. Interrogative 3. Declarative 4. Interrogative 5. Declarative 6. Imperative 7. Declarative 8. Imperative 9. Exclamatory)

8. Inform students they are going to use these sentence types in a piece of their own about weather.

9. Brainstorm with the class different kinds of weather conditions such as snowy, foggy, hailing, sunny, and windy. Write the examples on the board.

10. Have students choose a partner and select one of the weather conditions as the subject for a piece of writing they will work on together: song lyrics to promote the positive qualities of the type of weather they chose.

11. Brainstorm with the class a list of familiar songs such as "Mary Had a Little Lamb," "Row, Row, Row Your Boat," The Hokey Pokey," "Old McDonald Had a Farm," and "B-I-N-G-O." Write these songs on the board and ask partners to pick one.

12. Tell partners to write out new lyrics for one verse of the song they chose, using as many of the sentence types as they can: declarative, imperative, interrogative, and exclamatory. Remind them that their song is going to be used to "sell" their type of weather, so they should include as much interesting information about it as possible.

13. When partners have completed a draft, ask them to assess their lyrics for sentence fluency and revise as necessary.

14. When students have finished revising their lyrics, ask them to put the new verse on a poster. Hang up the posters in a prominent place, and then sing all the songs as a class.

15. Ask students which songs contain the best sentence variety and vote for the song that best advertises a particular kind of weather. Discuss how sentence fluency makes the ideas more interesting.

16. Encourage students to write out their songs and send them to a local TV or radio station for use during an upcoming weather broadcast.

Sentence Fluency Script

Adapted from *Come On, Rain!* by Karen Hesse

READER 1: I hold my breath, waiting. A breeze blows the thin curtains into the kitchen, then sucks them back against the screen. (Declarative)

READER 2: "Is there thunder?" Mamma asks. (Interrogative)

READER 3: "No thunder," I say. (Declarative)

READER 4: "Is there lightning?" Mamma asks. (Interrogative)

READER 1: "No lightning," Jackie-Joyce says. (Declarative)

READER 2: "Stay where I can find you," Mamma says. (Imperative)

READER 3: "We will," I say. (Declarative)

READER 4: "Go on then," Mamma says, lifting the glass to her lips to take a sip. (Imperative)

ALL: "Come on, rain!" I cheer, peeling out of my clothes and into my suit, while Jackie-Joyce runs to get Liz and Rosemary. (Exclamatory)

Getting Started With the Traits: Grades 3–5 © 2009 Ruth Culham and Raymond Coutu, Scholastic.

Sentence Fluency Cards

Interrogative

Declarative

Imperative

Exclamatory

Lesson #4 **BREAKING THE "RULES" TO CREATE FLUENCY**

I n *One Tiny Turtle* (2001), Nicola Davies uses fluid, descriptive language to explain the life cycle of loggerhead sea turtles. And, as with her books on whales, bats, and polar bears, she drops in "factlets" throughout—interesting, well-researched bits of information that provide the reader with another way to interact with her beautifully written text. In this lesson, while listening to *One Tiny Turtle* read aloud, students determine whether sentences are complete or fragments. Then they use what they learn to write picture captions that present facts about loggerhead sea turtles.

> **MATERIALS:**
>
> ❋ a copy of *One Tiny Turtle* by Nicola Davies
>
> ❋ writing paper
>
> ❋ pens, pencils, markers, crayons
>
> ❋ chart paper

WHAT TO DO:

1. Ask students if they have ever heard of loggerhead sea turtles and, if so, to explain what they know.

2. Tell them you are going to read a book about loggerhead sea turtles and as you read, you'd like them to listen not only for fascinating pieces of information, but also for the author's sentence fluency—how she makes the text easy to listen to.

3. Read the book, pausing to show the pictures as you go. When you come to a page that has informational notes, or "factlets," show students how the author sets factlets apart from the running text. Ask if they hear any difference in the sentence fluency of factlets versus the running text.

4. Explain to students that complete sentences have a subject and a verb (a doer and an action). Fragments are only parts of sentences. Tell students that writers use complete sentences most often, but occasionally they use a fragment to change the way a passage sounds. Fragments can change the rhythm and tempo of the writing to make it pleasing to the ear. They can also be used to make important ideas stand out in the text.

5. Tell students you are going to reread some sentences from the book, and they are going to determine whether the sentences are complete or not by listening to them carefully.

6. Read the following sentences aloud to the students. Tell them to put a thumb up if they think a sentence is complete and down if they think it is not. If you wish, make an overhead to show after students have made their decisions.

   ❋ She's a baby, so her shell is soft as old leather. (thumb up)

   ❋ Safe in her world of weed (thumb down)

✻ Fish breathe underwater, but turtles are reptiles. (thumb up)

✻ She pokes her pinprick nostrils through the silver surface to take a quick breath, so fast, blink and you'd miss it! (thumb up)

✻ When you look for her (thumb down)

✻ Rides out the storm (thumb down)

✻ Her head is tough as a helmet. (thumb up)

✻ A glimpse of her (thumb down)

✻ Left behind, under the sand, her eggs stay deep and safe. (thumb up)

✻ And before the summer's over they wriggle from their shells. (thumb up)

✻ Swims and swims! (thumb down)

✻ One day, she'll remember this beach and come back. (thumb up)

7. Tell students they are going to try writing complete and incomplete sentences of their own. Ask them to recall a fact about loggerhead turtles from the text and write it out in a complete sentence.

8. Have students draw a picture to go along with their sentence and write a short caption underneath it that is a fragment.

9. Compare the two pieces of writing, pointing out for students what makes one a complete sentence and the other a fragment. Discuss how students can use fragments in their writing to change how the fluency sounds to the reader.

FOLLOW-UP ACTIVITIES:

✻ During the discussion of the book, students most likely had questions about loggerhead sea turtles that the book couldn't answer. Help them to write these questions out and use the Internet to find answers. Then, write the questions and answers on chart paper for all to see. Use complete sentences for the questions and fragments for the answers, explaining that writers do this all the time when they want to fit a lot of information into a small space.

✻ Read and enjoy other books by Nicola Davies, such as *Bat Loves the Night; Extreme Animals; White Owl, Barn Owl; Ice Bear; Big Blue Whale;* and *Surprising Sharks.* You and your students will delight in how beautifully Davies writes, and how fascinating she makes each animal.

Conventions Lessons

When it comes to teaching conventions, it's important to start simply and put students in control as quickly as possible. You can edit for students or you can teach them how to do it themselves. It's not a hard decision when put that way, is it? A word of warning, though: young writers won't edit as well, work as quickly, or be as thorough as mature writers. But if they learn new skills gradually, perhaps one each week, and practice until these skills become second nature, they will progress. Have faith in your students and in your teaching. The lessons that follow are called "warm-ups," quick reproducible activities designed to help you teach a range of skills, at the start of writing time:

* Checking Spelling

* Punctuating and Paragraphing Effectively

* Capitalizing Correctly

* Applying Grammar and Usage

To get to the point where students are truly in charge of their own editing, we have to abandon time-honored methods of correcting with a red pencil, giving students practice worksheets, and only publishing work that is perfect. These warm-ups will help you get your students to that point.

MATERIALS:

* overhead transparencies and photocopies of one of the Warm-Ups on pages 78–82, editor's marks on page 107

* a blank transparency

* photocopies of the Student-Friendly Scoring Guide for Conventions on page 112

WHAT TO DO:

1. Choose one of the Warm-Ups on pages 78–82. Make an overhead transparency of it, and the editor's marks on page 109. Also, make enough photocopies of both pages for each student in your class.

2. Project the Warm-Up transparency and briefly discuss the Check It! box at the bottom so students understand questions they should be asking themselves as they edit.

3. Distribute the photocopies of the Warm-Up and editor's marks. Tell students to complete the Warm-Up by themselves or with a partner, following the directions at the top of the sheet.

4. When they're finished, ask students to help you mark the errors on the Warm-Up transparency, using editor's marks. If you like, check their responses against the answer key on pages 83–84.

Lesson #2 **Warm-Up**

Use the editor's marks to correct the sentences below. The number of errors you should try to find is indicated after each sentence. Then use your corrected sentences to create a well-edited paragraph on a separate sheet.

Skateboarding to get around some people In 2002, a sports' data in the world

Eigty perce & 74 perc

Skate Boo 20 yeers,

Lesson #1 **Warm-Up**

Use the editor's marks to correct the sentences below. The number of errors you should try to find is indicated after each sentence. Then use your corrected sentences to create a well-edited paragraph on a separate sheet of paper.

A individual from History I realy admire is abraham lincoln (6)

he is an intresting person and a Great president, to. (5)

It musta been very hard back in the 1860S to fight aganst all the people which wanted to kepe slavery. (6)

But if lincoln hadnt be strong and stood up for his beleifs, we wood not have abolished slavery. (5)

he was the rite man to be President of the united states' at the time. (6)

Check It!

Is the punctuation correct and does it guide the reader through the text?
Did I capitalize all the right words?
Is my spelling accurate—especially for words I read and write a lot?
Did I follow grammar rules to make my writing clear and readable?
Did I indent paragraphs in all the right places?

See answers, page 83, and editor's marks, page 109.

78

5. From there, have students share the well-edited paragraphs they created on a separate sheet of paper. Write a well-edited paragraph of your own on a blank transparency.

6. If time allows, encourage students to choose pieces from their writing folders to edit for spelling, punctuation, capitalization, and grammar and usage. Then have them assess their work using the Student-Friendly Scoring Guide on page 112. Linking Warm-Ups to their own work builds independence.

For scores of reproducible warm-ups to share with your students, see *Daily Trait Warm-Ups: 180 Revision and Editing Activities to Kick Off Writing Time* (Scholastic, 2009).

Warm-Up

Use the editor's marks to correct the sentences below. The number of errors you should try to find is indicated after each sentence. Then use your corrected sentences to create a well-edited paragraph on a separate sheet of paper.

A individual from History I realy admire is abraham lincoln (6)

he is an intresting person and a Great president, to. (5)

It musta been very hard back in the 1860S to fight aganst all the people which wanted to kepe slavery. (6)

But if lincoln hadnt be strong and stood up for his beleifs, we wood not have abolished slavery. (5)

he was the rite man to be President of the united states' at the time. (6)

Check It!

❋ Is the punctuation correct and does it guide the reader through the text?

❋ Did I capitalize all the right words?

❋ Is my spelling accurate—especially for words I read and write a lot?

❋ Did I follow grammar rules to make my writing clear and readable?

❋ Did I indent paragraphs in all the right places?

See answers, page 83, and editor's marks, page 109.

 Getting Started With the Traits: Grades 3–5 © 2009 Ruth Culham and Raymond Coutu, Scholastic.

Warm-Up

Use the editor's marks to correct the sentences below. The number of errors you should try to find is indicated after each sentence. Then use your corrected sentences to create a well-edited paragraph on a separate sheet of paper.

Skatebording can be an Art a Hobby a Sport, or just a way to get around conveniently. (6)

some peopl call it a extreem sport because it is so creativ. (5)

In 2002, a report from the marketing research firm american sports' data revealed that their were 12.5 million skateboarders in the world. (5)

Eigty percent of those Skateboarder's were under the age of 18, & 74 percent is mail. (6)

Skate Boarding are a sport that has really taken of in the last 20 yeers. (5)

Check It!

❋ Is the punctuation correct and does it guide the reader through the text?

❋ Did I capitalize all the right words?

❋ Is my spelling accurate—especially for words I read and write a lot?

❋ Did I follow grammar rules to make my writing clear and readable?

❋ Did I indent paragraphs in all the right places?

See answers, page 83, and editor's marks, page 109.

Warm-Up

Use the editor's marks to correct the sentences below. The number of errors you should try to find is indicated after each sentence. Then use your corrected sentences to create a well-edited paragraph on a separate sheet of paper.

Becomeing a Teacher is alot of hard work and takes meny year's of Study. (6)

They are a wonder ful job, however, 'cuz you get to help kids' lern. (6)

what culd possibly be moore rewarding then that (5)

Although their are many difficult things to learn to be a good Teacher, its a very worthwhile Profesion. (5)

helping a New Generation learn how to read & rite is an awesome responsibility and alot of fun, to. (7)

Check It!

❋ Is the punctuation correct and does it guide the reader through the text?

❋ Did I capitalize all the right words?

❋ Is my spelling accurate—especially for words I read and write a lot?

❋ Did I follow grammar rules to make my writing clear and readable?

❋ Did I indent paragraphs in all the right places?

See answers, page 83, and editor's marks, page 109.

Getting Started With the Traits: Grades 3–5 © 2009 Ruth Culham and Raymond Coutu, Scholastic.

Warm-Up

Use the editor's marks to correct the sentences below. The number of errors you should try to find is indicated after each sentence. Then use your corrected sentences to create a well-edited paragraph on a separate sheet of paper.

last year there was two earthquakes you could really feel in san Francisco. (3)

I know because my friends cusin lives their. (3)

She calls california the shaek-n-bake state because they are so many earthquakes and it was so hot. (4)

buildings has to be bilt to a special code to make sure their stable. (4)

Otherwise, theyl just crumbled into dust (3)

Check It!

* Is the punctuation correct and does it guide the reader through the text?
* Did I capitalize all the right words?
* Is my spelling accurate—especially for words I read and write a lot?
* Did I follow grammar rules to make my writing clear and readable?
* Did I indent paragraphs in all the right places?

See answers, page 84, and editor's marks, page 109.

Warm-Up

Use the editor's marks to correct the sentences below. The number of errors you should try to find is indicated after each sentence. Then use your corrected sentences to create a well-edited paragraph on a separate sheet of paper.

Its so hard togo to bed wen my parents tell me too (5)

i try hard to fall asleep, but its not easy when its still light out or when im not tyred. (5)

Sometimes I hid a book under the covers and read latee in to the nyght (5)

I turns the light out really fast if I here my Mom or dad comming to chek on me (6)

with the covers puled up, I try to breathe normaly until them have left the room, and than I go back to reading untill I fall asleep. (6)

Check It!

❋ Is the punctuation correct and does it guide the reader through the text?

❋ Did I capitalize all the right words?

❋ Is my spelling accurate—especially for words I read and write a lot?

❋ Did I follow grammar rules to make my writing clear and readable?

❋ Did I indent paragraphs in all the right places?

See answers, page 84, and editor's marks, page 109.

Answer Key

LESSON #1

An individual from History I really admire is abraham lincoln.
he is an intresting person and a Great president, to.
It musta been very hard back in the 1860s to fight against all the people which wanted to kepe slavery.
But if lincoln hadnt be strong and stood up for his beleifs we wood not have abolished slavery.
he was the rite man to be President of the united states at the time.

> An individual from history I really admire is Abraham Lincoln. He was an interesting person and a great president, too. It must have been very hard back in the 1860s to fight against all the people who wanted to keep slavery. But if Lincoln hadn't been strong and stood up for his beliefs, we would not have abolished slavery. He was the right man to be president of the United States at the time.

LESSON #2

Skateboarding can be an Art, a Hobby, a Sport, or just a way to get around conveniently.
some people call it a extreem sport because it is so creativ.
In 2002, a report from the marketing research firm american sports data revealed that their were 12.5 million skateboarders in the world.
Eigty percent of those Skateboarders were under the age of 18, & 74 percent is mail.
Skate Boarding are a sport that has really taken of in the last 20 yeers.

> Skateboarding can be an art, a hobby, a sport, or just a way to get around conveniently. Some people call it an extreme sport because it is so creative. In 2002, a report from the marketing research firm American Sports Data revealed that there were 12.5 million skateboarders in the world. Eighty percent of those skateboarders were under the age of 18, and 74 percent were male. Skateboarding is a sport that has really taken off in the last 20 years.

LESSON #3

Becomeing a Teacher is alot of hard work and takes meny years of Study.
They are a wonder ful job, however, cuz you get to help kids lern.
what culd possibly be moyre rewarding then that?
Although their are many difficult things to learn to be a good Teacher, its a very worthwhile Profesion.
helping a New Generation learn how to read & rite is an awesome responsibility and alot of fun, to.

Becoming a teacher is a lot of hard work and takes many years of study. It is a wonderful job, however, because you get to help kids learn. What could possibly be more rewarding than that? Although there are many difficult things to learn to be a good teacher, it's a very worthwhile profession. Helping a new generation learn how to read and write is an awesome responsibility and a lot of fun, too.

LESSON #4

last year there was two earthquakes you could really feel in san Francisco.
I know because my friends cusin lives their.
She calls california the shaek-n-bake state because they are so many earthquakes and it was so hot.
buildings has to be bilt to a special code to make sure their stable.
Otherwise, theyl just crumbled into dust

Last year there were two earthquakes you could really feel in San Francisco. I know because my friend's cousin lives there. She calls California the shake-n-bake state because there are so many earthquakes and it is so hot. Buildings have to be built to a special code to make sure they're stable. Otherwise, they'll just crumble into dust.

LESSON #5

Its so hard togo to bed wen my parents tell me too.
i try hard to fall asleep, but its not easy when its still light out or when im not tyred.
Sometimes I hid a book under the covers and read later in to the nyght.
I turns the light out really fast if I here my Mom or dad comming to chek on me.
with the covers puled up, I try to breathe normaly until them have left the room, and than I go back to reading untill I fall asleep.

It's so hard to go to bed when my parents tell me to. I try hard to fall asleep but it's not easy when it's still light out or when I'm not tired. Sometimes I hide a book under the covers and read late into the night. I turn the light out really fast if I hear my mom or dad coming to check on me. With the covers pulled up, I try to breathe normally until they have left the room, and then I go back to reading until I fall asleep.

Publishing Tips

After students have gotten what they want to say down on paper, they are ready to publish. Publishing is an important step because, finally, it makes the writing available to the audience for which it is intended. Student writing may be put on bulletin boards, made into books, shared with other classes or audiences, or sent home as "finished." When students are ready to have their work go public, consider these tips.

* Keep available plenty of writing supplies such as pens, pencils, markers, and paper of different types and colors, as well as scissors, tape, glue, and stickers. Take time to show students how to make books by folding paper and, if they are ready, cutting and stapling the books. Keep models available for students to follow.

* Encourage students to practice making neat letters in their own writing, not on worksheets. Ask students to select a sentence or passage to rewrite in their best handwriting.

* Remind students to leave plenty of space between lines in drafts to allow room for revisions and edits.

* Show students interesting text layouts as you discover them. One of our favorites is the Geronimo Stilton chapter-book series from Scholastic. Key words and phrases throughout the texts are presented in color and creative shapes for emphasis. Encourage students to try writing this way.

* Hang students' work in the room, in the hallway, and all around the school.

* Attach a photo of the student to his or her work to make a powerful connection between the writing and the writer. If possible, add a photo of a parent or guardian with the child to reinforce the fact that writing should extend beyond school walls.

* Help students keep writer's notebooks all year. At the end of the year, collect them, gift-wrap them over the summer, and return them to students at the start of the following school year. After clearing their minds over the summer and then reading their entries from the year before, chances are students will be amazed by their progress in all traits and be excited to dive back in.

Concluding Thought

You know better than anyone that working with upper-elementary students can be messy. Holding their attention, keeping them on task, and moving them forward is a challenge. But with the right routines in place, it's not impossible. In fact, it can be extremely satisfying for you and your students. Carrying out whole-class lessons on a regular basis is an essential routine. Another one is providing practice opportunities through independent and small-group work. In the next chapter, you'll find a host of activities that are perfect for doing just that.

Chapter 4

Trait-Based Activities for Independent and Small-Group Work

Once you've had a chance to work on a trait as a whole group, it's important to give students a chance to practice the trait on their own. This chapter contains activities designed to get them started. You'll find eight activities for each trait, organized by key quality—fun, classroom-tested activities that are sure to get your students drafting, revising, editing, and sharing their finished work with great pride.

We've also included student-friendly scoring guides for each trait (pages 110–112), so students can easily assess their work as they write and look for places to revise and edit. These scoring guides can be used in conjunction with the revision checklist (page 108) and the list of editor's marks (page 109), which contain handy reminders of things all writers need to think about as they bring their work to completion.

Ideas Activities

FINDING A TOPIC

Free Ideas

The topics we enjoy writing about most are the ones that matter to us. So help students look for experiences and ideas they really care about. Here are some ways to do that:

* *Free writing:* Ask students, "What's on your mind? What have you been thinking about lately? What are you feeling right now?" Then suggest they "Start writing to find out! One idea will lead to others."

* *Flashback:* Have students look through their journal entries or family photographs for ideas. Or have them dig out old toys, collections, or souvenirs at home. Encourage them to look for things that stimulate memories and feelings.

✳ *Favorite places:* Invite students to think about some place they love to go: the beach, the mountains, their grandparents' house, a tree house, a playing field, or an amusement park. Make a class list of favorite places to go and things to do there. From there, start writing.

Corral Ideas

Jotting down interesting tidbits as we encounter them is a good way to find ideas. And a writer's notebook is an excellent tool for doing that. As students ask questions about something the class is reading, something they heard on the news, or as you help them make the links between what they are studying and what they still want to know, have them write these kernels of ideas down in a notebook. These kernels can be big or small, old or new. Students just need a place to capture what intrigues them, issues that cause them to question things, and observations they make that fascinate them. Then later, when it is time to write, they can look back in their notebook and find things they have probably forgotten, but may make for interesting ideas for study, research, and writing. With notebooks, you may never hear "I don't know what to write about" again!

FOCUSING THE TOPIC

Call It Out

Pick a category such as "animals." Call out questions and encourage students to chime in with different answers. Go from general questions to narrow ones, such as "What kind of animal is it? Where does it live? What does it eat? Does it do anything interesting? What is a predator of this animal?" It should only take three to five minutes to work through a whole cycle, from a general topic to a narrow one. Keep asking questions until the category has been examined from many possible views. Then record some of the narrowed topics on the board and let students do a quick write, about five minutes long, on one of them.

Picture This

Bring in a poster-sized art print of a complex and interesting work that you think your students will enjoy analyzing, such as Pablo Picasso's *Guernica*. Display the print and ask students to write down what they see in a series of statements (complete or not). Next, take six precut pieces of paper, which together would cover the entire picture, and cover five-sixths of the print. Now, ask students to look closely at what they see and describe it. Continue moving the paper so that students get a chance to describe all six parts of the poster out of context. Finally, uncover the whole picture again and ask them to describe it one more time. Not only will they be more focused and use better descriptions, but they will also create a richer variety of work as a class.

DEVELOPING THE TOPIC

Ask Me a Question

Divide students into groups of three. Each student tells the group a short story of a memorable event in his or her life. The listeners cannot comment during or after. Instead, they write on a piece of paper three questions for the storyteller. They hand questions to the storyteller. That way, the storyteller becomes aware of details he or she might have left out, which can be included next time the story is told, either orally or in writing.

Leave It Out

Rewrite a familiar story—a simple story your students have read and enjoyed, such as "Rumpelstiltskin." Take out some of the juicy details, ones that are important to the central idea of the story, such as the guessing of the name or the wishes. Share the story as you rewrote it and ask students what is missing. Now read the original. Discuss which version makes more sense, is more interesting, and why. Help students discover that taking time to elaborate and fill in the blanks for the reader is an important step in making their ideas clear.

USING DETAILS

Observe Closely, Then Write

Ask students to observe their surroundings while hiking in the park, having a snack in the playground, or enjoying a day at the beach, and record their observations on a chart. (See example at right.) Be sure they sit long enough to observe details—small creatures scurrying by or clouds high above, for instance. Make students dig deep and use their senses. Ask them to report to their classmates things that were most interesting, important, and unusual. As a final step, students can write longer pieces about their experiences. Encourage them to show, not just tell. Teach them how to expand their ideas by including lively details. Compile these writings into a book.

Name MATT K.	Date	Location Forest Park	
What I:	Interesting	Important	Unusual
Saw SMALL YOUNG BUSHES DIFFERENT SIZES. GROWING IN THE OPEN BURNED SPACES. LOTS OF PRETTIE T. TREES	BIG DEAD TREES, BURNED SCARRED TRUNKS		
Heard AT LEAST 3 DIFFERENT KINDS OF BIRDS – SOME ALL THE TIME, SOME JUST A FEW CHIRPS			BIG TRUCKS, MAYBE LOGGING OVER THE HILLS OUT OF SIGHT – CONSTANT DRONING
Felt UNEVEN FOREST FLOOR, UNDER MY SHOES, MAKES IT	SUNSHINE ON MY FACE WARM HARD TO WALK FAST. DEAD CRUMBLY PINE NEEDLES.		
Smelled	DEEP BREATHES, FEELS GOOD, NO POLLUTION, CRISP, FRESH		
Tasted			PB&J SANDWICH REALLY TASTES GOOD THE WALK MADE ME HUNGRY, BUT FOOD TASTES BETTER THAN USUAL.

Pick the Postcard

Find a set of postcards on a single topic such as dogs, beach scenes, or city buildings. (You'll find them at most stores that sell greeting cards, as well as museum stores and stationery stores.) Give one postcard to each student and ask them to write a paragraph about the image that is so descriptive, readers will be able to identify the postcard in the set. Once students have finished writing, collect and display all the postcards. Have students read their paragraphs aloud and see if classmates can guess the card. Discuss the techniques that some writers used that made the matching of the text to the card easier—the more specific the details, the quicker the match.

Organization Activities

CREATING THE LEAD

Share Student Leads

Ask students to share just the leads from their work. As they read them in small groups or in a large circle, their classmates get ideas of different ways to begin their work.

After everyone has read, brainstorm a general list of different techniques to begin writing, and then identify those techniques a writer would use for specific kinds of writing. Encourage students to try several different leads before settling on the final one.

Share Examples From Literature

Share short excerpts from a variety of different sources so students can see how professional writers choose to begin their work. Here are some examples of beginnings that work tremendously well:

"What they don't understand about birthdays and what they never tell you is that when you're eleven, you're also ten, and nine, and eight, and seven, and six, and five and four, and three, and two and one."
—Sandra Cisneros, *Woman Hollering Creek*, from "Eleven," 1991

"Gramps says that I am a country girl at heart, and that is true. I have lived most of my thirteen years in Bybanks, Kentucky, which is not much more than a caboodle of houses rooting in a green spot alongside the Ohio River."
—Sharon Creech, *Walk Two Moons*, 1994

> ### WAYS TO BEGIN A PIECE OF WRITING
>
> ❖ A thought-provoking question to make the reader wonder
>
> ❖ A little "sip" of the conclusion to get the reader's attention and pique his or her interest
>
> ❖ A funny story or personal anecdote to set a humorous or individual tone
>
> ❖ A list of main points to introduce the topic in a serious, logical, and straightforward manner
>
> ❖ A dramatic, sweeping, or eye-opening statement
>
> ❖ An expert quotation to establish credibility from the start
>
> ❖ The student's own angle— one that readers have never seen before

"It was not that Omri didn't appreciate Patrick's birthday present to him. Far from it. He was really very grateful—sort of. It was, without a doubt, very kind of Patrick to give Omri anything at all, let alone a secondhand plastic Indian that he himself had finished with."
—Lynne Reid Banks *The Indian in the Cupboard*, 1980

USING SEQUENCE WORDS

Mix It Up

To reinforce sequencing, reorder a poem, magazine article, literature story, recipe, student paper, or any other kind of continuous text and ask students to reassemble it in the correct order. Cut the text into pieces so students can play with it like a puzzle. Ask them to look for transition words, the lead sentence, then the conclusion. It is important to start with a concrete, linear piece of writing and then move on to pieces that are more abstract.

Putting It in Order

Read aloud a familiar story to a group. When you're finished, choose a child to stand and tell the beginning of the story. Then choose another child to stand and tell the ending. Next, have another child tell the middle of the story, while standing between the children who told the beginning and ending. Have more volunteers add to the story, placing them in their logical position in line.

STRUCTURING THE BODY

Teach Organizational Options

Information can be organized in many ways. Helping students choose the best way is a little like picking out shoes. Sometimes they might want dressy and formal; other times, more relaxed and casual. Maybe one of these organizational "shoes" fits their topic and purpose— or perhaps they can find another style or structure that's a better fit. It's our job to help students try things on, to guide them.

* **Organizing by Space.** If students were describing, say, a room, they might begin with the big impression—size or color—then move gradually to smaller details: furniture, windows, lighting, rugs; then toys, pictures, figurines; then the spider on the window ledge, the half-eaten candy bar, the open book, the sock on the rug.

* **Organizing by Time.** If students are writing stories, or explaining events, they might organize chronologically. Be sure they include specific events, but not every one, because their papers will grow too big, sprawling, and unmanageable. This can happen if students begin too far before the real story even starts. They shouldn't keep going too long after the real story ends, either. Encourage students to keep their stories small—begin with what matters, and when the story ends, stop.

* **Organizing by Content.** Let's say a student is writing an informational piece on black bears. The student could begin by listing all the important things he or she knows. For the body of the paper, he or she might group details together into subcategories; for example, what black bears eat, where they live, their natural enemies, and so on. From there, the student would write paragraphs developing these categories. This approach keeps a writer from skipping around. Then, encourage the student to end with a surprise or an important tidbit: "Though often feared, black bears rarely attack people." Discourage him or her from "pre-organizing" the writing into nice, little five-paragraph themes. If there are more than five subcategories, great. If there are fewer, but with more details, that's fine, too.

* **Organizing by Perspective.** For a persuasive essay, it is important to keep everything focused on the main issue. Have students begin with a clear statement of their position. Then, tell them to lay out the arguments in favor of and against the issue. Students should give the best evidence they can to support the side they feel is right. Urge them to end with a strong conclusion that focuses on the advantages of their position.

ENDING WITH A SENSE OF RESOLUTION

Look to Authors

Probably the best way to study endings is to read a bunch of them. There are so many pieces of fiction and nonfiction available—pieces that you and your students will enjoy reading as you observe how the writers crafted their conclusions. Select a few models from literature that show the variety of techniques authors use. Here are a few to get you started:

A Profound Thought—to take a bit of common knowledge to a new level
> Example: "Miss Honey was still hugging the tiny girl in her arms and neither of them said a word as they stood there watching the big black car tearing round the corner at the end of the road and disappearing forever into the distance."
> —Roald Dahl, *Matilda*, 1988

A Surprise—to close on an unexpected note, inspired by an important moment or recurring theme in the text
> Example: "Once again, the tarot cards lay before him. Once again, he heard the cathedral bells ring twelve times. At the stroke of midnight, he flipped over the first card. It was THE SERVANT. Smiling broadly, Fabrizio turned the next card. . . ."
> —Avi, *Midnight Magic*, 1999

Scoring Guides

Sample Papers

Lessons

Activities

FAQs

A Quote—to reinforce key points made in the text

> Example: "Very softly, she half sang, half hummed a song that her grandmother used to sing . . . 'If only, if only, the moon speaks no reply; Reflecting the sun and all that's gone by. Be strong my weary wolf, turn around boldly, Fly high, my baby bird, My angel, my only.'"
> —Louis Sachar, *Holes*, 1998

A Tie-Up—to take care of loose ends and answer lingering questions the reader may still have about key points

> Example: "Then I ran ahead to put the plates on the table."
> —Jean Fritz, *Homesick: My Own Story*, 1982

A Question or Open-Ended Statement—to leave the reader on an uncertain note

> Example: "And soon, they were rolling on again, leaving Treegap behind, and as they went, the tinkling little melody of a music box drifted out behind them and was lost at last far down the road."
> —Natalie Babbitt, *Tuck Everlasting*, 1975

A Challenge—to take action

> Example: "Be smarter than I was: Go talk to Grandma and Grandpa, Mom and Dad and other relatives and friends. Discover and remember what they have to say about what they learned growing up. By keeping their stories alive you make them, and yourself, immortal."
> —Christopher Paul Curtis, *Bud, Not Buddy*, 1999

A Summary—to make key points one more time

> Example: "And because so many of them were always begging him to tell and tell again the story of his adventures on the peach, he thought it would be nice if one day he sat down and wrote a book. So he did. And that is what you have just finished reading."
> —Roald Dahl, *James and the Giant Peach*, 1961

A Literary Device—to create a lasting image using, for example, a metaphor

> Example: "This is why, walking across a school campus on this particular December morning, I keep searching the sky. As if I expected to see, rather like hearts, a lost pair of kites hurrying toward heaven."
> —Truman Capote, *A Christmas Memory,* 1956

A Laugh—to make the reader smile at the end

> Example: "'Oh, I will,' said Harry, and they were surprised at the grin that was spreading over his face. 'They don't know we're not allowed to use magic at home. I'm going to have a lot of fun with Dudley this summer. . . .'"
> —J. K. Rowling, *Harry Potter and the Sorcerer's Stone*, 1997

Practice What You See

Ask students to choose one of the techniques and try it on a piece of their own writing to see if it works. Have them share their endings in small groups and offer suggestions for revisions to one another. Don't forget to include picture books as resources. Since picture books are so short, you can examine many different techniques rather quickly. Another good way to look for well-crafted endings is to read through nonfiction sources such as encyclopedias, research articles, letters, and memos.

Voice Activities

ESTABLISHING A TONE

Illustrate the Trait

Students will enjoy the challenge of drawing visual representations of voice (or any of the traits, for that matter). They can write out their own explanation of the trait, or draw a picture or icon they feel represents the trait. Creating a visual representation of the trait enables students to think deeply about the central meaning of the trait.

Voice Out, Voice In

This is a simple activity, but it works well. Find a sample of writing that is devoid of voice. They are everywhere. Manuals and textbooks are often a good source; memos are, too. Have students, working individually or in pairs, rewrite the piece, trying to put in as much voice as possible. Read the revisions aloud to appreciate the contrast.

Try this activity in reverse, too. Strange as it may seem, taking voice out of a piece is also a good activity for building students' awareness of this trait, since to remove it, they must understand what it is!

CONVEYING THE PURPOSE

Voice in Art

Gather four or five art prints that depict the same subject, such as fruit, people, scenery, or buildings. Make sure you choose artists whose styles differ significantly. Your school's media center may have study prints, or your local art museum may have pictures that it loans to schools for art education programs. Don't forget the Internet. Images of art through the centuries, from old-world to modern, are readily available online.

Ask students to compare the prints and make lists of the ways they are alike and how they are different. If you choose images of people, for instance, ask students to give you specific examples of how a picture of a man by Picasso is different from one by Michelangelo. Help students see that each artist develops a distinctive voice through his or her work and, over time, that voice becomes recognizable to others.

Compare and Contrast

Find two or three books on the same topic, but by authors with different styles. For young children, a good place to begin is with folk or fairy tales—two versions of "Cinderella," for instance. There are wonderful examples of fairy tales that have been written in traditional narrative form and also as scripts for plays.

Older students might like to look at the differences in an expository text on the same topic. Find an encyclopedia entry on, say, spiders. Now look in other places, such as a museum guide that accompanies an exhibit on spiders, or a science magazine such as *Ranger Rick*, to find other examples of writing about the creature. Where else might you go? How about an excerpt from a novel such as *Spider Boy* (1997) by Ralph Fletcher? Now look at the different ways the author of each piece writes about spiders. Trust us, there will be a significant difference in voice.

CREATING A CONNECTION TO THE AUDIENCE

Make a Book of Books You Love

The books we love most are often those that ring with voice. Make lists of favorites and share them aloud. Keep a class book of favorites and ask students to add names and titles to it regularly. And be sure to tell students what you've been reading. Share favorite passages and let them see how good writing affects you. Give students time to do the same, either in small groups, in large groups, or with younger students. Listen carefully to what they have to say. What a refreshing alternative to the standard book report. And, look, no papers to correct!

New Voices, New Choices

Have students write the first sentence of a letter to five different audiences. If students are studying the effects of global warming, for instance, ask them to write to the local newspaper, their grandmother, an anti-environmentalist, a friend, and the president of a local consumer-rights group. Discuss how the voice in the writing will change depending on the intended audience. Students can also share other places to which they might write letters and who the audience would be. Now ask them to describe the voice that would be appropriate for each of those audiences.

TAKING RISKS TO CREATE VOICE

Historically BOLD?

Think back to the people and events that really stick in your mind. What makes this person or event so memorable? Talk to students about it. If the event changed history, or if the person accomplished something extraordinary, point out that history is determined by people who are bold and willing to stand up for what they believe in. This is what we want students to do in their writing, after all: take a stand, defend a position, think about things in new ways, astound and amaze us. Voice will help them do that.

You can extend this activity, too. After the discussion, ask students to assume the point of view of an important historical figure, such as Albert Einstein, Rosa Parks, or Sacagawea, and write a letter of application for a job. Brainstorm with the students what kinds of jobs each person might want to pursue. In their letters, encourage students to assume the powerful voice of this person in such a way that he or she would surely get the job.

The Old Switcheroo

Ask students to think about a favorite story, such as "Goldilocks and the Three Bears" or "Cinderella." Allow time for them to tell the story to a partner. Next, challenge students to change their story by telling it from the point of view of one of the other characters, or from someone who might have a different perspective on the event. After students have told and retold their stories, ask them if the voice changed. If so, why? If not, why not?

Word Choice Activities

APPLYING STRONG VERBS

Active and Passive Verbs

Nothing works harder in a sentence than the verb. Pound for pound, students get their money's worth by paying attention to the power that verbs bring to the piece. Other word forms carry a great deal of impact, such as precise nouns and modifiers. But in our book, it's the verbs that earn the most respect. And the use of active verbs over passive verbs makes the writing more vigorous. Consider the following:

While running, Frankie passed Johnny. (*active voice*)
While running, Johnny was passed by Frankie. (*passive voice*)

Ask students to find an example of each in one of their textbooks, and give them this advice: If the subject is the doer, the verb is in the active voice. If the subject is the receiver, the verb is in the passive voice.

Here's to Adverbs—or Not!

Want to have some fun with parts of speech? Try this. Divide the class into an even number of groups: pros and cons. Review the list of parts of speech students should know, and ask a set of two groups to debate the pros and cons—to use it or not, how to use it well in writing, how to abuse it. Make sure there is a pro and a con to each part of speech—one group that's for using it, another that's against using it. Use these jewels of examples from Mem Fox and Stephen King to get students started.

> Pro: "In the same way that weak nouns require adjectives to pep them up, weak verbs scream out for adverbs to help them along."
> —Mem Fox, (1993)

> Con: "I believe the road to hell is paved with adverbs . . . they're like dandelions. If you have one on your lawn, it looks pretty and unique. If you fail to root it out, however, you find five the next day . . . fifty the day after that. . . ."
> —Stephen King, (2000)

SELECTING STRIKING WORDS AND PHRASES

Rice Cakes or Salsa?

As students discover some of the less interesting words in their work, teach them to ask, "Is this a 'rice cake' word or a 'salsa' word?" Every paper should have salsa words! Use this analogy frequently, and students will begin to use it every day. One teacher shared that at the end of the day, as she was dismissing class, she said, "Have a nice afternoon and evening." To which a few students replied, *"Nice is a rice cake word!"*

Words, Words Everywhere

One year Ruth was assigned to a classroom that had no windows. It was truly awful. The students and she missed seeing the first snow, the brilliant blue sky, the bursts of rain that would soak them to the skin in just a minute or two—all the beauty of the outside world. During these long, sensory-deprived years in the classroom, she discovered a way to help students with words.

1. On 4- x 6-inch strips of bright neon paper that doesn't fade over time (you can buy it at an office supply store), print in bold the words you are discovering during reading and writing activities. Be sure to include precise nouns, descriptive adjectives, and energetic verbs.

2. Write each word on a slip of paper that is color coded according to part of speech: for example, red for verbs, green for nouns, and blue for adjectives. With the help of the students, pin the slips to the ceiling.

3. As you read and find new words to add throughout the year, have students look them up and write them on the color-coded slips of paper. Not only will they get practice spotting new and interesting words, determining their parts of speech, and building a collection, they will use the words in their writing.

4. Everyone needs to tune out and daydream occasionally, and since Ruth's students had no window to gaze out, she gave them words to stare at. She was surprised at how many of those words found their way into student writing. They were bright, colorful, and useful. It helped.

USING SPECIFIC AND ACCURATE WORDS

The More Detail, the Better

Have all students study the same object to see who can observe the most details—and the most *unusual* details. If possible, use a live (and lively!) subject for this activity—a chameleon or tarantula, for instance. Give students one minute to study the object you have selected, then put it away. Now allow one minute for students to write down everything they can remember about the object. Share ideas as a group and make one big list of details for the object. Repeat this activity several times until students begin seeing details easily and are able to record quite a few in the time allowed.

Describe It, Then Build It

Create two identical collections of building materials—blocks, sticks, cardboard, paper, pipe cleaners, corks, buttons, paper clips, and so forth. Then have students work in teams of three. One student builds something from the collection while a second student waits in another room or behind a barrier with the same collection of building materials. The third student observes the first construction, then describes it in detail to the second builder, who tries to replicate the creation of the first builder. The second builder must work only from the description without looking at the first builder's creation. After about fifteen minutes, tell the teams to stop and get together to observe their constructions. As a class, discuss the role of specific and accurate details, particularly when giving directions or instructions.

CHOOSING WORDS THAT DEEPEN MEANING

Is More Always Better?

If your students have discovered descriptive language and are trying just a little too hard to make sure every sentence is chock full of it, you might show them the other side of the coin. We want students to try new ways of saying things—even if, at first, it isn't very successful. But we don't want them to think that more is necessarily better all the time. Try rewriting common signs such as road signs, warning signs, business signs, and so forth, using flowery and highly descriptive language. Compare the original to the rewrite and challenge students to be specific about why one is more effective than the other. For example: "Caution: Children Crossing" could be overwritten to: "You better slow down a little. There are some pretty nice kids who go to school here and they often walk or ride their bikes along here. Sometimes they aren't listening and looking for traffic, and it could be dangerous for them if you didn't slow down." That would be quite a road sign, wouldn't it? Sometimes one or two words work more effectively than longer, more descriptive sentences.

What's in a Word?

Choose a word that everyone uses when things are going well or to describe a good situation, such as *cool.* Ask students to write a list of other everyday words and phrases that mean the same thing—things they might hear in conversation or find in stories. Also, have students go home and interview one or two people from an earlier generation for more synonyms for *cool.* Gather as many examples as possible as a class. Here are some starters to seed the list if necessary:

bad	*outta sight*	*terrific*
super-duper	*rad*	*hip*
awesome	*groovy*	*happenin'*
fantabulous	*excellent*	*hot*
tight	*far out*	*phat*

Sort the words into three categories: (1) the way I say it, (2) the way my parents say it, and (3) the way my grandparents say it. Make a chart to hang in the room. As students hear new ways to express the idea, invite them to add those words to the list. By examining contemporary language use, students find that every generation develops its own way to express itself, even when the expressions themselves wind up being similar. Cool, dude.

Sentence Fluency Activities

CAPTURING SMOOTH AND RHYTHMIC FLOW

I've Got Rhythm

Hearing good language read aloud builds fluency even in young writers who are themselves not yet ready to begin writing complex sentences. Share a piece of poetry that's fun to read aloud. Some poems work so hard at rhyming that much of the natural flow is lost, so pick one that is easy to read aloud and emphasizes the use of comfortable, natural language. Some prose pieces, such as Mem Fox's *Tough Boris* (1994) and *Koala Lou* (1989), also have natural rhythm and repeating refrains that students pick up and repeat on their own.

Music to Our Ears

Use the music of classic works such as "Peter and the Wolf" and "Carnival of the Animals" to develop sentence fluency skills. As you play a piece of music, let students close their eyes and enjoy it. Then, play it a second time; only this time, invite them to pick a section and write a description of what they think is happening. Challenge students to capture the same fluidity of the music in their descriptions. From "Peter and the Wolf," one sixth-grade student wrote: "I could really tell when the scary part was coming. The music sped up and got faster and faster and I felt myself tensing up until BAM, the wolf pounced."

CRAFTING WELL-BUILT SENTENCES

Which Is Better?

Share two versions of a piece of writing. They will have the same content, but very different sounds. One should be made up of short, choppy sentences; for example:

> We went to the beach. It was sunny. It was warm. We had fun.
> We flew kites and ate hot dogs.

And the other, one continuous sentence:

> We spent a warm, sunny day at the beach eating hot dogs and flying kites.

Ask students which version they prefer and why. Discuss how the flow of the sentence can enhance meaning. You may have to share a number of examples before students begin to hear the differences.

Extra, Extra, Read All About It

Teach students the types of sentences they can use in their writing by exploring the newspaper. First, explain that reporters need to make sense of the information they receive. When they tell their readers what was said, they may restate the questions and even quote some of the answers. Reporters will use various kinds of sentences in their articles. Second, hand out sections of the newspaper to small groups and ask them to find examples of different sentence patterns: declarative (makes a statement of fact or argument), interrogative (asks a question), imperative (gives a direct command), or exclamatory (makes a more forceful statement than the declarative). Then ask students to circle an example of each kind of sentence from their section of the newspaper. Share examples with the class. Discuss which types of sentences they would use in their writing for a story, an essay, or a piece of persuasion.

VARYING SENTENCE PATTERNS

End With a Noun

One of the best tips a teacher ever shared with Ruth to make her sentences more powerful was to end them with a noun. As Ruth reads other texts and revises her own, she finds the passages she believes to be the strongest do exactly that—they end with a noun. It's perfectly correct to use verbs, pronouns, and adjectives, but nouns seem to pack the most punch. Not in all cases, of course, but it is advice worth considering when you struggle with just the right way to say something. Take a sentence, such as the first one below, and play around with it. Try ending it with different parts of speech and decide which is the most effectively written sentence.

> A rolling stone gathers no moss. (noun)
> If a stone rolls, hardly any moss will be gathered. (verb)
> If you are concerned about moss gathering on a stone, roll it. (pronoun)
> When trying to get rid of moss, roll the stone quickly. (adverb)
> If you roll the stone, the moss will become smooth. (adjective)

Pass It On

Give students a short beginning sentence—"The night was dark and stormy," for example. They'll then take the last word of the sentence and begin the next sentence with that word: "Stormy, that wasn't even the half of it." Keep going until the stories or essays are finished:

> "It hadn't been this windy and rainy in years, and I felt a little scared all
> alone. Alone in my grandparents house for the first time, my common sense
> told me I had nothing to be frightened of, but every time the wind rattled
> the windows, I jumped."

Don't let it go on too long because the writing tends to get silly. Linking words from sentence to sentence helps students stay with the topic and gives the piece an almost poetic quality.

BREAKING THE "RULES" TO CREATE FLUENCY

Sentences and Fragments Bee

This game helps students develop an ear for hearing the difference between sentences and fragments. It can be played at all grade levels and is especially helpful to English language learners.

Line up a group of students. Ask the student at the front of the line: "Is this a sentence or a fragment?" Then, give an example:

> My cousin Luke (fragment)
> Come inside, now. (sentence)
> Here is your umbrella. (sentence)
> Who didn't want (fragment)
> The ugly old witch (fragment)

To remain standing, the student must give the right answer. If he or she misses, the student sits down, and the game continues. The last student standing is the winner.

Reading Aloud to Yourself

Reading their drafts aloud is a trick professional writers use to determine if they're breaking the rules effectively. However, getting students to do that hasn't been easy for us. At best, we've gotten mumbles, speed reads, or no reading at all. Our students were just too self-conscious to allow themselves the agony and the ecstasy of hearing how their words flowed across the page. It wasn't until we put a homemade phone in their hands that they successfully read their pieces without the concern of being overheard by others.

To make a simple "fluency phone" for your students, visit any home improvement store, go to the PVC plumbing pipe section, and describe what you need to a helpful salesperson: two to five short pieces of PVC pipe to fit together into the shape of a phone.

We decorate our fluency phones with stickers just to make them more fun, but the basic phone is simply a device, for students to read aloud and not feel conspicuous. And, as a bonus, when they read softly into the phone, not only can they hear every word and nuance, they can also hear the ocean.

Conventions Activities

CHECKING SPELLING

Reading Backwards

To check for spelling errors, have students read their pieces backwards. That way, they focus on each word and don't get caught up in the meaning of the words in the sentence. Be sure they start with the last word and work all the way to the beginning. You won't believe how effective this is!

Those Nasty Homophones

Students seem to handle homophones (words that sound alike but are spelled differently) better when they're not taught in clusters. Some perennial problem words are: *their*, *there*, and *they're*; *to*, *too*, and *two*; *bare* and *bear*; *break* and *brake*; *deer* and *dear*; *I'll*, *aisle*, and *isle*; *pair*, *pear*, and *pare*; and *your* and *you're*. Teach one word at a time. For example, teach the word *pair*, a noun meaning two of a kind, and stop. When the student needs to spell the word *pare*, a verb meaning to trim down, teach them how to spell it and use it correctly.

PUNCTUATING EFFECTIVELY

Punctuation Walkabout

While editing for punctuation (periods, mainly), have students walk while reading one of their drafts. When they intend to insert a stop (a period), they must physically stop and stamp their feet. Expand to other punctuation marks by adding new motions, such as shooting a hand up in the air for an exclamation point or curling one arm around their head for a question mark. This kinesthetic approach helps students realize the importance of punctuation for indicating the end and tone of a thought.

Look Who's Talking

For students just learning to write dialogue, showing a change of speaker can be a big challenge. To teach them how to use quotation marks around spoken words, instruct students to highlight who is speaking in one color and what he or she is saying in another color. To get the students started, show them how to punctuate dialogue in one sentence and ask them to do the next. Remind them that every time there is a change of speaker, there should be a new paragraph.

CAPITALIZING CORRECTLY

Bouncing Ball

Give each student a super ball. (You may have to establish some ground rules for these—they have a way of flying out of control.) Call upon students to read a paragraph of their writing aloud to a partner. Every time there is a capital letter (or should be one), have them bounce their balls. If both students bounce balls at the same point, they should carry on. But if not, make sure the difference gets resolved so the capitals are in the right places. Switch roles so that both partners have their pieces edited for capitalization.

Context Capitals

Review the rules for using capitals in titles of books, magazines, headlines, and so forth. Your school reference collection may have an up-to-date style handbook, or perhaps your textbook contains the information. You can always check the Internet by searching "capital letters" or "capitals in titles."

Ask students to observe the way capitals are used on road signs, billboards, business signs, and other kinds of environmental text and find at least three examples of incorrect capitalization. Notice how businesses write their names or how slogans are capitalized. Discuss why a writer of signs might break the rule to create a look or feel.

APPLYING GRAMMAR AND USAGE

Pass It Back

Seat students in rows. The person at the front of each row writes a simple sentence (or takes one that you provide) and passes it back. The second person adds an appositive (a definition of someone or something), the third person adds internal punctuation.

* ❋ Charlie took his dog for a walk.

* ❋ Charlie my best friend since the third grade took his dog for a walk.

* ❋ Charlie, my best friend since the third grade, took his dog for a walk.

The rest of the row checks the sentence for corrections. From there, students rotate positions. This activity can be used to practice certain sentence parts, depending on what you ask students to add.

Use Literature

Read aloud Rick Walton's *Pig, Pigger, Piggest* (1997). Then have each student pick a word and add "er" and "est" to it. Illustrate by giving several examples, such as "cranky," "crankier," and "crankiest." You may wish to bring in objects such as stuffed animals to spur students' imagination: "teddy bear," "larger teddy bear," "largest teddy bear." This technique helps to teach comparative and superlative forms.

Concluding Thought

We hope the activities described in this chapter serve you and your students well. And to that end, we have one last piece of advice: Be fearless. The energy you bring to your work, your faith in your students, and your willingness to try new things right along with them will make all the difference. Commit to leaving no stone unturned in your quest to inspire young writers. Use these activities as starting points to stretch the bounds of your imagination. The writing lives of your young students are at stake.

Chapter 5

Answers to the Questions Intermediate Teachers Ask Most

Teachers are inquisitive. We know because we are bombarded with good questions from them every day. Here are some of the most common ones about using the writing traits. Read through them for additional information on and clarification of points raised in this book. The answers will help you apply the traits to your teaching.

Are the traits a writing curriculum?

No. The traits have no scope and no sequence that unfold from year to year. We use the traits for assessment and as a shared vocabulary to describe what good writing looks like, whether the child is 5 or 15.

The traits should unfold as lessons and activities embedded in the writing curriculum. To be most effective, these lessons and activities should spring out of the grade-level curriculum and connect to important concepts found in literature, science, social studies, math, fine arts, and health (see Chapters 3 and 4 for examples). As you examine your curriculum with "trait eyes," you'll see the connections. Seize on them.

Use the traits to assess writing so you'll understand what students know and what they can do. Then focus your writing lessons and activities on improving their writing within the curriculum you're expected to teach. Use all the traits all the time. Forget any misguided notion that you should teach only a few traits to younger students or that you should assign different traits to different grades. Students in all grades need all traits every time they write. The traits bring the writing curriculum to life. But they are *not* the curriculum.

In what order should I cover the traits?

We start with the ideas trait because most writing begins with figuring out what to say and we end with conventions because most writing finishes with figuring out how it will look. However, there is no "right order" in between. You should cover the traits in the order that makes the most sense for your students and their needs. Once students have drafted a few pieces and you've assessed those papers using the scoring guides on pages 24–29, let their scores determine the sequence in which you cover the traits.

Isn't it punitive to give a score of 1?

A score of 1 is not a final summative evaluation. It's a message to the writer that he or she has work to do to show strength in the trait. It's an indicator of where the piece is right now and how much work it will need to become stronger in the trait, but nothing more. It's okay to give 1s as long as you give students the tools and support they need to move beyond them. Over time, as students get scores of 2, 3, and higher, they will notice and appreciate the improvement. And they will recognize you as an honest assessor. That's important.

Doesn't a score of 6 send a message that there's absolutely no room for improvement?

It's sometimes hard to give 6s out of fear that students will think their work is perfect and, thus, stop trying. It's important to remember that a 6 doesn't mean perfect. It means, "Good for you. You show control in the trait." That's it. There's always room for more. Challenge the student to write in a different mode, for instance, to stretch him or her as a writer.

How often should I use prompts to help students get started?

The best rule of thumb is fifty-fifty. About half the time students should write on topics of their own choosing, and about half the time they should be given relevant, stimulating, open-ended prompts.

How should I teach spelling?

There is no one way to teach spelling that will help every child. Like every other complex task, you need a variety of ways to approach it. For example, you may want to teach students how to use phonics and orthographic features (word parts) to help them spell. At the same time, be sure to let students know that there are some words that don't sound one bit like the way they are spelled, so they'll just have to learn them. Students should have lists of commonly spelled words at their desks or in their writing notebooks. Teach them how to use spell check on the computer. Finally, allow students to ask, "How do you spell . . . ?" so they don't get hung up on a word and lose track of what they're writing about. For more on teaching spelling, see page 102.

Why do parents worry so much about conventions?

Parents probably got feedback mostly on conventions during their school years, so it only makes sense that they are looking for the same emphasis on conventions from their children's teachers. However, if you teach conventions in the context of real writing (preferably the students' own writing), you need to explain that to parents. Parents will be supportive if they understand the plan. Explain to them that their child will receive focused and explicit help in conventions, but will be applying them to real writing, not to words and sentences in isolation. Also, explain that learning to apply conventions correctly takes time. Although their child may not be using commas and spelling words like *because* correctly, perhaps he or she is capitalizing the first letter of each sentence and spelling words like *from* correctly. This is cause for celebration. In time, the child will learn the more sophisticated matters.

PROFESSIONAL RESOURCES CITED

Culham, R. (2009). *Daily trait warm-ups: 180 revision and editing activities to kick off writing time.* New York: Scholastic.

Culham, R. & Coutu, R. (2009). *Getting started with the traits: K–2.* New York: Scholastic.

Fox, M. (1993). *Radical reflections: Passionate opinion on teaching, learning, and living.* New York: Harcourt.

King, S. (2000). *On writing: A memoir of the craft.* New York: Scribner.

CHILDREN'S LITERATURE CITED

Abercrombie, B. (1995). *Charlie Anderson.* New York: Simon & Schuster.

Avi. (1999). *Midnight magic.* New York: Scholastic.

Babbitt, N. (1975). *Tuck everlasting.* New York: Farrar, Straus.

Banks, L. R. (1980). *The Indian in the cupboard.* New York: Avon.

Bloom, B. (1999). *Wolf!* New York: Orchard.

Capote, T. (1956). *A Christmas memory.* New York: Random House.

Christelow, E. (1995). *What do authors do?* New York: Clarion.

Cisneros, S. (1991). *Woman hollering creek.* New York: Random House.

Cobb, V. (1997). *Blood & gore like you've never seen!* New York: Scholastic.

Creech, S. (1994). *Walk two moons.* New York: HarperCollins.

Curtis, C. P. (1999). *Bud, not Buddy.* New York: Delacorte.

Dahl, R. (1961). *James and the giant peach.* New York: Alfred A. Knopf.

Dahl, R. (1988). *Matilda.* New York: Viking.

Davies, N. (2001). *One tiny turtle.* Cambridge, MA: Candlewick.

Duke, K. (1992). *Aunt Isabel tells a good one.* New York: Dutton.

Fletcher, R. (1997). *Spider boy.* New York: Clarion.

Fox, M. (1989). *Koala Lou.* New York: Harcourt.

Fox, M. (1994). *Tough Boris.* New York: Harcourt.

Frame, J. A. (2003). *Yesterday I had the blues.* Berkeley, CA: Tricycle.

Fritz, J. (1982). *Homesick: My own story.* New York: Bantam Doubleday Dell.

Hesse, K. (1999). *Come on, rain!* New York: Scholastic.

Lester, H. (1997). *Author: A true story.* New York: Houghton Mifflin.

Liao, J. (2006). *The sound of color: A journey of the imagination.* Boston: Little, Brown.

Moss, M. (2006). *Amelia's Notebook.* New York: Simon & Schuster.

Muth, J. J. (2002). *The three questions.* New York: Scholastic.

Nobisso, J. (2004). *Show, don't tell! Secrets of writing.* Westhampton Beach, NY: Gingerbread House.

O'Connor, J. (2006). *Fancy Nancy.* New York: HarperCollins.

O'Neill, M. (1961). *Hailstones and halibut bones.* Garden City, NY: Doubleday.

Reynolds, P. H. (2004). *Ish.* Cambridge, MA: Candlewick.

Rose, D. L. (2001). *Into the a, b, sea.* New York: Scholastic.

Rowling, J. K. (1997). *Harry Potter and the sorcerer's stone.* New York: Scholastic.

Sachar, L. (1998). *Holes.* New York: Farrar, Straus.

Schotter, R. (2006). *The boy who loved words.* New York: Schwartz & Wade.

Schotter, R. (1997). *Nothing ever happens on 90th Street.* New York: Orchard Books.

Teague, M. (1996). *The secret shortcut.* New York: Scholastic.

Walton, R. (1997). *Pig, pigger, piggest.* Layton, UT: Gibbs Smith.

Watt, M. (2006). *Scaredy Squirrel.* Toronto, ON: Kids Can Press.

Watt, M. (2007). *Scaredy Squirrel makes a friend.* Toronto, ON: Kids Can Press.

White, E. B. (1952). *Charlotte's web.* New York: HarperCollins.

Wisniewski, D. (1998). *The secret knowledge of grown-ups.* New York: William Morrow.

Wong, J. S. (2002). *You have to write.* New York: Margaret K. McElderry.

Revision Checklist

I've revised for:

☐ **Ideas:** I've selected one topic, focused it, and used specific details to describe it.

☐ **Organization:** I've written an attention-grabbing lead, organized my details in a logical way, and wrapped it all up in the conclusion.

☐ **Voice:** I've written in a way that sets the right tone for my piece, targets my audience, and sounds fresh and original.

☐ **Word Choice:** I've used strong verbs and other specific and accurate words that add sparkle to my writing.

☐ **Sentence Fluency:** I've used sentences with different lengths and patterns to add rhythm to my writing, and I've taken some risks and tried some new ways to write sentences.

☐ **Conventions:** I've checked my spelling, capitalization, punctuation, and grammar and usage for accuracy. My use of conventions will help to guide the reader through the text.

Traits in my writing that still need attention and my plan for improving them:

☐ Ideas: _____   ☐ Word Choice: _____

_____   _____

☐ Organization: _____   ☐ Sentence Fluency: _____

_____   _____

☐ Voice: _____   ☐ Conventions: _____

_____   _____

Editor's Marks

for Beginning Writers

Mark	Meaning	Example
℘	Delete material.	The writing is is good.
(sp)	Correct the spelling or spell it out.	We are learning 2 traits this week. sp / week
◠	Close space.	To day is publishing day.
∧	Insert a letter, word, or phrase.	My teacher has books. wonderful
∧	Change a letter.	She is a great writer.
⋕	Add a space.	Don't forget agood introduction.
∿	Transpose letters or words.	She raed the piece with flair!
≡	Change to a capital letter.	We have j.k. Rowling to thank for Harry Potter's magic.
/	Change to a lowercase letter.	The "Proof is in the Pudding" was his favorite saying.
¶	Start a new paragraph.	"What day is it?" he inquired. "It's Christmas," returned Tiny Tim.
⊙	Add a period.	Use all the traits as you write ⊙

Student-Friendly Scoring Guide
Organization

I've Got It!

* I included a bold beginning.
* I've shown how the ideas connect.
* My ideas are in an order that really works.
* My ending leaves you with something to think about.

On My Way

* There is a beginning, but it's not particularly special.
* Most of my details fit logically; I could move or get rid of others.
* Sections of my writing flow logically, but other parts seem out of place.
* My ending is not original, but it does clearly show where the piece stops.

Just Starting

* I forgot to write a clear introduction to this piece.
* I have the right "stuff" to work with, but it's not in order.
* The order of my details are jumbled and confusing.
* Oops! I forgot to end my piece with a wrap-up.

Student-Friendly Scoring Guide
Ideas

I've Got It!

* I picked a topic and stuck with it.
* My topic is small enough to handle.
* I know a lot about this topic.
* My topic is bursting with fascinating details.

On My Way

* I've wandered off my main topic in a few places.
* My topic might be a little too big to handle.
* I know enough about my topic to get started.
* Some of my details are too general.

Just Starting

* I have included several ideas that might make a good topic.
* No one idea stands out as most important.
* I'm still looking for a topic that will work well.
* My details are fuzzy or not clear.

Getting Started With the Traits: Grades 3–5 © 2009 Ruth Culham and Raymond Coutu, Scholastic.

Student-Friendly Scoring Guide
Word Choice

I've Got It!

* I used strong verbs to add energy.
* My words are specific and are colorful, fresh, and snappy.
* My words help my reader see my ideas.
* My words are accurate and used correctly.

On My Way

* Only one or two verbs stand out in this piece.
* I've used many ordinary words; there's no sparkle.
* My words give the reader the most general picture of the idea.
* I've misused some words or overused others.

Just Starting

* I haven't used any verbs that convey energy.
* I've left out key words.
* Many of my words are repetitive or just wrong.
* I'm confused about how to use words as I write.

Student-Friendly Scoring Guide
Voice

I've Got It!

* I used a distinctive tone that works with the topic.
* I was clear about why I was writing, so my voice is believable.
* The audience will connect with what I wrote.
* I tried some new ways of expressing myself to add interest.

On My Way

* I played it safe. You only get a glimpse of me in this piece.
* I wasn't always clear about my purpose, so my voice fades in and out.
* I'm only mildly interested in this topic.
* I didn't try to express myself in new ways.

Just Starting

* I didn't share anything about what I think and feel in this piece.
* I'm not sure what or why I'm writing.
* This topic is not interesting to me at all.
* I'm bored and it shows.

Student-Friendly Scoring Guide
Conventions

I've Got It!

❈ My spelling is magnificent.

❈ I put capital letters in all the right places.

❈ I used punctuation correctly to make my writing easy to read.

❈ I used correct grammar and indented paragraphs where necessary.

On My Way

❈ Only my simpler words are spelled correctly.

❈ I used capital letters in easy spots.

❈ I have correct punctuation in some places but not in others.

❈ There are a few places where the grammar isn't quite right, and I've forgotten to indicate paragraphs except at the beginning.

Just Starting

❈ My words are hard to read and understand because of the spelling.

❈ I've not followed the rules for capitalization.

❈ My punctuation is missing or in the wrong places.

❈ The grammar needs a lot of work. I forgot about using paragraphs.

Student-Friendly Scoring Guide
Sentence Fluency

I've Got It!

❈ My sentences are well-built and have varied beginnings.

❈ I've tried to write using interjections or fragments to create variety.

❈ My sentences read smoothly.

❈ I've varied the length and structure of my sentences.

On My Way

❈ My sentences are working pretty well.

❈ I've tried a couple of ways to begin my sentences differently, but could do more.

❈ When I read my piece aloud, there are a few places that need smoothing.

❈ I might put some sentences together or I could cut a few in two.

Just Starting

❈ My sentences aren't working well.

❈ The beginnings of my sentences sound the same.

❈ I'm having trouble reading my piece aloud.

❈ I've used words like "and" or "but" too many times.

Getting Started With the Traits: Grades 3–5 © 2009 Ruth Culham and Raymond Coutu, Scholastic.

"An ultimately useful collection of plays for both children and adults, presented with both humor and intelligence…"
—*School Library Journal*

The Plays
of the

Songs of Christmas

The Plays of the Songs of Christmas is very highly recommended for the family, and the church, that is looking for instructive, entertaining and inspiring literature for the Christmas season. The plays are sure to delight, and they are especially suitable for sharing with children. They are well written, often amusing, and short enough for family reading on the busy night before Christmas. Stage designs and directions are clear and simple, so that they could easily be produced even by a quite small church community. Each play brings to life the situation in which the corresponding song was composed. Most of the songs are old favorites. A few were new to me—and welcome additions indeed! You can enrich the religious life of your own family by sharing this fine book with them this year, and for many years, at Christmas.

—*Fred Berthold, Professor of Religion, Emeritus, Dartmouth College*

Smith and Kraus *Books For Actors*

YOUNG ACTORS SERIES

Great Scenes and Monologues for Children

Great Scenes for Young Actors from the Stage

Great Monologues for Young Actors

Multicultural Monologues for Young Actors

Multicultural Scenes for Young Actors

Monologues from Classic Plays 468 BC to 1960 AD

Scenes from Classic Plays 468 BC to 1970 AD

New Plays from A.C.T.'s Young Conservatory Vol. I

New Plays from A.C.T.'s Young Conservatory Vol. II

Plays of America from American Folklore for Young Actors K-6

Plays of America from American Folklore for Young Actors 7-12

Multicultural Plays for Children Grades K-3

Multicultural Plays for Children Grades 4-6

Seattle Children's Theatre: Six Plays for Young Actors

Short Plays for Young Actors

Villeggiatura: A Trilogy by Carlo Goldoni, *condensed for Young Actors*

Loving to Audition: The Audition Workbook for Young Actors

Movement Stories for Young Children Ages 3-6

An Index of Plays for Young Actors

Discovering Shakespeare: A Midsummer Night's Dream; *a workbook for students*

Discovering Shakespeare: Romeo and Juliet; *a workbook for students*

Discovering Shakespeare: The Taming of the Shrew; *a workbook for students*

CAREER DEVELOPMENT SERIES

The Job Book: 100 Acting Jobs for Actors

The Job Book II: 100 Day Jobs for Actors

The Smith and Kraus Monologue Index

The Great Acting Teachers and Their Methods

The Actor's Guide to Qualified Acting Coaches: New York

The Actor's Guide to Qualified Acting Coaches: Los Angeles

The Camera Smart Actor

The Sanford Meisner Approach

Cold Readings: Some Do's and Don'ts for Actors at Auditions

If you require prepublication information about upcoming Smith and Kraus books, you may receive our semi-annual catalogue, free of charge, by sending your name and address to *Smith and Kraus Catalogue, P.O. Box 127, One Main Street, Lyme, NH 03768. Or call us at (800) 895-4331, fax (603) 795-4427.*

The Plays
of the
Songs *of* Christmas

by L.E. McCullough

Young Actors Series

SK
A Smith and Kraus Book

A Smith and Kraus Book
Published by Smith and Kraus, Inc.
One Main Street, PO Box 127, Lyme, NH 03768

Copyright ©1996 by L.E. McCullough All rights reserved
Manufactured in the United States of America
Cover and Text Design by Julia Hill
Cover Art and Text Illustration by Irene Kelly
First Edition: August 1996
10 9 8 7 6 5 4 3 2 1

Library of Congress Cataloging-In-Publication Data
McCullough, L.E.
The plays of the songs of Christmas / by L.E. McCullough.
p. cm. — (Young actors series)
Summary: Twelve plays, each of which illustrates the theme of a well-known Christmas carol.
ISBN 1-57525-062-4
1. Christmas music—Juvenile drama. 2. Children's plays, American. 3. Christmas plays, American.
[1. Christmas music—Drama. 2. Christmas—Drama. 3. Plays.] I. Title. II. Series.
PS3563.C35297P587   1996
812'.54—dc20   96-22834
CIP
AC

Acknowledgments

The author wishes to thank the following:
Claude McNeal and the American Cabaret Theatre, Art Aban, Carol and Jeffrey Cohen, George Bailey, Daphna Czernobilsky, Kris Kringle, Jay Ungar and Molly Mason, John Canoe, Kent Hooper & Aileen Kane, Père Noël, Marci Lynne, Jules Venn, Ann Sloan and her great-great uncle Charles, Lam Khoong-Khoong, Gioia Timpanelli, Hotei Osho, Pauline Oliveros & Ione, Grandfather Grost, Monsignor Richard Kavanaugh, Viejo Pascuero, Israel Baline, Star Man, Will Porter, Mrs. Schmidt of Eagledale—who taught me my first Christmas carols on the piano—and my beloved Jane, who brings Christmas into my life every day of the year.

Dedication

To everyone everywhere
who makes Christmas
the most wonderful time
of the year.

Foreword

"The night was made radiant like the day, filling men and animals with joy. The crowds drew near and rejoiced...As they sang in praise of God, the whole night rang with exultation."

— *Thomas of Celano describing St. Francis of Assisi's*
Christmas celebration at Greccio, Italy, 1223 A.D.

"Nobody can tell you the whole true story of that incredible Christmas truce of the First World War...A British officer suggested a songfest. The Germans agreed eagerly, both sides singing in turn...A truce was agreed upon until midnight on Christmas Day."

— *an eyewitness account of the Christmas Eve meeting between British*
and German soldiers in No Man's Land, France, 1914 A.D.

The songs of Christmas have come to us over several centuries and from many cultures throughout our world. Their singular power to inspire, cheer and comfort—even during the darkest days of war and disaster—is unsurpassed by any other musical idiom. Be they lighthearted frolic or pious religious hymn, the songs of Christmas offer a tantalizing glimpse of the colorful legends and lore that have made December 25 the most festive day on Earth. Many of the most popular songs of Christmas commemorate historical figures and events that are strikingly dramatic, hence this book, *The Plays of the Songs of Christmas.*

It is possible to combine *Plays of the Songs of Christmas* with studies in other disciplines: history, costume, language, dance, music, geography, etc. Each play has enough real-life historical and cultural references to support a host of pre- or post-play activities that integrate easily with related curriculum areas. Using authentic ethnic or period music is another great way to enhance your production; plenty of additional seasonal music can be inserted between scenes or at the start and end of the play. If you have questions about where to find recordings or written music of the tunes or genres included in these plays, or want some tips on performing them, I would be happy to assist you and may be reached by calling Smith & Kraus.

Besides those children enrolled in the onstage cast, others can be included in the production as lighting and sound technicians, prop masters, script coaches and stage managers. *Plays of the Songs of Christmas* is an excellent vehicle for getting other members of the school and community involved in your project. Maybe there is an accomplished performer of English Morris music in your area; ask them to play a few dance tunes for *Here We Come A-Wassailing.* Perhaps someone at your local historical society or library can give a talk about early Christmas customs. Try utilizing the talents of local school or youth orchestra members to play incidental music...get the school art club to paint scrims and backdrop...see if a senior citizens' group might volunteer time to sew costumes...inquire whether a French restaurant might bring samples of Provençal cuisine for *Bring a Torch, Jeannette, Isabella.*

Most of all, have lots of fun. Realizing that many performing groups may have limited technical and space resources, I have kept sets, costumes and props minimal. However, if you do have the ability to rig up an entire 19th-century Boston street scene for *Jingle Bells* or build a facsimile palace and wilderness for *Good King Wenceslas*—go for it! Adding more music, dance and visual arts and crafts into the production involves a greater number of children and makes your play a genuinely multi-media event. There are numerous books that can be consulted for details on period costumes, traditional foods and national Christmas customs guaranteed to give your show an extra richness and appeal.

Similarly, I have supplied only basic stage and lighting directions. Blocking is really the province of the director; once you get the play up and moving, feel free to suit cast and action to your available population and experience level of actors. When figuring out how to stage these plays, I suggest you follow the venerable UYI Method—Use Your Imagination. If the play calls for a hearth and chimney, one can be fashioned from cardboard and wood frame or have children draw a hearth and chimney and hang as a scrim behind where the actors perform. If your fire code permits, angels and Wise Men can hold live candles, as is the custom in the Mexican *posada* ritual alluded to in *Let Us Go, O Shepherds*. Keep in mind the spirit of the old Andy Hardy musicals: "C'mon, everybody! Let's make a show!"

Age and gender. Obviously, your purpose in putting on the play is to entertain as well as educate; even though in the historical reality of 10th-century Germany, Teuton warriors would all have been male, there is no reason these roles can't be played in your production by females. After all, the essence of the theatrical experience is to suspend us in time and ask us to believe that anything may be possible. Once again, UYI! Adult characters can be played by children costumed or made up to fit the part as closely as possible, or they can actually be played by adults. While *Plays of the Songs of Christmas* are intended to be performed chiefly by children, moderate adult involvement will add validation and let children know this isn't just a "kid project." A highly choreographed and musically intensive play like *The Twelve Days of Christmas* would, in fact, benefit from a strategically placed onstage adult or two to keep things moving smoothly.

At this point in human history, nearly two thousand years after a man named Jesus of Nazareth announced his remarkable message of love and forgiveness to the world, Christmas has come to represent much more than a religious holiday. Christmas has become an opportunity for people of all faiths to express good will, peace, the sharing of prosperity, joy at our very humanness—a short breathing space in our onrushing lives when we attempt to make the Earth more closely resemble the Paradise from which we came and to which we aspire to return.

It is my hope that these plays will provide plenty of Christmas all year round. Not the Christmas you buy at the mall, but the Christmas you find in your heart and see in the eyes of children who know for a fact that Christmas is truly the greatest miracle there ever was.

L.E. McCullough, Ph.D.
Mt. Laurel, New Jersey

Contents

Here We Come A-Wassailing

The art of mumming–dressing up in costumes and acting out plays based on seasonal themes–has been common in Europe for over two thousand years. Mumming still survives in modern times, the annual Mummers' Parade in Philadelphia on New Year's Day being the most well-known example. Mumming was especially popular during the Middle Ages, and even King Henry VIII was known to join reveling bands of Christmas mummers. "Wassail" derives from the old Anglo-Saxon phrase "waes hael," meaning "be well" or "hale," and originated in an ancient agricultural festival designed to help fruit orchards grow by sprinkling the trees with a mixture of mulled ale or cider carried in a "wassail bowl." With the advent of Christianity, the custom evolved into a roving Christmas party, with "wassailers" carrying a wassail cup or bowl from house to house, putting on plays and performing music and carols–such as *Here We Come A-Wassailing*–before asking for food and money to ensure good luck to the household for the coming year.

Here We Come A-Wassailing

TIME: Christmas Eve, 1599

PLACE: The Holcomb Family cottage,
                                             Scarborough, County
                                             Yorkshire, England

CAST:
    Miles Holcomb   Squire Bradford
    Captain Mummer   Susan Holcomb
    Lady Bradford   Old Father Christmas
    Bess Holcomb   Anastasia Bradford
    Divily Doubt   Ben Holcomb
    Archibald Bradford   Fanny Funny
    Big Head   Doctor Brown
    Tom Foolery   Sir Slickity Slack

STAGE SET: wooden dining table set with food dishes and pans containing pies, cookies, beef, vegetables; two dining table chairs; fireplace with hearth, chimney and mantle trimmed with evergreens and stockings; a sprig of mistletoe hanging at stage center; cooking pot on metal frame; wooden bench

PROPS: chess board; ladle; cooking pot; firewood; letters; jugs; leather purse; tambourines; handbells; simple noisemakers; ribbons; buttons; plums; pears; dolls; balls; water bottle; coins; wallet

SPECIAL EFFECTS: sound—door opening and closing; wind whistling; church bells

MUSIC: recorder or tinwhistle playing melody to *Here We Come A-Wassailing*

COSTUMES: Holcombs and Bradfords dress in Elizabethan-era garb, the Holcombs plain and homespun, the Bradfords fancy and foppish with a ruff for the Squire and Archibald and lace cuffs and dress lining for the Lady and Anastasia; Mummers dress in masks and costumes—Old Father Christmas: a long, deep green robe trimmed with red, a white beard, a holly wreath on his head; Captain Mummer: pseudo-military dress, cape and wooden sword; Tom Foolery: a court jester with a dunce cap; Sir Slickity Slack: a court jester carrying a burlap bag from which Father Christmas pulls out gifts; Divily Doubt: a black smock, black horns and red tail and carries a small broom and a small pan and a small wooden sword in his belt; Big Head: a large horse head or mask; Doctor Brown: white robe and a white pillbox cap; Fanny Funny: a woman's dress and shawl, straw stuffed under her head kerchief; all Mummers wear green sashes around their waist, red ribbons around necks and hats and carry tamborines, handbells and kazoo-like noisemakers

PERFORMANCE NOTE: Every moment they are onstage, Mummers caper, strut, grovel, simper, nudge, etc.; they are figures of fun and mischief, and their speeches are punctuated by silliness and exaggeration.

☆ ☆ ☆

(MUSIC: "Here We Come A-Wassailing" played offstage by recorder or tinwhistle. LIGHTS UP FULL on the interior of the Holcomb Family cottage. At the hearth, SUSAN HOLCOMB stirs a cooking pot with a ladle, occasionally tasting the contents. Two children, BESS AND BEN HOLCOMB, play chess at the table. MUSIC FADES OUT. SOUND: Door opening, closing, wind whistling as MILES HOLCOMB enters from stage right carrying a bundle of firewood. Bess and Ben leap up excitedly and run to him.)

BESS & BEN HOLCOMB Father, Father, have you seen him? Have you seen him?

MILES HOLCOMB *(Lays firewood next to hearth and assumes a puzzled expression.)* Have I seen who?

BEN HOLCOMB Old Father Christmas! Have you seen him anywhere about?

MILES HOLCOMB *(Hands his cloak to Bess, who puts it on bench at up right.)* Old Father Christmas? What an odd-sounding name that is! Why would a chap with a name like Old Father Christmas be wandering around the likes of Scarborough town in this bitter cold?

BEN HOLCOMB Because it is Christmas Eve, and he visits all the children in Scarborough, all the children in Yorkshire, nay, all the children in England and everywhere in the world!

MILES HOLCOMB Visit children? What on earth for?

(Ben stares open-mouthed at his father, who breaks into a big laugh and ruffles Ben's hair.)

BESS HOLCOMB Oh, he is teasing again, Ben! You know how childish grownups can be at holidays.

(Bess and Ben sit at table.)

SUSAN HOLCOMB Now, children, calm yourselves. Your cousins will be here any time now. Then there will be plenty of amusement for all.

BESS HOLCOMB Mother, the Bradfords are the most un-amusing people I know. They are too proper to enjoy themselves.

BEN HOLCOMB Even the children are sticks in the mud.

BESS HOLCOMB With their noses stuck in the air.

BEN HOLCOMB And their backsides—

MILES HOLCOMB Enough of that now, if you want Old Father Christmas to pay a visit!

SUSAN HOLCOMB I admit the Bradfords can be a bit reserved. And I am told that city people often do not celebrate Christmas as gaily as we in the provinces. But they have journeyed all the way from London to share Christmas with us. We must show them some good Yorkshire country fun!

(SOUND: KNOCKING AT DOOR OFFSTAGE RIGHT)

SUSAN HOLCOMB Here they are now! Show them in, Miles!

(Miles greets SQUIRE BRADFORD, LADY BRADFORD and their children ANASTASIA and ARCHIBALD, who enter slowly from stage right; they are extremely formal in manner.)

MILES HOLCOMB Come warm yourselves by the fire! Bess, Ben, take their cloaks!

(Bess and Ben take the Bradfords' cloaks and put them on bench.)

SUSAN HOLCOMB Welcome to our home. Please, sit down.

(Squire and Lady Bradford sit in chairs; Anastasia and Archibald stand stiffly beside them.)

SUSAN HOLCOMB Anastasia, Archibald. How you have grown since we last saw you! Come hug your Auntie Susan!

ANASTASIA *(To Lady Bradford.)* Mother, may we hug Auntie Susan?

LADY BRADFORD You may. But delicately, delicately.

(Anastasia and Archibald advance in drillstep to Susan Holcomb, permit themselves to be hugged, then step back beside their parents.)

MILES HOLCOMB Squire Bradford, would you care for a jug of mull punch?

SQUIRE BRADFORD Thank you, Holcomb. That would be most—

LADY BRADFORD Perhaps later. The Squire has to watch his diet most carefully. He is not permitted anything that might excite his digestion.

MILES HOLCOMB Or his palate, I daresay.

LADY BRADFORD I beg your pardon?

SUSAN HOLCOMB The palace. Is there any news from the palace?

SQUIRE BRADFORD Nothing much. The Queen is in good health. And that clever fellow Will Shakespeare has written a delightful new play. What was it called, my lady?

LADY BRADFORD *Romeo and Juliet.* About two young Italians who decide to get married because they fall in love. Of all the silly reasons for one to marry!

SQUIRE BRADFORD It will never happen in England!

(Bess and Ben have gone to the fireplace and are sealing letters, then throwing them up the chimney.)

BEN *(Shouts.)* Hurrah! I get my wish!

LADY BRADFORD What on earth?

BESS On Christmas Eve, you write a letter to Old Father Christmas, asking him for a gift.

BEN Then you throw the letter into the chimney, and if the draft takes it up, your wish is granted! My letter went up!

BESS Archibald, Anastasia! Come send a letter of your own!

ARCHIBALD *(To Lady Bradford.)* Mother, may we?

LADY BRADFORD I suppose so. As long as you keep out of the ashes. Children and their silly games!

(Bess and Ben show Anastasia and Archibald how to seal letters and toss them up the chimney.)

MILES HOLCOMB Dear sister, I remember when we were children, you made silly games and Christmas rhymes a-plenty.

LADY BRADFORD I never!

MILES HOLCOMB Tis true. In fact, you taught me this very riddle:
Flower of England, fruit of Spain
Met together in a shower of rain
Put in a bag and tied with a string
If you guess the answer, I'll give you a pin

BESS HOLCOMB I know the answer! Plum pudding!

SUSAN HOLCOMB Come children, have some plum pudding and gingerbread. And some frumety cake as well. *(To Lady Bradford.)* May they, my lady?

LADY BRADFORD Oh, very well.

(Children grab up pudding and gingerbread.)

LADY BRADFORD But, brother Miles, Christmas is different in these modern times. It has become such a display...such a...spectacle of uncivilized excess.

SQUIRE BRADFORD A veritable circus of emotional riot, I should say.

MILES HOLCOMB And, pray sister dear, what is excessive about displaying good will and affection toward your fellow men and women one day a year? Can there ever be too much happiness in this world?

LADY BRADFORD But look at all this food! Cakes, pies, pudding, meat and garden bounty of every description!

SUSAN HOLCOMB Oh, not all of this is for eating. Much of it is for luck.

SQUIRE BRADFORD Luck?

SUSAN HOLCOMB A loaf of bread left on the table after Christmas Eve ensures your family will have bread for the next twelve months.

BEN HOLCOMB Eating an apple at midnight gives good health.

BESS HOLCOMB And you had better eat a slice of mince pie at Christmas, or it is bad luck you will have for a full year.

LADY BRADFORD Superstitious nonsense, my dear!

SQUIRE BRADFORD Country people...where do they get these notions?

(SOUND: LOUD CHURCH BELLS RINGING OFFSTAGE)

SQUIRE BRADFORD The Spanish Armada! Run for your lives! *(Dashes to the door, stage right.)*

MILES HOLCOMB *(Grabs him.)* Stay, squire! Tis but the village church bells ringing in Christmas, as they do each year. Now, the true celebration of Our Lord's birthday may begin!

(SOUND: LOUD, RAUCOUS KNOCKING AT DOOR OFFSTAGE RIGHT)

LADY BRADFORD Zounds! Intruders! Squire, draw your sword and save us! Children, hide beneath the table!

MILES HOLCOMB Nonsense, my lady. Tis unlucky to refuse strangers calling on Christmas. *(Calling:)* Enter, pilgrims!

(A TROUPE OF MUMMERS dances in, striking tambourines, shaking handbells and blowing crude noisemakers. The Bradfords cower at left as the Holcombs smile with delight at right.)

BESS Tis the Mummers! Hurrah!

BEN And Old Father Christmas!

(The Mummers scamper through the room making general mischief—picking up chess pieces, stirring the pot, messing with the stockings, making faces at the Bradfords—then gather at center stage.)

ANASTASIA BRADFORD Mother, father! Make them go away! They frighten me!

ARCHIBALD BRADFORD See here, you ruffians, my father is a personal friend of Sir Walter Raleigh, and—

MUMMERS *(Chant.)*
Wassail, wassail, all around the town;
Our bread is white, our ale is brown.
We come not to your door to beg or borrow;
We come to your door to drive away all sorrow

LADY BRADFORD Such impertinence!

SQUIRE BRADFORD *(Confronts TOM FOOLERY.)* And who, sir, are you?

TOM FOOLERY (*Bows exaggeratedly.*)

Tom Foolery of Foolton is my name,
Just fooling about is my game.
Come meet my friend with the burlap sack,
A boon companion, Sir Slickity Slack.

(*SIR SLICKITY SLACK comes up behind Squire Bradford, taps his shoulder roguishly
and ducks away, calling out to all.*)

SIR SLICKITY SLACK

Here comes I, Sir Slickity Slack,
A bag of burlap upon my back.
Some say I'm woozy, a little bit daft,
But I came this eve for to make you laugh.

TOM FOOLERY

Room, room, give us room,
Come give us room to rhyme.
We've come to show activity
Upon this Christmas time.

SIR SLICKITY SLACK

Acts of young and acts of age,
The like was never acted on the stage.
If you don't believe in what I say,
Enter Captain Mummer, and he'll clear the way!

(*CAPTAIN MUMMER steps forward with a flourish, twirling his cape and brandishing
a sword.*)

CAPTAIN MUMMER

Here I am, Captain Mummer brave,
I lead a mighty throng.
With a chosen band of heroes grand
To Yorkshire we belong.
For mirth and sport we do resort
And for diversion play.
And with our skill all people thrill,
So pay attention to what we say.

(*OLD FATHER CHRISTMAS steps forward.*)

OLD FATHER CHRISTMAS

I am Old Father Christmas, the man upon the hour;
I bring gifts of warmth and cheer to every family's bower.

(Sir Slickity Slack hands his sack to Old Father Christmas, who goes around the room laying out little bits of ribbon, buttons, plums, pears, dolls, balls.)

OLD FATHER CHRISTMAS
And now I turn to my appointed task,
Is there any present who must need ask:
What brings us here this wintry eve
Our hearts with those of heaven to weave?

(BIG HEAD steps forward.)

BIG HEAD
Here comes I who didn't yet;
My head is big, but with little wit.
Though my rhyme is slight and small,
I'll do my best to please you all.
If you don't believe in what I say,
Here comes Divily Doubt to clear the way.

(DIVILY DOUBT rudely shoves his way to front brandishing a small broom and a small pan.)

DIVILY DOUBT
Here comes I, cruel Divily Doubt;
I'm the devil himself, I'll sweep you all out.
Some call me Beelzebub,
And on my shoulder I carry a club,
In my hand a dripping pan
Pleased to steal all the good I can.

(Divily Doubt begins grabbing up the presents Old Father Christmas has just set down)

MUMMERS
Hallo, haroo! Hallo, haroo!
Stop the devil and give him his due!

OLD FATHER CHRISTMAS *(Turns and faces Divily Doubt.)*
How dare you upset the good I've spread,
With your horns of black and tail of red!
I'll spend my blood for childrenkind;
Come fight with me in battle, swine!

(Divily Doubt pulls a sword from his belt, and Captain Mummer hands his sword to

Old Father Christmas. Divily Doubt and Old Father Christmas duel, and Divily Doubt stabs Old Father Christmas, who falls to the floor.)

MUMMERS

Ohhhhhhhh!

CAPTAIN MUMMER

A doctor grand, I do demand
If one here can be found.
For to restore Old Father Christmas
He shall have full fifty pound.

(DOCTOR BROWN steps forward.)

DOCTOR BROWN

Here comes I, wee Doctor Brown,
The best wee doctor in all the town.
I can cure the plague within, the plague without,
The itch, the scratch, palsy and gout.

BIG HEAD

Pray, before you cure, desist
And tell us of what does your medicine consist?

DOCTOR BROWN

My medicine is made of hens' pens and snails' tails,
Grey cat feathers and the teeth of a whale.
Green juice of beetle, a smidgen of kippers,
Bumble bee oil and a footman's slippers.
Wit of a weasel, wool of a frog,
Fifteen ounces of last October's fog.

(Takes a bottle of water from his pocket and hands it to Big Head.)

DOCTOR BROWN

Put three drops of that in his ear
And watch him rise and sing a cheer.

(Big Head shakes bottle all over Old Father Christmas, who revives and leaps up shouting as Divily Doubt falls to floor.)

MUMMERS

Hurrah! Hurrah! Hurrah!

OLD FATHER CHRISTMAS

    Hallo! Hallay! The devil flay!
    I live again, this precious day.
    Restored to life by a Savior born
    In a humble stable this very morn.
    Let all to whom joy and mirth are inclined,
    Hear this good news for to pleasure your mind.

(Mummers lift up Divily Doubt, and Old Father Christmas places a wreath on his head.)

OLD FATHER CHRISTMAS

    With this garland of green, the devil I leaven
    And bring him under the power of heaven.
    Where every soul on earth rejoices
    Singing His praise with angel voices.

MUMMERS

    Hurrah! Hurrah! Hurrah!

(FANNY FUNNY steps forward shaking a leather purse and tambourine.)

FANNY FUNNY

    Here comes I, Miss Fanny Funny
    With a big leather purse to lift up the money
    Give us all silver and give us no brass;
    Open the till now and get us the cash!

(Fanny Funny accosts Miles Holcomb, who throws a few coins in the purse, and Squire Bradford, who refuses to give anything; Tom Foolery sidles up beside the Squire.)

TOM FOOLERY

    If you haven't got sixpence, thruppence will do;
    If you haven't got any, then God's blessings on you.

(He pulls out a wallet from the Squire's back pocket and waves it aloft.)

MUMMERS

    For we are Christmas Mummers
    And jolly folk are we.
    All out and gaily rambling
    In your houses for to see.
    And it's all for the money that we sing, too-ra-loo!

ANASTASIA BRADFORD Mother, may we sing with the Mummers?

ARCHIBALD BRADFORD Please, mother. After all, it is Christmas.

LADY BRADFORD (*Pause.*) I suppose so. But, please, do not strain your voicessssssssss!

(*Old Father Christmas grabs Lady Bradford and dances with her.*)

MILES HOLCOMB Now, that's the spirit of an English Christmas!

(*MUSIC: Mummers begin singing "Here We Come A-Wassailing."*)

MUMMERS (*Sing.*)
Here we come a-wassailing
Among the leaves so green
Here we come a-wandering
So fair to be seen

(*All other characters join in on choruses.*)

CHORUS:
Love and joy come to you
And to your wassail, too
And God bless you and send you
A happy new year
And God send you
A happy new year

MUMMERS (*Sing.*)
We are not daily beggars
That beg from door to door
But we are your own good neighbors
Whom you have seen before

ALL (*Sing.*)

CHORUS

MUMMERS (*Sing.*)
Call up the butler of this house
Put on his golden ring
Let him bring us a glass of ale
And better we shall sing

ALL (*Sing.*)

CHORUS

MUMMERS *(Sing.)*

    We have got a little purse
    Of stretching leather skin
    We want a little money
    To line it well within

ALL *(Sing.)*

CHORUS

MUMMERS *(Sing.)*

    Bring us out a table
    And spread it with a cloth
    Bring us out a moldy cheese
    And some of your Christmas loaf

ALL *(Sing.)*

CHORUS

MUMMERS *(Sing.)*

    God bless the master of this house
    Likewise the mistress, too
    And all the little children
    That round the table go

ALL *(Sing.)*

CHORUS

    (LIGHTS OUT.)

THE END

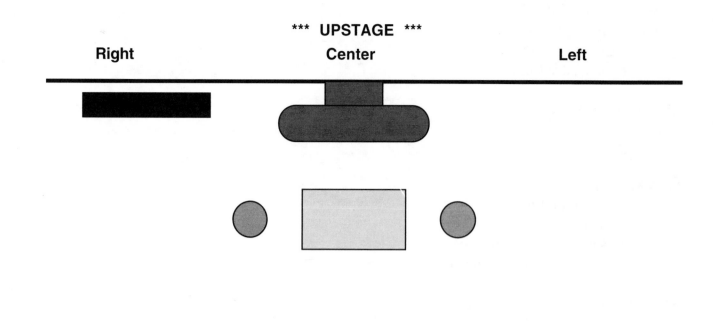

Stage Plan—*Here We Come A-Wassailing*

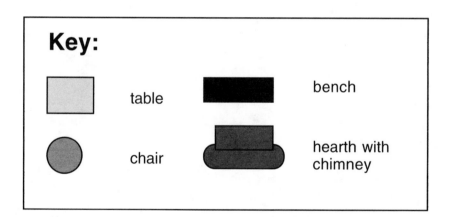

Key:

table

chair

bench

hearth with chimney

Here We Come A-Wassailing

(traditional, arranged by L.E. McCullough)

Silent Night

Almost as interesting as the circumstances surrounding the creation of *Silent Night* is the trail of the song's subsequent dissemination into the world beyond Oberndorf, Austria. After its premiere performance at Midnight Mass in 1818, the song was forgotten until the following spring when the manuscript was discovered by the repairman who came to fix the church's rusted organ. He sang the untitled song on his travels until it was heard by two professional folk singing families, the Rainers and the Strassers, who each made *The Song from Heaven* part of their regular repertoire. In 1834 the Strassers sang the song for the King of Prussia who liked it so much he ordered it sung by his own choir every Christmas Eve. The Rainers first sang the song in the United States in 1839 in New York City. Franz Gruber did not hear the song again until 1854; he shocked the music authorities of the day by announcing that he, a small-town music teacher, had composed the music to this by now world-famous song. Fr. Mohr died in 1848 without ever knowing the song had been sung again. In 1863 *Stille Nacht! Heilige Nacht!* was translated into English by Reverend John Freedman Young, the Episcopal bishop of Florida.

Silent Night

TIME: Christmas Eve, 1818

PLACE: Church of St. Nicholas,
                                         Oberndorf, Austria

CAST:
    Fr. Josef Mohr   Sexton Sirker
    Franz Gruber   Altar Boy
    Herr Hummel   Guitar Student
    Frau Schmidt   4 Congregation Members
    Choir Members

STAGE SET: church interior with altar and 2 pews (or benches); Gruber's music studio with table and 2 chairs

PROPS: Psalm book; baton; shovel; guitar; music paper; quill pen; ink pot

COSTUMES: characters dress in early 19th-century German peasant garb; Fr. Mohr wears standard black cassock and a wide-brimmed hat, for Mass he wears a chasuble — a white blouse over his cassock; Herr Hummel could wear fancy frock coat and breeches; Gruber and other men wear more common vests, trousers and boots; women wear plain dresses and bonnets

☆ ☆ ☆

(LIGHTS UP RIGHT AND CENTER ON CHURCH INTERIOR. An old woman, FRAU SCHMIDT, kneels in a pew, head bowed and hands folded in prayer.)

FRAU SCHMIDT And please, oh Lord, a special prayer for those in our village suffering from hunger and hardship this Christmas Eve.

(She blesses herself, rises and turns to exit right as FR. JOSEF MOHR enters from right, blessing himself; he carries a Psalm book.)

FR. MOHR Good afternoon, Frau Schmidt. How are you today?

FRAU SCHMIDT I am in good health, Father. Though my cottage may be washed away with all this rain and melting snow.

FR. MOHR It has been raining quite a bit lately.

FRAU SCHMIDT Six weeks, Father. Six weeks it has either rained or snowed every day. Is God trying to drown us? Have we people of Oberndorf so offended him that he is going to flood our sins away?

FR. MOHR *(Chuckles.)* I do not know if it is time yet to build an ark, Frau Schmidt. But you may be right about God sending us a message. He is always speaking to us, even in the most humble ways. We must train ourselves to listen.

FRAU SCHMIDT Yes, Father. Good day. *(Blesses herself, exits right.)*

FR. MOHR Good day. And keep dry.

(Fr. Mohr crosses to altar platform, where he genuflects and then kneels, praying.)

FR. MOHR Dear God, I ask that you not only hear our prayers, but open our ears to hear your voice as well. Open our ears to the needs of our fellow men and women. Open our ears to the sounds of music and laughter celebrating the birthday of your only son, Jesus. And open our ears... to the silence... yes, the silence... so we can better hear the sound of your divine, majestic voice as it speaks to us through the world you have created for us to enjoy.

(HERR HUMMEL enters excitedly from right, waving a baton, and crosses to center.)

HERR HUMMEL Father Mohr! Father Mohr!

FR. MOHR *(Stands.)* Yes, Herr Hummel?

HERR HUMMEL Father, the organ is ruined!

FR. MOHR Ruined?

HERR HUMMEL The dampness from this rain has rusted the pipes. The pedals are stuck. And the bellows have been nibbled by mice. The entire instrument is ruined!

FR. MOHR Is it beyond repair?

HERR HUMMEL I don't know about that. But for mass tonight, there will be no organ.

FR. MOHR And without the organ, there will be no choir.

HERR HUMMEL No choir, no music. And how can there not be music for Midnight Mass at St. Nicholas Church?

(SEXTON SIRKER rushes in from right, carrying a muddy shovel.)

FR. MOHR Sexton Sirker! You look exhausted!

SEXTON SIRKER Bad news, Father! The river has run over its banks. I have been digging since daybreak to keep it out, but water is flowing under the church.

FR. MOHR Will it get worse?

SEXTON SIRKER In a few hours the entire building could tear away from the foundation — and collapse!

HERR HUMMEL Ach! We have no organ, no choir and now no church!

SEXTON SIRKER What shall I do, Father?

FR. MOHR *(Holds up the Psalm book, reflects for a moment.)* "I will sing a new song to you, O God; upon a ten-stringed harp I will play to you." *(Pause.)* There is nothing we can do about the river, gentlemen. But there *is* something we can do about the music. Meet me here at nine o'clock—with the choir.

(LIGHTS OUT. Sirker and Hummel exit right. Fr. Mohr crosses to stage left. LIGHTS UP LEFT ON MUSIC STUDIO where FRANZ GRUBER sits teaching a GUITAR STUDENT who holds a guitar. Some music paper and a quill pen and ink pot are on the table. Fr. Mohr stands to their right behind Gruber.)

FRANZ GRUBER Very good, Anna. The Bach minuet in G is a difficult piece to interpret with proper feeling. You are well on your way to mastering it.

GUITAR STUDENT Thank you, Herr Gruber. *(Notices Fr. Mohr.)* Father Mohr!

(Gruber and the Student stand.)

FR. MOHR Please, please, I do not wish to disturb your lesson.

FRANZ GRUBER A visit from you is an honor, not a disturbance. Come, enter.

(Gruber offers his chair to Fr. Mohr, who sits; Student sits.)

FR. MOHR Herr Gruber, the organ at St. Nicholas has been ruined by the damp. Herr Hummel cannot play his Christmas music for the Midnight Mass.

FRANZ GRUBER That is a tragedy. Herr Hummel is a fine organist.

FR. MOHR And you are a fine guitarist.

FRANZ GRUBER *(Chuckles.)* You are too kind, Father. I am an untrained musician. I play nothing of significance—only a few folk tunes.

FR. MOHR Like that minuet by the folk musician Johann Sebastian Bach? *(Laughs.)* Herr Gruber, you are much too modest. I know that the instrument you play, the guitar, is not used in the church.

FRANZ GRUBER *(Bitterly.)* "Too common," say the authorities. "A peasant instrument." Not "noble enough" for serious worship.

FR. MOHR When the humblest peasant speaks with the voice of God, he is as noble as any duke or prince. Herr Gruber, I need you— and your guitar—to perform music at Midnight Mass.

FRANZ GRUBER Midnight Mass!

FR. MOHR We must compose a song for the choir. This afternoon.

FRANZ GRUBER Impossible!

FR. MOHR It is your chance to make music that is truly divine.

(Gruber says nothing for a moment, then takes the guitar from his Student.)

FRANZ GRUBER Anna, take pen and paper. You will be our scribe.

(Anna pulls her chair to table and readies herself to write.)

FRANZ GRUBER Have you any verses, Father?

FR. MOHR I am afraid my desperation has not produced inspiration. Have you a melody?

FRANZ GRUBER I cannot write a melody without a picture.

FR. MOHR A picture?

FRANZ GRUBER A picture in my mind. If I write a song about a person, I must see that person. A house, I must see that house. A Savior... *(Shrugs.)* I have never seen a Savior, Father. Have you?

(Fr. Mohr nods "no." Gruber paces with guitar. Fr. Mohr stares away toward audience. No one speaks for several seconds.)

FRANZ GRUBER *(Stops pacing, looks toward audience.)* Listen to that rain. It is so persistent.

FR. MOHR Yet so gentle. Almost like a lullaby.

FRANZ GRUBER Yes, a lullaby. A mother and her child. Asleep in the still of the night.

FR. MOHR Surrounded only by silence. The silence of peace.

FRANZ GRUBER Can you imagine that holy night in Bethlehem? How quiet it must have been after the Christ child was born!

GUITAR STUDENT They say not even the animals made a sound.

FRANZ GRUBER *(Crosses to Fr. Mohr, outlines the scene with his hands.)* Yes, in the stable! In the moonlight flooding down upon the stable.

FR. MOHR All is calm. All is bright.

FRANZ GRUBER Shepherds and animals gathered around the Virgin Mother and her child.

FR. MOHR Holy infant. So tender.

GUITAR STUDENT So mild.

FRANZ GRUBER Sleeping. Sleeping.

FR. MOHR In heavenly peace.

FRANZ GRUBER Anna, take down this melody...a lullaby...not too fast...three-four time...

(Gruber begins playing first few notes of "Silent Night." LIGHTS OUT FOR TEN SECONDS, THEN UP RIGHT AND CENTER ON CHURCH where the town is gathered for Midnight Mass. THE CHOIR stands against back curtain with Franz Gruber and his guitar to their right, Herr Hummel and his baton in front; THE CONGREGATION including Frau Schmidt and Anna sit in the two pew rows; Fr. Mohr and AN ALTAR BOY are at the altar.)

FR. MOHR My friends, this is a troublesome time in the world. A troublesome time in Austria. A troublesome time in our own small village of Oberndorf. But we must not fall victim to fear. For fear is a temptation to sin. Instead, let us remember words from today's gospel: "And the angel said to them, 'Do not be afraid, for behold, I bring you good news of great joy which shall be to all the people. For today in the town of David, a Savior has been born to you who is Christ the Lord. And this shall be a sign to you: you will find an Infant wrapped in swaddling clothes and lying in a manger.'" Let us raise our voices in song, and sing of this good news.

(He points to Herr Hummel, who cues Franz Gruber to begin playing guitar; Choir sings "Silent Night.")

CHOIR *(Sings.)*
  Silent night, holy night
  All is calm, all is bright
  Round yon Virgin Mother and child
  Holy Infant so tender and mild
  Sleep in heavenly peace
  Sleep in heavenly peace

(Choir is joined by Congregation.)

CHOIR & CONGREGATION *(Sing.)*
  Silent night, holy night
  Shepherds quake at the sight
  Glories stream from heaven afar
  Heavenly hosts sing alleluia
  Christ the Savior is born
  Christ the Savior is born

(Sexton Sirker bursts in from right.)

SEXTON SIRKER The river! The river! It's gone down!

(Congregation sighs, exclaims with relief.)

GUITAR STUDENT The town is saved!

FRAU SCHMIDT It is a miracle! God has heard our prayers!

FR. MOHR Now let Him hear our thanks! *(Turns to audience.)* Everyone! Lift up your voice in thanks!

ALL *(Sing.)*

    Silent night, holy night
    Son of God, love's pure light
    Radiant beams from Thy holy face
    With the dawn of redeeming grace
    Jesus, Lord, at Thy birth
    Jesus, Lord, at Thy birth

    Silent night, holy night
    All is calm, all is bright
    Round yon Virgin Mother and child
    Holy Infant so tender and mild
    Sleep in heavenly peace
    Sleep in heavenly peace

(LIGHTS OUT.)

THE END

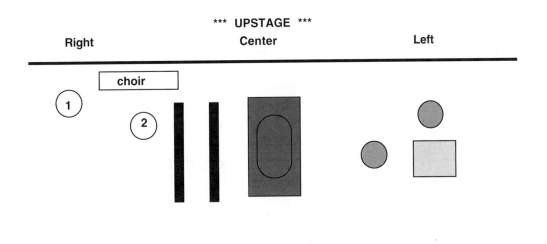

Stage Plan—*Silent Night*

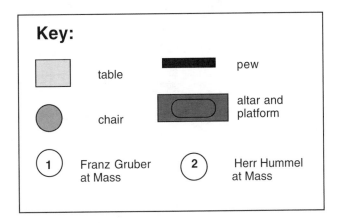

Silent Night

(Words: Joseph Mohr / Music: Franz Gruber / Arranged: L.E. McCullough)

The Twelve Days of Christmas

The Twelve Days of Christmas is perhaps the best known example of the "counting song," a type of song very popular in the Middle Ages. Counting songs were often used to teach as well as entertain. The version of *The Twelve Days of Christmas* known today was first published in England in 1842. Of course, if all the presents were actually delivered each time they were mentioned in the song, the total numbers would be: 12 drummers drumming, 22 pipers playing, 30 lords a-leaping, 36 ladies dancing, 40 maids a-milking (and their 40 cows), 42 swans a-swimming, 42 geese a-laying, 40 gold rings, 36 calling birds, 30 French hens, 22 turtle doves and 12 partridges in a dozen pear trees—quite a houseful even for the holidays!

The Twelve Days of Christmas

TIME: Christmas Season in the Olden Time

PLACE: The Royal Palace, Kingdom of Pfeffernüsse

CAST:
Narrator
Princess Harmonia
Prince Hasalot
Myopia, the Princess' Maid
Flaccido, the Prince's Manservant
Royal Trumpeter

12 Drummers Drumming
11 Pipers Piping
10 Lords A-Leaping
9 Ladies Dancing
8 Maids A-Milking

STAGE SET: a large sofa at center stage

PROPS: 5 gold rings; a ring tray; cardboard cutouts or stuffed fabric representations of a partridge glued to a potted pear tree, 2 turtle doves in a bird cage, 3 French hens, 4 calling birds in a cage, 6 geese, 7 swans, 8 cows; parchment scroll; woman's hair brush; hand mirror; handkerchief; boombox; 11 kazoos for pipers; percussion instruments for 12 drummers

SPECIAL EFFECTS: sound—trumpet fanfare; a boombox tune

MUSIC: *Scotland the Brave* played on Highland bagpipes or kazoo

COSTUMES: characters dress in medieval costume appropriate to their occupation and social status; some characters could add modern touches: pipers could dress in tartan kilts, ladies in ballet outfits, maids in milkman uniforms or cowhorns, drummers with sunglasses, and so forth.

PERFORMANCE NOTE: For greater comical effect, the trumpet fanfare should be played badly or jazzily, or sounded by a kazoo or group of kazoos.

☆ ☆ ☆

(LIGHTS UP FULL. NARRATOR stands at stage right holding a scrolled piece of parchment; ROYAL TRUMPETER stands at left holding trumpet.)

NARRATOR

Welcome to the royal palace
Where we start our Christmas tale.
We bid you all a pleasant time
And a hearty, bold "Wassail!"

(PRINCESS HARMONIA enters quickly from stage left holding a hair brush and is followed by her maid, MYOPIA, who squints and bumps into things; Princess Harmonia plops onto the sofa at center stage and begins brushing her hair as Myopia holds the mirror.)

NARRATOR

Here in the Kingdom of Pfeffernüsse
There lived a Princess fair,
Who spent her days in leisure
Mostly brushing her hair.

Harmonia was this royal's name,
Myopia, her trusty maid,
Whose eyesight was so awfully poor
She'd mistake mashed potatoes for marmalade.

(SOUND: ROYAL TRUMPETER sounds fanfare. PRINCE HASALOT strides in from stage left, followed by his slow-moving servant, FLACCIDO; the Prince crosses to the sofa and bows before the Princess as Myopia squints at him.)

NARRATOR

But on this first day of Christmas
There came a trumpet blast.
And in strode Prince Hasalot
With his entire supporting cast.

PRINCE HASALOT

My dearest lovely Princess,
I come to win your hand.
I will shower you with presents
And hope you understand

That I, Prince Hasalot,
The richest suitor in the realm
Will prove his love's true value
And your shyness overwhelm.

Go now, Flaccido,
And fetch the first day's gift

While I sit with the Princess
And watch her spirits uplift.

(Prince sits on sofa next to Princess as Flaccido lopes to stage left, goes behind curtain and re-enters carrying a potted plant with a partridge glued to a leaf. Princess stands and sings.)

PRINCESS HARMONIA *(Sings.)*
On the first day of Christmas
My true love gave to me:
A partridge in a pear tree.

(Prince stands and receives the potted plant from Flaccido; the Prince presents it to Princess, who nods and hands it to Myopia, who takes it to the right of the sofa and puts it on the floor.)

PRINCESS HARMONIA
Why thank you, for your kindly thought,
A partridge I've long desired.
I suppose I'll find a place for it
Someday when I'm retired.

PRINCE HASALOT
Oh, but Princess, you've seen nothing yet,
That tree is just a twig.
Flaccido, bring the next day's gift!
And get ready to flip your wig!

(SOUND: ROYAL TRUMPETER sounds fanfare. Princess and Prince sit; Prince gestures for Flaccido to bring in another gift; Flaccido shuffles left, goes behind curtain and re-enters carrying a bird cage with two turtle doves. Princess stands and sings.)

PRINCESS HARMONIA *(Sings.)*
On the second day of Christmas
My true love gave to me:
Two turtle doves
And a partridge in a pear tree.

(Prince stands and receives the bird cage from Flaccido; the Prince presents it to Princess, who nods and hands it to Myopia, who takes it to the right of the sofa and puts it on the floor next to the potted plant.)

PRINCESS HARMONIA
These turtle doves are truly fine;
I adore their constant cooing.

MYOPIA

I wonder if they ever sleep?
Or for supper they'll soon be stewing!

PRINCE HASALOT

Harmonia, your very name
Excites within me passion!
Flaccido, bring the third day's gift!
It's the very latest fashion!

(SOUND: ROYAL TRUMPETER sounds fanfare. Princess and Prince sit; Prince gestures for Flaccido to bring in another gift; Flaccido trots left, goes behind curtain and re-enters carrying three French hens in his arms. Princess stands and sings.)

PRINCESS HARMONIA *(Sings.)*

On the third day of Christmas
My true love gave to me:

PRINCE HASALOT *(Stands, sings.)*

Three French hens,
Two turtle doves
And a partridge in a pear tree.

(Prince Hasalot directs Flaccido to present the hens to the Princess, who gestures for them to be given to Myopia, who receives them from Flaccido and takes them to the right of the sofa and arranges them on the floor next to the potted plant and bird cage.)

PRINCESS HARMONIA

Once again, my Prince,
Your generosity is grand.
But to live inside a hen house,
I really hadn't planned.

PRINCE HASALOT

My Princess dear, a special treat
I have for you in store.
Flaccido, bring the fourth day's gift
And be quick about the chore!

(SOUND: ROYAL TRUMPETER sounds fanfare. Princess and Prince sit; Prince gestures for Flaccido to bring in another gift; Flaccido lumbers left, goes behind curtain and re-enters carrying a cage with four calling birds in his arms. Princess stands and sings.)

The Twelve Days of Christmas 29

PRINCESS HARMONIA *(Sings.)*
On the fourth day of Christmas
My true love gave to me:

PRINCE HASALOT *(Stands, sings.)*
Four calling birds
Three French hens

PRINCESS HARMONIA *(Sings.)*
Two turtle doves

MYOPIA *(Sings.)*
And a partridge in a pear tree.

(Prince Hasalot directs Flaccido to present the cage to the Princess, who gestures for it to be given to Myopia, who receives it from Flaccido and takes it to the right of the sofa and puts it on the floor next to the potted plant, turtle dove bird cage and French hens.)

PRINCE HASALOT
Now, Princess dear, I think you see
How I'd love you for all eternity.
All this and more are yours to keep.
Nay, my darling, how come thou weep?

(Princess has begun sniffling; Myopia wipes her nose with a handkerchief.)

PRINCESS HARMONIA
My Prince, oh please, do hear me well
Your kindness has me taken aback.
But whatever you choose to bring out next
Make sure it does not quack?

(SOUND: ROYAL TRUMPETER sounds fanfare. Prince gestures for Flaccido to bring in another gift; Flaccido lumbers left, goes behind curtain and re-enters carrying a tray with five golden rings.)

PRINCESS HARMONIA *(Sings.)*
On the fifth day of Christmas
My true love gave to me:

PRINCE HASALOT *(Sings.)*
Five golden rings

PRINCESS HARMONIA *(Sings.)*
Four calling birds
Three French hens

PRINCE HASALOT *(Sings.)*
Two turtle doves

MYOPIA *(Sings.)*
And a partridge in a pear tree.

(Prince Hasalot receives tray from Flaccido and presents it to Princess, who delightedly puts on all the rings and gestures for the tray to be given to Myopia, who tosses it behind the sofa.)

PRINCESS HARMONIA
That, sir Prince, is a vast improvement
Running more to a woman's style.

MYOPIA
Bring on the gold, the silver, the gems
Forget all those feathery piles!

(SOUND: ROYAL TRUMPETER sounds fanfare. Prince gestures for Flaccido to bring in another gift; Flaccido stumps left, goes behind curtain and re-enters carrying/dragging six geese, dropping them, booting them along to center stage. Narrator and Royal Trumpeter make goose-squawk noises.)

PRINCESS HARMONIA *(Sings.)*
On the sixth day of Christmas
My true love gave to me:
Six geese a-laying

PRINCE HASALOT *(Sings.)*
Five golden rings

PRINCESS HARMONIA *(Sings.)*
Four calling birds
Three French hens

PRINCE HASALOT *(Sings.)*
Two turtle doves

MYOPIA *(Sings.)*
And a partridge in a pear tree.

(Prince Hasalot directs Flaccido to present the geese to the Princess, who gestures for them to be given to Myopia, who receives them from Flaccido and shoves them to the right of the sofa next to the other gifts.)

MYOPIA *(Squinting at the geese.)*
All these children squawking about!
They seem so short and awfully stout!

PRINCESS HARMONIA
Please, dear Prince, your giving stay;
I think we've run out of room today!

(SOUND: ROYAL TRUMPETER sounds fanfare. Prince gestures for Flaccido to bring in another gift; Flaccido slumps left, goes behind curtain and re-enters carrying/dragging seven swans, dropping them, booting them along to center stage. Narrator and Royal Trumpeter make swan-call noises.)

PRINCESS HARMONIA *(Sings.)*
On the seventh day of Christmas
My true love gave to me:

PRINCE HASALOT *(Sings.)*
Seven swans a-swimming

PRINCESS HARMONIA *(Sings.)*
Six geese a-laying

PRINCE HASALOT *(Sings.)*
Five golden rings

PRINCESS HARMONIA *(Sings.)*
Four calling birds

PRINCE HASALOT *(Sings.)*
Three French hens

PRINCESS HARMONIA *(Sings.)*
Two turtle doves

MYOPIA *(Sings.)*
And a partridge in a pear tree.

(Prince Hasalot directs Flaccido to present the swans to the Princess, who gestures for them to be given to Myopia, who receives them from Flaccido and dumps them to the right of the sofa next to the other gifts.)

PRINCESS HARMONIA (*Throws up her hands.*)
> I can't believe it!
> This Prince is insane!
> He's taken every bird
> From its forest domain!

PRINCE HASALOT
> My dearest Harmonia,
> Pray, feel no alarm.
> No palace would be complete
> Without a working dairy farm.

(SOUND: ROYAL TRUMPETER sounds fanfare. Prince gestures for Flaccido to bring in another gift; Flaccido drags left, goes to curtain and whistles: EIGHT MAIDS A-MILKING enter and cross to center stage, each carrying her own cow as Flaccido herds them along. Narrator and Royal Trumpeter make cow-moo noises.)

PRINCESS HARMONIA (*Sings.*)
> On the eighth day of Christmas
> My true love gave to me:

PRINCE HASALOT (*Sings.*)
> Eight maids a-milking

FLACCIDO (*Sings.*)
> Seven swans a-swimming

PRINCESS HARMONIA (*Sings.*)
> Six geese a-laying

PRINCE HASALOT (*Sings.*)
> Five golden rings

FLACCIDO (*Sings.*)
> Four calling birds

PRINCE HASALOT (*Sings.*)
> Three French hens

PRINCESS HARMONIA (*Sings.*)
> Two turtle doves

MYOPIA & EIGHT MAIDS (*Sing.*)
> And a partridge in a pear tree.

(The maids curtsey to the Princess, who staggers back onto the sofa in shock; Myopia pushes the maids off to the right of the sofa where they sit and milk their cows.)

PRINCE HASALOT
Aha! I see by the look in your eyes
You've been dazzled by my gifts!
Well, Princess dear, have no fear
This next offering will give you a lift!

(SOUND: ROYAL TRUMPETER sounds fanfare. Prince gestures for Flaccido to bring in another gift; Flaccido remains at center stage and shouts:)

FLACCIDO
Yo! Bring in the dancers!

(SOUND: Royal Trumpeter holds out a boombox playing some sort of contemporary Top 40 dance tune for five-ten seconds as NINE LADIES DANCING enter and twirl to center stage; Narrator and Royal Trumpeter vocalize with boombox music, which stops when singing starts.)

PRINCESS HARMONIA *(Sings.)*
On the ninth day of Christmas
My true love gave to me:

NINE LADIES *(Sing.)*
Nine ladies dancing

EIGHT MAIDS *(Sing.)*
Eight maids a-milking

FLACCIDO *(Sings.)*
Seven swans a-swimming

PRINCESS HARMONIA *(Sings.)*
Six geese a-laying

PRINCE HASALOT *(Sings.)*
Five golden rings

FLACCIDO *(Sings.)*
Four calling birds

PRINCE HASALOT *(Sings.)*
Three French hens

PRINCESS HARMONIA *(Sings.)*
Two turtle doves

MYOPIA, EIGHT MAIDS & NINE LADIES *(Sing.)*
And a partridge in a pear tree.

(The dancers curtsey to the Princess, who hides her head in hands; Myopia pushes the dancers off to the right of the sofa behind the maids.)

PRINCE HASALOT
And how lonely ladies dancing are,
Unless they have their beaus;

MYOPIA
If you bring one more gift in here
I'll punch you in the nose!

(SOUND: ROYAL TRUMPETER sounds fanfare. Prince gestures for Flaccido to bring in another gift; Flaccido remains at center stage and bellows:)

FLACCIDO
Ten lords a-leaping! Move it!

(TEN LORDS A-LEAPING enter and somersault to center stage, as ladies dance in place.)

PRINCESS HARMONIA *(Sings.)*
On the tenth day of Christmas
My true love gave to me:

TEN LORDS *(Sing.)*
Ten lords a-leaping

NINE LADIES *(Sing.)*
Nine ladies dancing

EIGHT MAIDS *(Sing.)*
Eight maids a-milking

FLACCIDO *(Sings.)*
Seven swans a-swimming

PRINCESS HARMONIA *(Sings.)*
Six geese a-laying

PRINCE HASALOT *(Sings.)*
Five golden rings

FLACCIDO *(Sings.)*
Four calling birds

PRINCE HASALOT *(Sings.)*
Three French hens

PRINCESS HARMONIA *(Sings.)*
Two turtle doves

MYOPIA, EIGHT MAIDS, NINE LADIES & TEN LORDS *(Sing.)*
And a partridge in a pear tree.

(The lords bow to the Princess, who waves at them weakly; Myopia and Flaccido arrange the lords behind the sofa. Prince takes the Princess' hand.)

PRINCE HASALOT
Alas, I feel I have not yet
Wiped away that royal frown
Flaccido, send in day eleven's gift
And we shall party down!

(SOUND: ROYAL TRUMPETER sounds fanfare. Prince gestures for Flaccido to bring in another gift; Flaccido remains at center stage and bellows:)

FLACCIDO
Piperssssssssss, ho!

(ELEVEN PIPERS PIPING enter playing on kazoo [or miming to an offstage tape of] a few seconds of "Scotland the Brave" and march to center stage, as ladies dance and lords leap around stage, maids milk, Princess puts hands over her ears and cowers on sofa.)

PRINCESS HARMONIA *(Sings.)*
On the eleventh day of Christmas
My true love gave to me:

ELEVEN PIPERS *(Sing.)*
Eleven pipers piping

TEN LORDS *(Sing.)*
Ten lords a-leaping

NINE LADIES *(Sing.)*
Nine ladies dancing

EIGHT MAIDS *(Sing.)*
Eight maids a-milking

FLACCIDO *(Sings.)*
Seven swans a-swimming

PRINCESS HARMONIA *(Sings.)*
Six geese a-laying

PRINCE HASALOT *(Sings.)*
Five golden rings

FLACCIDO *(Sings.)*
Four calling birds

PRINCE HASALOT *(Sings.)*
Three French hens

PRINCESS HARMONIA *(Sings.)*
Two turtle doves

MYOPIA, EIGHT MAIDS, NINE LADIES, TEN LORDS & ELEVEN PIPERS *(Sing.)*
And a partridge in a pear tree.

(The pipers salute the Princess, who still holds her ears; Myopia and Flaccido send the pipers to left of sofa. The Prince kneels before the Princess, who looks away.)

PRINCE HASALOT
Now, my darling, tell me true,
Shall we live in wedded bliss?

PRINCESS HARMONIA
I'd give my kingdom for an aspirin
And to be miles away from this!

(Prince stands and gestures to Flaccido to call in the next gift.)

FLACCIDO
Rhythm Section! On the double!

(TWELVE DRUMMERS DRUMMING enter playing all sorts of percussion instruments and do a conga line to center stage, as ladies dance and lords leap around stage, maids milk, pipers toot kazoos.)

PRINCESS HARMONIA *(Sings.)*
On the twelfth day of Christmas
My true love gave to me:

TWELVE DRUMMERS *(Sing.)*
Twelve drummers drumming

ELEVEN PIPERS *(Sing.)*
Eleven pipers piping

TEN LORDS *(Sing.)*
Ten lords a-leaping

NINE LADIES *(Sing.)*
Nine ladies dancing

EIGHT MAIDS *(Sing.)*
Eight maids a-milking

FLACCIDO *(Sings.)*
Seven swans a-swimming

PRINCESS HARMONIA *(Sings.)*
Six geese a-laying

PRINCE HASALOT *(Sings.)*
Five golden rings

FLACCIDO *(Sings.)*
Four calling birds

PRINCE HASALOT *(Sings.)*
Three French hens

PRINCESS HARMONIA *(Sings.)*
Two turtle doves

MYOPIA *(Sings.)*
And a...

(Myopia starts to sing, stops when she notices no one else is singing, then finishes the line.)

MYOPIA *(Sings.)*
...partridge in a pear tree.

(The drummers salute the Princess and are sent by Myopia and Flaccido to join pipers at left of sofa. The Princess stands.)

PRINCESS HARMONIA
Stop now, everyone, and listen to me
And from all noise please do refrain.
Dear Prince, I'm afraid you've missed the point
To which Christmas does pertain.

Christmas is not about costly gifts
Or fancy fiddle-dee-dee.
It's about caring for other people
Not so fortunate as are we.

The greatest gift that one can give
Is from the heart and soul within.
For that is where true beauty lies
And not upon the skin.

The man I marry won't gain my heart
By trinkets and toys sublime.
But only if he learns that Christmas lives
In the love he shows all humankind.

PRINCE HASALOT
Oh, Princess dear, your words ring true;
I see the error of my role.
I hereby declare these gifts and more
To be given to the kingdom whole.

Bring in the poor, the aged, the sick
To share our bountiful feast.
Those without families or friends to join,
Let them be our guests in peace.

Now let us all raise voices high
And sing of Christmas plenty—

MYOPIA
And be glad Christmas has just twelve days
And not fifteen or twenty!

(All sing entire "The Twelve Days of Christmas" song.)

ALL *(Sing.)*
On the first (second, third, etc.) day of Christmas, my true love gave to me:
1.   A partridge in a pear tree
2.   Two turtle doves and a partridge in a pear tree

3. Three French hens, two turtle doves, etc.
4. Four calling birds, etc.
5. Five golden rings, etc.
6. Six geese a-laying, etc.
7. Seven swans a-swimming, etc.
8. Eight maids a-milking, etc.
9. Nine ladies dancing, etc.
10. Ten lords a-leaping, etc.
11. Eleven pipers piping, etc.
12. Twelve drummers drumming, etc.

(LIGHTS OUT.)

THE END

The Twelve Days of Christmas
(traditional, arranged by L.E. McCullough)

On the first day of Christ- mas my true love gave to me: a

par- tridge in a pear tree. On the sec-ond day of Christ- mas my

true love gave to me: two tur- tle doves and a part- ridge in a pear

tree. On the third day of Christ- mas my true love gave to me:

three French hens, two tur- tle doves and a part- ridge in a pear

tree. On the fourth day of Christ- mas my true love gave to me:

four cal- ling birds, three French hens, two tur- tle doves and a

The Twelve Days of Christmas

par- tridge   in   a   pear   tree.   On the   fifth   day   of   Christ- mas my

true love gave to   me: five   gold-   en   rings

fo- ur   cal- ling birds,   three French hens,   two___ tur- tle doves and a

par-   tridge___   in   a   pear   tree.   On   the

sixth   day of Christ-mas my   true love gave to me: six geese a- lay-ing (to #5)
seventh day, etc.   seven, etc. (to #6)

five   gold- en   rings   fo- ur   cal- ling birds,

D.S.

three French hens,   two___ tur- tle doves and a   par- tridge in a pear   tree.

O, Christmas Tree

Decorating a tree at Christmas is a custom that was first practiced in Germany in the early Middle Ages. Centuries before, in pre-Christian times, Northern Europeans made mid-winter sacrifices to evergreen trees such as firs in hopes of ensuring a bountiful harvest in the coming year. With the coming of Christianity, "paradise trees" were popular and accompanied by plays about Christ's birth. The first written reference to a fully decorated Christmas tree comes from 1605 in Strasbourg; Hessian soldiers from Germany introduced the custom to America in the 1770s. In 1856 Franklin Pierce decorated the first tree at the White House. St. Boniface was a Benedictine monk born in England about 680 A.D. and was the first Roman Catholic Bishop of Germany. He died a martyr in 754 A.D.

O, Christmas Tree

TIME: Christmas Eve, 720 A.D.

PLACE: The Dark Forest of Geismar,
                                                Germany

CAST:
   St. Boniface   Gundhar, Chief of the Teutons
   Brother Liam   Gruach the Druid
   Lovernios   6 Teuton Warriors

STAGE SET: scrim with forest scenery; large oak tree; small fir tree with low bushes around it; small kindling sticks scattered around down right and down center

PROPS: staff for St. Boniface; swords and spears for Teutons; long knife for Druid; rope for Lovernios; small kindling sticks

SPECIAL EFFECTS: sound—wind whistling, wolf howling in distance, thunder, lightning; visual—lightning flashes

COSTUMES: St. Boniface and Brother Liam dress as early monks: simple brown or black robe with rope belt, sandals, winter cloak, a crucifix around the neck, a rosary tied to belt; Gruach the Druid wears a long green robe with hood; Lovernios is dressed in white robe; Gundhar and his Teuton warriors dress in 8th-century barbarian garb: rough wool shirts, vests and trousers with leather leggings wrapped around legs, Viking-style helmet-type headgear; Gundhar might have a gold necklace or more ornate helmet or belt to show his status as chief

☆ ☆ ☆

(SOUND: WIND WHISTLING, WOLF HOWLING IN DISTANCE. SPOTLIGHT STAGE RIGHT as ST. BONIFACE, carrying a staff, enters from right, followed closely by BROTHER LIAM. St. Boniface stops, looks out toward audience as if straining to see something faraway. Sounds fade out.)

BROTHER LIAM *(Anxiously.)* Brother Boniface, what do you see? Are we in danger? Are we lost?

ST. BONIFACE *(Turns to Brother Liam, chuckles.)* We are men, Brother Liam, and men are always in danger. In danger of losing faith in God and yielding our eternal souls to the Tempter. But as long as we trust in the power and goodness of Christ the Lord born this very night seven centuries ago, we shall not be lost.

BROTHER LIAM Of course, Brother. But I was referring to the immediate danger of being immediately lost.

(SOUND: WOLF HOWLING IN DISTANCE.)

BROTHER LIAM We are still far from the abbey, I believe. Perhaps we should build a fire and rest for the night?

ST. BONIFACE If you wish.

BROTHER LIAM *(Folds hands in prayer, looks to sky.)* Thank you, Lord. *(To St. Boniface.)* I will gather wood, Brother.

(Brother Liam scampers around down right and center gathering firewood kindling as St. Boniface kneels at down right, facing audience, still in spotlight.)

BROTHER LIAM This is my first time as a missionary to Germania. Ireland seems so much more... civilized. They say the Teutons are a fierce and savage people. I have heard tales—terrible tales, Brother—of tribes here in the dark forest of Geismar who still live in trees and eat raw food uncooked by fire.

ST. BONIFACE We are here to bring fire.

BROTHER LIAM Bring fire? Yes, Brother, in a moment, in a moment, a few more sticks, I will bring the fire.

ST. BONIFACE You have already brought the fire, my son. It is the fire you carry within your soul that brings light to the minds and hearts of pagans... light that shows them the path to Heaven. Your fire must burn bright for all the world to see, even in these gloomy woods.

BROTHER LIAM (*Pauses, puzzled.*) Yes, Brother Boniface. That is true, very true. I will make a bright fire.

(*Brother Liam turns toward up center and gathers more wood. LIGHTS COME UP SLOWLY TO FULL revealing GUNDHAR, 6 TEUTON WARRIORS and GRUACH THE DRUID gathered silently around a large oak tree, to which is tied a young man, LOVERNIOS. Brother Liam notices them, pauses, then drops his kindling and shouts.*)

BROTHER LIAM Blessed Virgin, preserve us!

(*St. Boniface turns and faces the Teutons.*)

ST. BONIFACE I am Boniface of the Abbey of La Tène. This is my assistant, Brother Liam. We have come to bring the word of Christ to the Teuton people of Germania.

(*Gundhar strides forward, looks contemptuously at the quaking Brother Liam, and speaks to St. Boniface.*)

GUNDHAR I am Gundhar, chief of the Teutons. We listen to the word of Odin and to the many gods who serve him. Who is this Christ you speak of?

ST. BONIFACE He was a carpenter's son born in a humble stable in Palestine. As a man, he taught kindness and love for all, even one's enemies.

BROTHER LIAM And he made many miracles. He turned water into wine...and multiplied bread and fishes...and cured lepers and the blind.

ST. BONIFACE But the greatest miracle of all: he so loved his people that he allowed himself to be put to death in order to save humankind. He freed us from the darkness your gods revere.

(*Gundhar and the Warriors snicker.*)

GUNDHAR A god allowed himself to be killed? (*Laughs.*) What a weak god he must be! Our god, Odin, is strong! He teaches us to crush our enemies, not love them!

(*Warriors roar approval.*)

ST. BONIFACE But you do understand the idea of sacrifice. That boy you have tied to the tree. You intend to offer him to Odin?

(*St. Boniface approaches the tree as Brother Liam shrinks behind him; Gruach the Druid steps forward and faces St. Boniface.*)

GRUACH I am Gruach the Druid, priest of mighty Odin. *(Points to tree.)* That is Lovernios. He is one of our most promising young warriors. He must be killed at this oak, the sacred tree of Odin, so that the gods continue to favor our tribe with good hunting and success in battle.

ST. BONIFACE When Jesus Christ died on the cross at Calvary, he gave his life for all men.

GRUACH All men?

ST. BONIFACE He died so that all could live in the light that shows the way to the Paradise. There is no need for more sacrifice.

LOVERNIOS I am not afraid to die for Odin and for my people. Nay, I am proud to be the chosen one, much as your Christ. But if our sins have already been banished and darkness defeated, I wish to live and serve him.

ST. BONIFACE Free the boy and let him proclaim the glory of Christ the King.

GUNDHAR Gruach, what say you to this Christian's words?

(Gruach draws a long knife from his belt, walks to the tree and holds knife to Lovernios' neck.)

GRUACH I say, if this man's god has any power, he should perform one of his miracles and save Lovernios from his fate!

(SOUND: WIND WHISTLING. St. Boniface turns toward audience, looks skyward, bows head for a few seconds, then raises his staff and strikes the oak tree. SOUND: THUNDER CRASHING, LIGHTNING CRACKING. LIGHTS FLICKER AS LIGHTNING FLASHES. Warriors, Gruach, Gundhar jump away from tree as it crashes to the ground, freeing Lovernios who kneels at the feet of St. Boniface.)

WARRIOR #1 Odin's tree has been destroyed!

WARRIOR #2 That oak tree is the biggest tree in the forest!

WARRIOR #3 It is a miracle! No axe could ever fell it!

WARRIOR #4 Not even the axes of a hundred men!

WARRIOR #5 Yet there it lies, smashed to the roots!

WARRIOR #6 The Christian's God is a powerful god! More powerful than Odin!

ST. BONIFACE *(To Gundhar.)* Now will you kneel before the power of Jesus Christ, who came as a babe to save all men?

(Gundhar looks at Gruach, who slowly nods assent. Gundhar kneels, Warriors kneel and lay down weapons, Gruach steps back left and turns away, his hood shielding his face.)

GUNDHAR I, Gundhar, chief of the Teutons, forsake our belief in Odin and the gods of darkness. We will serve the Christian god of light and keep his birthday holy for all time.

LOVERNIOS But what of Odin's tree? It was a mighty symbol of strength to our people.

(Brother Liam points to a small tree standing at the left of the fallen oak.)

BROTHER LIAM Look! A fresh green sapling rises amid the ruins of Odin's oak!

ST. BONIFACE There, Lovernios. There is the new symbol of strength for Germania—the fir tree. With its branches ever green through the coldest winter and darkest storm, it will remind your people of Jesus Christ, the bringer of life eternal.

(Teutons gather around fir tree and look wonderingly upon it.)

ST. BONIFACE Now let us all join hands and sing a hymn of adoration.

BROTHER LIAM To Christ, Brother Boniface?

ST. BONIFACE To Christ, Brother Liam—and to his tree. May it always remind us of the blessed babe born upon this day and his gift of love for all.

(All join hands and sing "O Christmas Tree.")

ALL *(Sing.)*
O Christmas Tree, O Christmas Tree
How lovely are your branches
O Christmas Tree, O Christmas Tree
How lovely are your branches
In summer sun, in winter snow
A dress of green you always show
O Christmas Tree, O Christmas Tree
How lovely are your branches

O Christmas Tree, O Christmas Tree
With happiness we greet you
O Christmas Tree, O Christmas Tree
With happiness we greet you
When decked with candles once a year

You fill our hearts with yuletide cheer
O Christmas Tree, O Christmas Tree
With happiness we greet you

O Christmas Tree, O Christmas Tree
With faithful leaves unchanging
O Christmas Tree, O Christmas Tree
With faithful leaves unchanging
Not only green in summer's heat
But also winter's snow and sleet
O Christmas Tree, O Christmas Tree
With faithful leaves unchanging

O Christmas Tree, O Christmas Tree
You are the tree most loved
O Christmas Tree, O Christmas Tree
You are the tree most loved
How oft you've given me delight
With Christmas fires burning bright
O Christmas Tree, O Christmas Tree
You are the tree most loved

O Christmas Tree, O Christmas Tree
Your faithful leaves will teach me
O Christmas Tree, O Christmas Tree
Your faithful leaves will teach me
That hope and love and constancy
Give joy and peace eternally
O Christmas Tree, O Christmas Tree
Your faithful leaves will teach me

(LIGHTS OUT.)

THE END

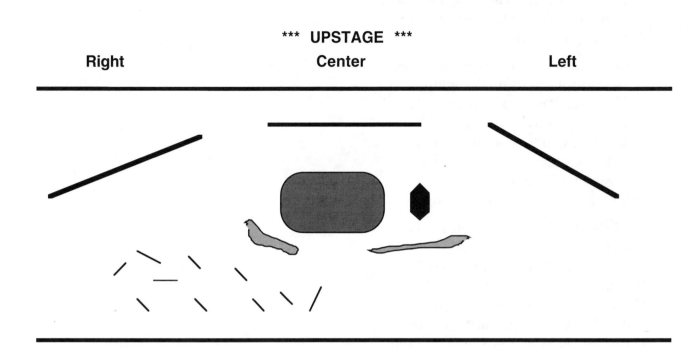

Stage Plan—*O Christmas Tree*

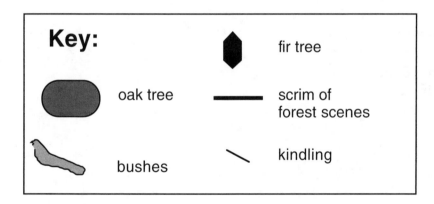

Key:

oak tree

bushes

fir tree

scrim of forest scenes

kindling

O Christmas Tree

(traditional, arranged by L.E. McCullough)

O Christ-mas Tree, O Christ-mas Tree how love-ly are your

bran-ches O Christ-mas Tree, O Christ-mas Tree how love-ly are your

bran-ches In sum-mer sun, in win-ter snow a dress of green you

al-ways show O Christ-mas Tree, O Christ-mas Tree how love-ly are your

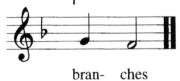

bran- ches

Diamonds in the Snow

In addition to charity, the qualities of faith and hope have come to play a very significant role in our modern Christmas celebration—children and adults convinced that something miraculous and wonderful will happen if only they believe strongly enough. After all, so much of what surrounded the first Christmas was truly miraculous; why can't other miracles happen now? If one trusted only in pure logic and provable fact, the family of *Diamonds in the Snow* would have no reason at all to hope that Santa Claus would visit their humble home and brighten their lives with the spirit of Christmas. Most people would say it just couldn't happen. But then again, most people have never met Aunt Leddy.

David Levine is a songwriter/performer of children's and family music who lives in Kingston, New York. *Diamonds in the Snow* appears on his new album, *Dance of a Child's Dreams* (Angel Records 656772), and also features the fine musicianship of Molly Mason and Jay Ungar.

Diamonds in the Snow

TIME: Christmas Present; Christmas
                                     Past (1945)

PLACE: Grandpa's living room; a
                                     mountain cabin in East
                                     Tennessee

CAST:
   Grandpa   Taylor (Grandpa as a Boy)
   Janice   Mother
   Jimmy   Sheriff Howard
   Jean   Aunt Leddy

STAGE SET: a chair; fireplace with mantle and 3 stockings; wooden dining table with one wooden chair; rocking chair

PROPS: guitar (or mandolin or banjo); story book; pair of maracas; set of paints and brushes; sock; darning needle and thread; 3 Christmas stockings; Aunt Leddy's book; sack of flour; a baseball; hard candy; ink pen; bow tie; harmonica; fistful of coins; scarf; gold lipstick dispenser and makeup case; hair barrette; sunglasses; wristwatch

SPECIAL EFFECTS: sound—door opening and closing; wind whistling

COSTUMES: Janice, Jimmy and Grandpa dress in contemporary clothes (Grandpa with suspenders, perhaps); 1940s characters dress in rural period garb—Taylor in overalls and plaid shirt; Mother in long brown dress, then night robe

☆ ☆ ☆

(LIGHTS UP STAGE RIGHT on GRANDPA sitting in chair, strumming a guitar. JIMMY, JANICE and JEAN enter from right carrying toys—Jimmy totes a pair of maracas, Janice a story book, Jean a set of paints and brushes—and gather around Grandpa.)

JIMMY Grandpa, Grandpa! Guess what I got for Christmas! *(Shakes maracas.)*

JANICE Grandpa, look at my story book!

JEAN Sit still, Grandpa, and I'll paint you with my new brushes!

GRANDPA That's wonderful, kids. Santa was very generous to you.

JIMMY He sure was. And we got so much more, too.

GRANDPA You must have all been very good this past year.

JANICE We were *extra* very good, Grandpa.

JEAN Even me!

GRANDPA *(Laughs.)* Well, I'm happy to hear that. I was pretty good, too. Grandma was able to talk Santa into bringing me some new strings for this old tunebox. *(Strums guitar.)*

JIMMY What kind of presents did you get when you were young, Grandpa?

JANICE Did they have big toy stores back then?

JEAN All decorated for Christmas by Halloween?

GRANDPA *(Chuckles.)* Christmas was pretty different when I was your age. Sit down, and I'll tell you a story about the best Christmas I ever had.

(The kids sit on the floor; LIGHTS DOWN RIGHT; LIGHTS UP CENTER AND LEFT on MOTHER sitting at the table darning a sock, AUNT LEDDY sitting in the rocking chair reading a plain, hardcover book, TAYLOR standing at the fireplace, staring at and occasionally touching the empty stockings, as if getting them ready to be filled.)

GRANDPA I was nine years old, and we were living in the Smoky Mountains of East Tennessee. It was a beautiful place, and I loved being around all the animals and trees. But it was a sad time for our family. My daddy had died at the Battle of the Bulge that year, and my mother had been laid off from her job at the textile mill in October. The food on our table, we grew in the garden patch behind the cabin. Pa's sister, Aunt Leddy, boarded with us and brought in a little money from her teacher's pension. But it didn't look like Santa Claus was going to visit our house this year.

MOTHER (*Sighs.*) Taylor, you might as well stop mooning over those stockings and finish the rest of your chores.

TAYLOR Yes, ma'am. I was just wishing—

MOTHER Wishing won't fill those stockings, son. I shouldn't have even let you put them up, they've become such a distraction.

AUNT LEDDY If wishes were fishes, I'd be Queen of the Deep Blue Sea. And all the little fishes—

(Taylor joins in.)

AUNT LEDDY & TAYLOR —with all their little wishes, would come wishing and fishing to me.

(Aunt Leddy and Taylor laugh.)

(SOUND: KNOCKING ON DOOR OFFSTAGE LEFT)

MOTHER Who's there?

SHERIFF HOWARD *(O.S.)* Sheriff Howard, ma'am! And it's mighty cold!

MOTHER Come in, Sheriff! Come in! *(Stands and puts sock and darning needle on chair.)*

(SOUND: Door opening, closing, wind whistling as SHERIFF HOWARD enters from left, stamping his feet and shaking snow from his hat and coat; he carries a sack of flour.)

SHERIFF HOWARD Hooo-eee! That is some blizzard!

MOTHER You shouldn't be out in this weather.

SHERIFF HOWARD I won't be out long. The road into the hollow is near closed up with snow. I can just about make it home for supper.

MOTHER What are you doing with that sack of flour?

SHERIFF HOWARD Well, ma'am, Parson Potter said you might be running short on essentials, and... after all, it is Christmas Eve. *(Lays sack of flour on table.)* From our family to yours. *(Tips his hat, backs away.)*

MOTHER No, no, we couldn't—

SHERIFF HOWARD (*Turns and heads for door, left.*) Merry Christmas, y'all!

MOTHER Sheriff, no! Taylor, pick up the Sheriff's flour and hand it back to him! Taylor!

(*Sheriff Howard exits; SOUND: Door opening, closing, wind whistling. Aunt Leddy turns a page in her book. Taylor has remained at the fireplace and watches his Mother, who stands and fingers the flour sack, eyes downcast. Taylor walks over to the flour, stands next to her and gazes at her expectantly, but she does not speak.*)

TAYLOR Now that we got flour, we can bake some cookies, can't we, Mother?

MOTHER (*Puts the flour sack under table, sighs.*) Maybe tomorrow. I'm going to turn in early. Good night. (*Kisses his head, turns and exits slowly right.*)

TAYLOR Good night.

AUNT LEDDY Don't let the bedbugs bite.

(*After his Mother exits, Taylor returns to the mantle, looking at and straightening the stockings.*)

TAYLOR Aunt Leddy, do you believe in miracles?

AUNT LEDDY Believe in miracles? Course I do... they happen all the time!

TAYLOR Really?

AUNT LEDDY Why, this very book is full of miracles!

(*Taylor rushes to her and grabs the book.*)

TAYLOR (*Reading the title.*) "The Wonderful World of Cats"?

AUNT LEDDY Why, surely! You ever watched a cat? Studied it real close? Watched it stretch out in the sun, or jump ten feet in the air, or climb a tree, or even sit and just purr, whiskers twitching like some invisible hand is brushing them to and fro? Why every one of those things is a miracle! Every thing any one of the Earth's creatures does is a miracle, every minute of every day. Taylor, the world is full of miracles, if you know where to look and how to see them.

TAYLOR (*Hands the book back.*) I reckon they've run out of miracles in *this* hollow. At least for *this* Christmas.

AUNT LEDDY I wouldn't be so sure. You haven't seen any diamonds yet, have you?

TAYLOR Diamonds? What diamonds?

AUNT LEDDY The diamonds in the snow. Come here to the window.

(He helps her out of the chair and walks with her to center stage, where she points toward the audience.)

AUNT LEDDY Look out there. What do you see?

TAYLOR *(Peers intently into audience.)* Can't see anything. Just snow. Miles of snow.

AUNT LEDDY That's right. And what do you see in the snow?

TAYLOR More snow?

AUNT LEDDY Look again! Close!

TAYLOR *(Peers.)* Gosh, Aunt Leddy, what am I supposed to see besides snow?

AUNT LEDDY *Diamonds* in the snow. Diamonds in the snow on Christmas Eve are the footsteps of where an angel is walking. And if you see them glitter, you might get a wish granted.

TAYLOR Real diamonds?

AUNT LEDDY I said, "might." And only if you really believe. Don't they teach children anything useful in school these days?

(She turns away and shuffles back to her chair as Taylor stares out the window.)

TAYLOR Diamonds in the snow... angel footsteps...

(LIGHTS FADE DOWN TO QUARTER-FULL; Aunt Leddy nods off in chair, as Taylor curls up in a sleeping position on the floor at down center.)

TAYLOR Diamonds...angels...all this snow...Santa is never going to find his way into the hollow with all this snow...

(LIGHTS FADE OUT. SOUND: five seconds of wind whistling, then a loud thump from offstage. SPOTLIGHT ON TAYLOR, who awakes with a start.)

TAYLOR Who's there?

(SOUND: more thumps. Taylor rises to his knees, crouches, looks around.)

TAYLOR Mother? Aunt Leddy? Who's there?

(SOUND: a flurry of wind whistling, then silence.)

TAYLOR *(Yawns, scratches his head.)* I had the strangest dream... something about diamonds and somebody walking in the snow...snow! *(Becomes fully alert and stares out the window.)* Look at that moon! It's so clear, so bright... *(Peers intensely.)* It can't be...no! Yes! There they are! The diamonds! The diamonds in the snow! Mother! Aunt Leddy! Come quick! Come see the diamonds in the snow!

(SPOTLIGHT OUT, LIGHTS UP CENTER AND LEFT TO HALF as Mother enters from right and Aunt Leddy rises from her chair.)

MOTHER Taylor! What in the world are you doing up? It's not even daybreak.

TAYLOR *(Turns and waves her toward him.)* Come see, Mother! Quick!

(Mother joins Taylor at center stage and looks out the window.)

TAYLOR All up the hill and down the hollow! Do you see them?

MOTHER I'm sorry, son. What am I supposed to see?

AUNT LEDDY The diamonds!

TAYLOR The diamonds in the snow!

(He turns and dashes to the mantle; LIGHTS UP CENTER AND LEFT TO FULL.)

MOTHER *(Staring out window.)* Leddy, I don't know why you fill his head with that nonsense. Taylor, you go back to bed now, and—my word!

(Taylor takes a stocking, now full, and empties its contents onto the table—a baseball, hard candy, ink pen, a bow tie, a harmonica, a fistful of coins.)

TAYLOR Santa Claus did come! He followed the diamonds in the snow!

(Mother rushes to the table; Taylor hands her a stocking.)

TAYLOR Here, Mother.

(She backs away.)

MOTHER No...I can't.

TAYLOR Please...please...

(He holds the stocking for her, and she tentatively reaches in, slowly pulling out a scarf, a gold lipstick dispenser and makeup case, hair barrette, sunglasses, wrist watch.)

MOTHER It's a miracle! *(Hugs Taylor.)*

AUNT LEDDY You all seem so surprised. Miracles didn't get invented yesterday, you know.

(Mother pulls Aunt Leddy to the table, and Taylor hands her the third stocking.)

AUNT LEDDY *(Shrugs, refusing the stocking.)* I already know what's inside my stocking.

(Taylor reaches into the stocking, but comes out empty-handed.)

TAYLOR Aunt Leddy! Your stocking is...empty!

(Aunt Leddy grabs the stocking and shakes it at him.)

AUNT LEDDY Silly boy! This stocking isn't empty! It's chock-full—full of *my* three Christmas wishes! And no use asking me what they are, because I'm not going to tell you! But you'll know what they are, the day they come true.

(Taylor and Mother hug Aunt Leddy and all laugh. LIGHTS FADE OUT CENTER AND LEFT, FADE UP RIGHT on Grandpa, Jimmy, Janice and Jean.)

JIMMY Golly, Grandpa, that's a really neat story!

GRANDPA It was one Christmas I never forgot.

JANICE Did Aunt Leddy ever get her three wishes?

GRANDPA I believe she did. You might say you three grandkids are living proof.

JEAN Did you ever see any more diamonds in the snow?

GRANDPA Well now, that's hard to say. It seems the older I got, my eyesight went a little bit weaker each Christmas Eve. But even if I can't see those diamonds anymore, that's not to say they're not there for somebody else to see.

(He points to audience, and children turn.)

GRANDPA Someone who believes in miracles.

(MUSIC: Grandpa begins singing "Diamonds in the Snow;" children join in on choruses.)

GRANDPA *(Sings.)*

Wood stove is a blazing; children, gather round
It's time for story telling; snow is on the ground
Put a log into the fire; and, lo, we'll warm our souls
Watch the night's full moon a-rising, see the diamonds in the snow

CHORUS:

And it's diamonds in the snow, wrap yourselves up tight
Spending Christmas with your loved ones as the stars they shine so bright
Time is oh so precious with family and friends
And it's diamonds in the snow, it's Christmas once again

Once there was a Christmas, it was many years ago
St. Nick couldn't see the houses of the families down below
He looked into the night sky, and he winked up at the moon
He followed the shining road map of the diamonds in the snow

CHORUS

He landed on the rooftops spreading lots of love and joy
To the people in many nations, all little girls and boys
And the magic of that Christmas still warms our hearts and souls
And if you look outside the window, you'll see the diamonds in the snow

REPEAT CHORUS TWICE

(LIGHTS OUT.)

THE END

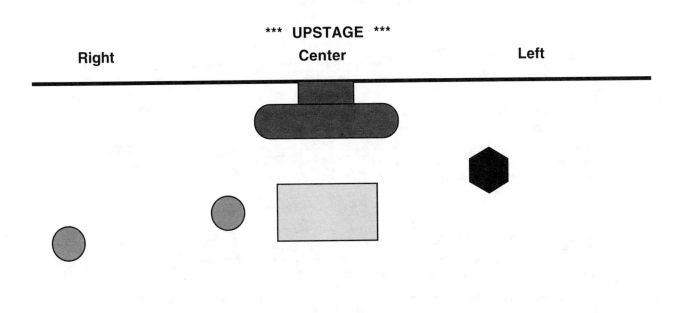

Stage Plan -- *Diamonds in the Snow*

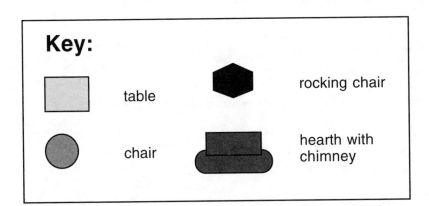

Key:

table

rocking chair

chair

hearth with chimney

Diamonds in the Snow

(Words & Music: David Levine / Arranged: L.E. McCullough)

Wood stove is a bla- zing; chil- dren ga- ther round It's time for sto- ry tell- ing; snow is on the ground Put a log in- to the fi- re, and, lo, we'll warm our souls Watch the night's full moon a- ri- sing; see the dia-monds in the snow And it's dia-monds in the snow ____ wrap your- selves up tight Spen-ding Christ-mas with your loved ones as the stars they shine so bright Time is oh so pre- cious with fa- mi- ly and friends And it's dia- monds in the snow, it's Christ-mas once a- gain

Jingle Bells

Jingle Bells was written for a family gathering in 1857 by James Pierpont of Boston. While it is one of the few popular Christmas songs that do not specifically mention Christmas, it has become a perennial holiday anthem due to its lively portrait of outdoor winter fun. James Pierpont was the son of an abolitionist but ended up moving to Georgia and fighting for the Confederacy in the Civil War. His nephew, John Pierpont Morgan, became a famous banker, financial speculator and philanthropist of the late 19th century whose New York City mansion is now a public museum and library.

Jingle Bells

TIME: Christmas Eve, 1857

PLACE: The Pierpont Home, Boston,
                               Massachusetts

CAST:
  Mr. James Pierpont   Liza Pierpont, Daughter
  Mrs. Martha Pierpont   Lucas Pierpont, Son
  Pettynoll the Horse   Mr. Robbins, a neighbor
  Mrs. Slater, a neighbor   Miss Bright, a neighbor
  Mr. Hoskins, a neighbor

STAGE SET: large four-wheel surrey-type carriage (optional scrims showing Boston houses, shops, street scenes)

PROPS: small valise; several gift boxes; snowball; lump of sugar; sack; blanket; jelly jar; green leaves; garland of small bells

COSTUMES: characters dress in mid-19th-century New England middle-class clothes (see Currier & Ives period paintings for details); Pettynoll can be one or two actors in a realistic horse costume or a costume that is silly, depending upon the director's decision; he should have standard dray horse equipment attached such as reins, bit and bridle bearing a colorful ribbon, sprig of Queen Anne's lace, juniper, or other floral decoration; a wreath, holly, some pine cones and a garland of small bells can be hung on the front carriage post on the driver's side (left)

☆ ☆ ☆

(LIGHTS UP FULL ON EXTERIOR FRONT OF PIERPONT HOUSE. A horse, PETTYNOLL, stands silent and immobile at center stage in front of a carriage. MRS. MARTHA PIERPONT enters from stage right carrying a small valise. She puts it down at center stage and looks around, exasperated.)

MARTHA Lucas! Liza! Come here this instant! Every time this family takes a simple day trip, it turns into a major continental expedition! James Pierpont, where are you?

(MR. JAMES PIERPONT enters from stage left, staggering under the weight of a half dozen gift-wrapped boxes.)

JAMES Coming, Martha dear.

MARTHA Oh, James, get the children to help you. Lucas! Liza!

(LUCAS and LIZA enter from stage right; Lucas has a snowball he is threatening to throw at Liza.)

LIZA If you throw that snowball, Lucas Pierpont, Santa Claus will put coal in your stocking for the rest of your life!

LUCAS Will not!

LIZA Will so!

LUCAS Will not! *(Gets ready to throw.)*

LIZA Maaaaaaaaaa!

MARTHA Children, stop that horseplay and help your father with the gifts. And be careful!

(Lucas drops snowball and joins Liza at center stage to help their father load packages into carriage.)

LIZA I love visiting Grandmother's farm. Millis is such a pretty little town. Especially at Christmas.

LUCAS When we will get there, pop?

JAMES Well, it's a twenty-mile ride. And if this old buggy holds up and we don't hit too many snow drifts, we can make about five miles an hour.

LIZA Then we'll be there in four hours. Just in time for dinner.

MARTHA *If* we ever manage to leave! James, are we ready *yet?*

JAMES Just waiting for you, my dear. Come on, children, hop aboard.

(Lucas and Liza jump in back seat; James helps Martha up into front passenger seat. He climbs up into driver's seat, takes up the reins and looks around.)

JAMES Everyone ready?

LUCAS I bet this new horse will get us there faster than ever. He sure is a beaut!

LIZA What's his name?

JAMES Pettynoll.

LUCAS Pettynoll? That's a peculiar name.

LIZA No more than Lucas. Now *that* is a peculiar name.

MARTHA Children!

JAMES It's what the man who sold him to me called him. Now, is everyone ready?

MARTHA We've been ready for an hour, James. Can you get this beast in motion?

JAMES Yes, dear. *(Tugs reins.)* Hyaaah!

(Pettynoll does not move.)

JAMES *(Tugs reins.)* Hyaaah!

(Pettynoll does not move.)

JAMES *(Tugs reins harder.)* Hyaaah! Hyaaah! Hyaaah!

(Pettynoll does not move.)

LUCAS Pop?

JAMES Yes, son.

LUCAS We haven't left yet, have we?

JAMES No, son. The horse isn't moving.

MARTHA James, why isn't the horse moving? He does know he's a horse, doesn't he?

JAMES I'm sure he does, Martha. I've yet to hear of a horse thinking he's the President of Harvard College.

LUCAS Maybe the reins are too loose.

JAMES I checked them this morning. The reins are fine.

LIZA Maybe he didn't eat his supper last night.

LUCAS I fed him good last night. And this morning, too.

LIZA Maybe you fed him too much, and he's too tired to go.

LUCAS Says who?

MARTHA Lucas and Liza! That's enough! James, why don't you try to get the horse moving again?

JAMES Would you like to drive, Martha?

MARTHA No, dear. I want *you* to drive.

JAMES Very well. I shall. *(Tugs reins.)* Hyaaah! Come on, Pettynoll! Come on, boy!

(Pettynoll does not move.)

JAMES *(Tugs reins.)* Hyaaah there, Pettynoll!

(Pettynoll does not move.)

JAMES *(Tugs reins harder.)* Hyaaah! Hyaaah! Hyaaah!

(Pettynoll does not move.)

JAMES Don't anybody say a word!

(James hops down from carriage and stands in front of Pettynoll, staring him in the face. A neighbor, MR. ROBBINS, enters from left and hails the Pierponts.)

MR. ROBBINS Hello, Pierponts!

LUCAS & LIZA Hello, Mr. Robbins!

MR. ROBBINS Happy Christmas Eve!

MARTHA It *would* be if we could get this carriage on the road.

MR. ROBBINS What's the problem?

JAMES It sounds silly, but the horse doesn't seem to...well, he doesn't seem to want to move.

MR. ROBBINS Horses can be mighty stubborn now and then. *(Digs in pocket, pulls out a lump of sugar.)* Here, I've got a lump of sugar. Let's see if this perks him up.

(Mr. Robbins feeds the sugar to Pettynoll. James gets back in carriage and tugs on reins.)

JAMES Hyaaah, Pettynoll!

(Pettynoll does not move.)

JAMES *(Tugs reins.)* Hyaaah, Pettynoll! Hyaaah, Pettynoll! Hyaaah, Pettynoll!

(Pettynoll does not move.)

JAMES You see! He just won't move!

MR. ROBBINS Now, that *is* a curiosity. A curiosity, indeed.

(A neighbor, MRS. SLATER, enters from right, carrying a small sack.)

LUCAS Look, it's Mrs. Slater, the candlemaker.

LIZA Hello, Mrs. Slater. Merry Christmas!

MRS. SLATER And a Merry Christmas to you! Going to Christmas dinner at Grandmother's farm?

MARTHA That was our plan. But this new horse James bought won't move an inch.

JAMES *(To Martha.)* It was my Christmas present to you, dear. *(Pause, as she glares at him.)* But not the only one.

MRS. SLATER Well, I've never heard of a horse not moving! Have you, Mr. Robbins? Maybe you need to change his blanket. *(Takes a blanket from her sack and puts it over Pettynoll's shoulders.)* Here, see if this makes him feel better.

JAMES *(Tugs reins.)* Come on, Pettynoll!

(Pettynoll does not move.)

MRS. SLATER It's a very fine blanket, you know. I wove it myself. And *my* horse always moves.

(A neighbor, MISS BRIGHT, enters from left.)

LIZA Hello, Miss Bright!

MISS BRIGHT Goodness, I thought you Pierponts had left hours ago!

MR. ROBBINS Their horse won't move.

MISS BRIGHT Won't move? Try some of this elderberry jam. My horse loves it!

(She pulls out jar, opens it and offers a fingerful to Pettynoll. A neighbor, MR. HOSKINS, enters from right.)

MR. HOSKINS What-ho, Pierponts! I hear you've got transportation trouble. Well, here's a lucky charm I picked up during my seagoing travels with Captain Ahab. It's a plant grows wild in Samoa, and it never fails to pick me up when I'm sluggish.

(He takes a few leaves from his jacket and sticks them under Pettnoll's nose; Pettynoll sneezes; everyone shouts and murmurs.)

JAMES Friends, neighbors, everyone, please. I appreciate your advice, but I think I'd better handle this myself.

MR. HOSKINS Just where did you get that horse, anyway?

JAMES From Claude Dupree. The horse trader from Quebec.

MR. ROBBINS Dupree is an honest man. He wouldn't give you a bum steer.

MR. HOSKINS Or a lame horse.

LIZA Maybe Pettynoll has another name.

MRS. SLATER Another name?

LUCAS Maybe he has a...a Christmas name.

MISS BRIGHT A Christmas name? What kind of name is that?

LIZA Well, it is almost Christmas. Maybe he was born on Christmas.

LUCAS And he only answers to his Christmas name.

JAMES Of all the ridiculous—and I suppose the horse only speaks French.

(Adults laugh, except for Martha.)

MARTHA You did say Mr. Dupree was from Quebec?

JAMES I did. And they speak plenty of French in Quebec.

MARTHA Then "Pettynoll" could also be pronounced "Pe-tit No-ël."

(Pettynoll whinnies and raises its head.)

MRS. SLATER The horse moved its lips!

MISS BRIGHT It speaks French!

MARTHA Petit Noël!

(Pettynoll whinnies.)

LUCAS That's Pettynoll's real name, mama! That's his Christmas name!

MARTHA Petit Noël!

(Pettynoll whinnies and stamps a hoof.)

LIZA That's French for "little Christmas."

ALL Hurrah! The horse speaks French! Petit Noël! Hurrah!

(Everyone quiets; James tugs reins; Pettynoll does not move.)

JAMES If we've found out his real name, how come he still doesn't move? This is absurd!

(He steps off the carriage and knocks down a garland of small bells hanging on the carriage post; Pettynoll whinnies loudly and stamps both front hooves.)

LIZA He seems to like the sound of bells, papa.

MARTHA I suppose he only responds to music. Does anyone know any horse songs?

(Adults laugh.)

LUCAS We could make up a song about riding a horse. Maybe he'll get the idea.

JAMES A horse that only speaks French and only moves to music? Well, why not? Here's a little tune that's been running around in my head the last few days.

(He hums the first two bars of "Jingle Bells.")

LIZA I've heard mama sing that tune!

MARTHA Da-da-da-da-da-da...*(Hums next two bars.)* Yes, I do believe I know that tune.

LUCAS *(Sings.)*
Dashing through the snow—

LIZA *(Sings.)*
In a one-horse open sleigh—

LUCAS *(Sings.)*
O'er the fields we go—

LIZA *(Sings.)*
Laughing all the way—ho-ho-ho!

JAMES *(Sings.)*
Bells on bobtails ring— *(Shakes bells.)*

MARTHA *(Sings.)*
Making spirits bright—

LUCAS *(Sings.)*
Oh, what fun it is to sing—

LIZA *(Sings.)*
A sleighing song tonight!

(Pettynoll whinnies and begins moving, pacing slowly; people follow him around the stage.)

ALL *(Sing.)*
Jingle bells, jingle bells
Jingle all the way
Oh, what fun it is to ride
In a one-horse open sleigh
Jingle bells, jingle bells
Jingle all the way
Oh, what fun it is to ride
In a one-horse open sleigh

MR. HOSKINS *(Sings.)*
> A day or two ago
> I thought I'd take a ride

MR. ROBBINS *(Sings.)*
> And soon Miss Fannie Bright
> Was seated by my side

MRS. SLATER *(Sings.)*
> The horse was lean and lank
> Misfortune seemed his lot

MISS BRIGHT *(Sings.)*
> He got into a drifted bank
> And then we got upshot

ALL *(Sing.)*
> Jingle bells, jingle bells
> Jingle all the way
> Oh, what fun it is to ride
> In a one-horse open sleigh
> Jingle bells, jingle bells
> Jingle all the way
> Oh, what fun it is to ride
> In a one-horse open sleigh

(Pettynoll races around stage.)

LUCAS Now look at him go! He's a regular Stewball!

LIZA Let's take him to Camptown Races!

MARTHA If he can just get us to Millis, he'll be fine! James, stop that horse!

(Pettynoll runs offstage left followed by James in pursuit. Everyone sings "Jingle Bells.")

ALL *(Sing.)*
> Dashing through the snow
> In a one-horse open sleigh
> O'er the fields we go
> Laughing all the way
> Bells on bobtails ring
> Making spirits bright
> Oh, what fun it is to sing
> A sleighing song tonight

Jingle bells, jingle bells
Jingle all the way
Oh, what fun it is to ride
In a one-horse open sleigh
Jingle bells, jingle bells
Jingle all the way
Oh, what fun it is to ride
In a one-horse open sleigh

(LIGHTS OUT.)

THE END

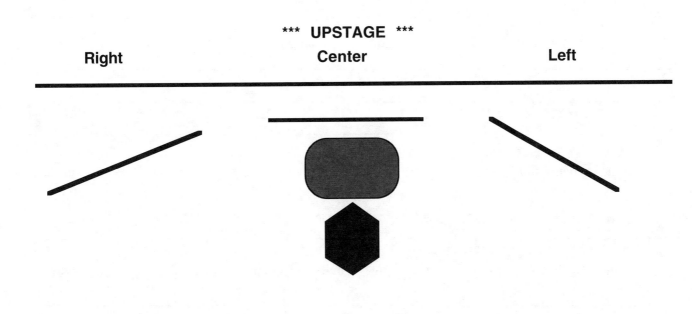

*** UPSTAGE ***

Right	Center	Left

Stage Plan—*Jingle Bells*

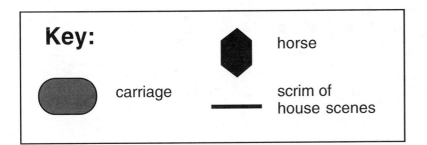

Key:

horse

carriage

scrim of
house scenes

Jingle Bells

(Words & Music: James Pierpont / Arranged: L.E. McCullough)

Dash- ing through the snow in a one- horse o- pen sleigh

O'er the fields we go laugh- ing all the way

Oh, what fun it is to sing a sleigh-ing song to- night

Jin- gle bells, jin- gle bells, jin- gle all the way

Oh, what fun it is to ride in a one-horse o- pen sleigh ____

Oh, what fun it is to ride in a one- horse o- pen sleigh

Good King Wenceslas

Wenceslas was the ruler of Bohemia in the early 10th century A.D. and presided over the conversion of that country to Christianity. He was murdered by his jealous brother, Boleslav, around the year 935. The legend of the page being saved from freezing by walking in Wenceslas' warming footsteps is very old and was only one of the many good deeds that led to Wenceslas being declared a saint. The modern version of *Good King Wenceslas* was composed by Reverend John Mason Neale, the warden of Sackville College in Sussex, England, sometime in the 1850s using music from a medieval Swedish carol.

Good King Wenceslas

TIME:	St. Stephen's Day (Dec. 26), 931 A.D.
PLACE:	The Castle of King Wenceslas in Bohemia

CAST:

King Wenceslas	Queen Marta
Duke Boleslav	Thaddeus the Page
Serf	The Angel Ezer
Serf's Wife	4 Castle Revelers
2 Serf Children	

STAGE SET: long table; four upholstered or high-backed chairs; double throne; 2 scrims depicting rich tapestry and palace furnishings; three stone slabs around a small makeshift fire

PROPS: ornate tablecloth; 4 bowls; 4 place knives; 7 drinking cups; turkey drumstick; tray; Wenceslas' staff; 2 baskets of food and gifts

SPECIAL EFFECTS: sound—wind whistling, wolves howling

COSTUMES: characters dress in early 10th-century Slavic clothes befitting occupation and social status—palace characters well-dressed and ornate, peasant family plain and ragged; Angel Ezer dresses in white robe; when Wenceslas and Thaddeus are outside they wear heavy cloaks, fur hats and boots

☆ ☆ ☆

(LIGHTS UP STAGE RIGHT AND CENTER ON DINING HALL OF KING WENCESLAS. The King sits on his throne with QUEEN MARTA by his side as FOUR CASTLE REVELERS eat and make merry at the long table. THADDEUS THE PAGE stands to the left of the table, holding a tray, while DUKE BOLESLAV, the King's brother, stands to the right.)

REVELER #1 And then the peasant says to the squire, "I do not know, sir. What *is* time to a pig?"

(Revelers laugh heartily; Duke Boleslav claps hands and calls for quiet.)

DUKE BOLESLAV In honor of the feast of St. Stephen, I propose a toast.

REVELER #2 I propose a leg! *(Holds up a turkey drumstick as Revelers laugh.)*

DUKE BOLESLAV Silence! *(Raises his drinking cup.)* I propose a toast to the glorious reign of my brother King Wenceslas, ruler of Bohemia! *(Drinks.)*

REVELERS Huzzah! *(Raise their cups and drink.)*

DUKE BOLESLAV And to his beautiful Queen, Marta! May they rule eternally! *(Raises his drinking cup, drinks.)*

REVELERS Huzzah! *(Raise their cups and drink.)*

(King Wenceslas stands; he and Queen Marta had sipped lightly from their cups.)

KING WENCESLAS The Queen and I appreciate your expression of esteem. But as my brother, Duke Boleslav, points out—this is the feast day of St. Stephen. It is his bravery and devotion we should honor, while remembering that the only monarch who shall rule eternally is Jesus Christ the Savior.

REVELERS Huzzah! *(Raise their cups and drink.)*

(Duke Boleslav moves closer to the throne as Revelers drink, laugh, drowse. Thaddeus the Page begins to look right, out the castle window.)

DUKE BOLESLAV Dear brother, you are too serious! You should enjoy life more! You have been blessed with wealth and good fortune! Revel in it!

QUEEN MARTA It is possible to enjoy one's blessings without flaunting them in the face of those less fortunate, Boleslav. Beginning with this new year I shall ask the King to suggest that our nobles spend less of their income on feasts and more on new oxen and tools for the serfs who work the fields.

DUKE BOLESLAV (*Shrugs.*) The Lord giveth and the Lord taketh away, my Queen. To us, he has giveth. To others, he taketh.

(*Thaddeus the Page points out the window and exclaims.*)

THADDEUS My lord! There is someone on the hillside!

KING WENCESLAS Outside on a night like this? In this bitter cold? You must be mistaken!

(*Revelers #3 and #4 rise and look out window beside Thaddeus.*)

REVELER #3 By St. Peter's beard, the boy is right! There is someone on the hillside!

REVELER #4 It looks like he is gathering kindling. He must be mad!

KING WENCESLAS (*Gazes out window.*) Or very cold. Not even the wolves are abroad this winter evening. Thaddeus, do you know him?

THADDEUS It is one of the serfs from the village near the forest gate. He lives a good league hence by the fountain of Saint Agnes.

DUKE BOLESLAV Stealing the King's firewood! What nerve! I will send the guard to seize him at once!

KING WENCESLAS Stay, brother. There is plenty of wood to spare. King Wenceslas begrudges no comfort to a subject in want. Let him forage. (*Sits.*)

QUEEN MARTA Husband, any man away from home and hearth on such a night as this must be desperately cold. Hungry as well. I suspect he may perish on his journey back.

THADDEUS Perhaps he should be invited into the palace?

DUKE BOLESLAV Invited into the palace? A serf? You might as well invite a dog! Charity is a waste of time on those who cannot earn their daily bread.

REVELERS Huzzah! (*Raise cups and drink.*)

KING WENCESLAS Thaddeus!

THADDEUS Yes, my lord?

KING WENCESLAS Have the cook prepare a generous assortment of food and drink for this serf. And gifts for his family.

THADDEUS Yes, my lord. I will have the cook's helper deliver it right away.

KING WENCESLAS No. *I* will deliver it. Come, Thaddeus, let us celebrate St. Stephen's feast in the forest.

(LIGHTS OUT. SOUND: WIND WHISTLING, WOLVES HOWLING. SPOTLIGHT UP DOWN RIGHT ON KING WENCESLAS AND THADDEUS. They face left, trudging slowly through the snowy night against the wind, King Wenceslas in the lead carrying a staff and a basket, Thaddeus carrying a basket. SOUND FADES OUT.)

KING WENCESLAS *(Struggling.)* I think this storm has quickened its hand against us, young page. It rages like a wave of Scythian horsemen.

THADDEUS *(Gasping.)* If the moon would but...shed her cloak of clouds...it is so dark...and the wind...the wind...

(Thaddeus falls to one knee as King Wenceslas continues on to down left, moving out of spotlight that is now completely on Thaddeus.)

THADDEUS Sire, I fail...*(Drops other knee.)* I fail...

(The ANGEL EZER enters from right behind Thaddeus.)

ANGEL EZER Loyal page, you have not failed your king. And he will not fail you.

(Thaddeus turns and sees the Angel.)

THADDEUS An angel! Are you Gabriel? Come to ferry me heavenward?

ANGEL EZER I am Ezer, son of Hur, firstborn of Ephrathah, the father of Bethlehem. I come not to take your life but to preserve it. *(Points left.)* Your king awaits around the bend. *(Points toward ground.)* See his path? Mark his footsteps good, my page. Tread in them boldly, and thou shalt find the winter's rage freeze thy blood less coldly.

(The Angel exits right. Thaddeus slowly rises and walks in the footsteps of King Wenceslas.)

THADDEUS The Angel speaks true! Heat is in each sod the King has printed! Nay, this fire burns from no mere king—but a saint!

(Thaddeus steps more strongly and crosses to serf's hut where King Wenceslas stands; LIGHTS UP LEFT where THE SERF, SERF'S WIFE and TWO SERF CHILDREN sit on rough stone slabs and huddle around a small fire.)

KING WENCESLAS God save all here!

(Serf family exclaims and cowers in fear.)

SERF It is the King!

SERF'S WIFE *(Kneels.)* Spare us from your wrath! We are but starving serfs and throw ourselves upon your mercy!

KING WENCESLAS Rise, Christians! There is no need to prostrate yourselves before your fellow brothers in Christ. Look! We have brought gifts in His name. Share the bounty of His birthday with us!

(King Wenceslas and Thaddeus lay down baskets in front of astonished Serfs.)

SERF Thank you, my lord! Bless you!

SERF'S WIFE Bless you!

THADDEUS My lord, even with this small fire it remains killing cold.

KING WENCESLAS Right you are, my page. Let us bring them to the castle, where they may dine with us in full faith and fellowship.

(King Wenceslas and Thaddeus put their arms around the Serfs and guide them right toward center stage. LIGHTS UP RIGHT AND CENTER on Revelers standing at the table starting to sing "Good King Wenceslas." As song progresses, all actors join hands and face audience.)

REVELER #1 *(Sings.)*
Good King Wenceslas looked out
On the feast of Stephen

REVELER #2 *(Sings.)*
When the snow lay round about
Deep and crisp and even

REVELER #3 *(Sings.)*
Brightly shone the moon that night
Though the frost was cruel

REVELER #4 *(Sings.)*
When a poor man came in sight
Gathering winter fuel

KING WENCESLAS *(Sings.)*
"Hither, page, and stand by me
If thou knowest it telling

Yonder peasant, who is he?
Where and what his dwelling?"

THADDEUS *(Sings.)*
"Sire, he lives a good league hence
Underneath the mountain
Right against the forest fence
By Saint Agnes' fountain"

QUEEN MARTA *(Sings.)*
"Bring me flesh and bring me wine
Bring me pine logs hither
Thou and I will see him dine
When we bear them thither"

DUKE BOLESLAV *(Sings.)*
Page and monarch forth they went
Forth they went together
Through the rude wind's wild lament
And the bitter weather

ALL *(Sing.)*
"Sire, the night is darker now
And the wind blows stronger
Fails my heart, I know not how
I can go no longer"

"Mark my footsteps good, my page
Tread thou in them boldly
Thou shalt find the winter's rage
Freeze thy blood less coldly"

ALL *(Sing.)*
In his master's steps he trod
Where the snow lay dinted
Heat was in the very sod
Which the Saint had printed
Therefore, Christian men, be sure
Wealth or rank possessing
Ye who now will bless the poor
Shall yourselves find blessing

(LIGHTS OUT.)

THE END

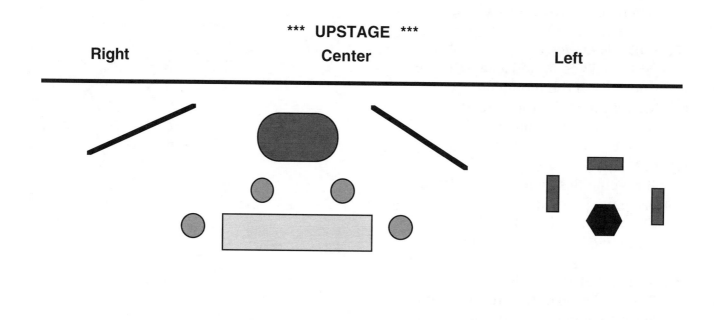

*** UPSTAGE ***

Right   Center   Left

Stage Plan—*Good King Wenceslas*

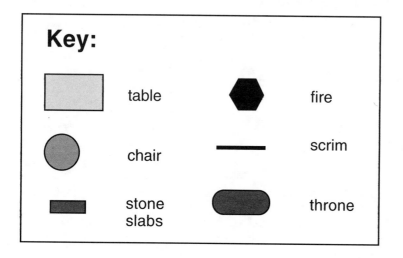

Key:

▭	table	⬡	fire
●	chair	—	scrim
▬	stone slabs	⬭	throne

Good King Wenceslas

(traditional, arranged by L.E. McCullough)

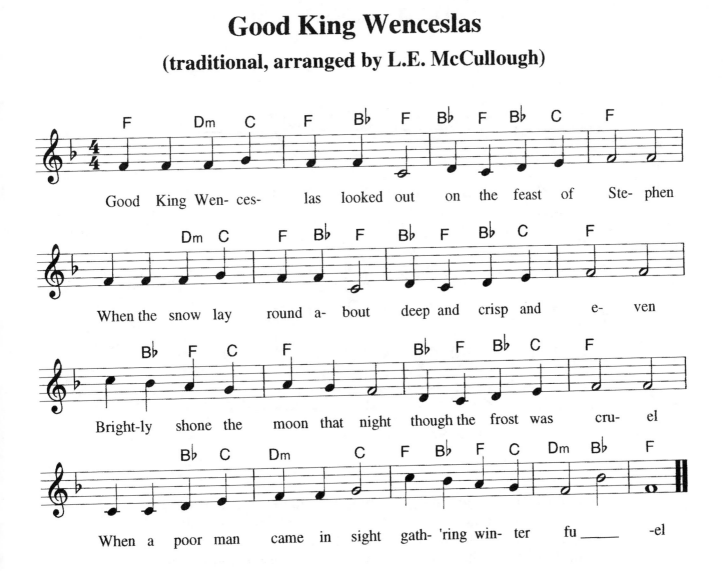

Good King Wen- ces- las looked out on the feast of Ste- phen

When the snow lay round a- bout deep and crisp and e- ven

Bright-ly shone the moon that night though the frost was cru- el

When a poor man came in sight gath- 'ring win- ter fu____ -el

O Thou Joyful Day

One of the many ancient figures who became part of our modern legend of Santa Claus is a real person, St. Nicholas, the bishop of Myra, Asia Minor. Born around 280 A.D., he died in 343 A.D., and a number of his relics are housed in the Greek Orthodox Shrine of St. Nicholas in Flushing, New York. Several of the miracles ascribed to him during his life involved helping and caring for children and distributing his family fortune to the needy. The tune to which *O Thou Joyful Day* is sung is a very old Sicilian folk melody, and the original words were written and sung in Latin.

O Thou Joyful Day

TIME: December, 320 A.D.

PLACE: A village in Sicily

CAST:
    Bishop Nicholas of Myra   Antonio
    2 Clothsellers   Andrea
    Slave Buyer   Francesca
    Tax Collector   Lucretia

STAGE SET: two stone slabs, one larger; a table with two chairs; a hearth and chimney

PROPS: drinking bowl; some cloths; a pouch of money; parchment scroll; quill pen; three small bags of gold with notes in the bottom; gold coins; chimney net; torch

SPECIAL EFFECTS: sound—wind whistling, clumping noises, rooster crowing for daybreak

COSTUMES: characters dress in costume of the ancient Mediterranean world—plain robes and sandals, with a more embroidered robe and perhaps jewelry for Slave Buyer and Tax Collector

☆ ☆ ☆

(LIGHTS UP STAGE RIGHT. TWO CLOTHSELLERS sit on a large stone slab in the marketplace hawking their wares.)

CLOTHSELLER #1 Panno! Panno bello! Cloth! I have beautiful cloth for sale!

CLOTHSELLER #2 Salutos, amicos! I, Befana of Adrano, too, have the most beautiful cloth in all Sicily, taken from the luxurious silk of the Orient! Come, buy from me, and you will not be disappointed!

(BISHOP NICHOLAS OF MYRA enters from right; he is dressed as an ordinary traveler. He stops when hailed by Clothseller #1.)

CLOTHSELLER #1 Signore, signore, you look tired. Sit and rest.

(She directs him to the smaller stone slab, where he sits.)

CLOTHSELLER #1 I see you have been traveling far. Yes, and your robe, signore. It is old and thin. Perhaps you would like to make another? I have some very beautiful cloth. Ah, but you are thirsty. Have some water.

(She hands him a bowl of water.)

BISHOP NICHOLAS Grazie, signora.

CLOTHSELLER #2 Josefina, you waste your breath. This man is too poor to buy your shabby wares. Nor does he possess the vanity to do so even had he the money. Can you not tell he is a *mendicante?* He wanders the countryside in the service of God.

BISHOP NICHOLAS No kindness is ever wasted upon a stranger, signora. Especially in this season of the birthday of our Savior, Jesus Christ.

CLOTHSELLER #1 Ah, it is a happy time for some. But in this village, hard times have befallen. Many are hungry. Many go without shelter. The children's faces are streaked with tears of want. And our rulers do nothing.

BISHOP NICHOLAS Truly! Tell me more of these difficulties.

CLOTHSELLER #2 Times are so bad that one man, the widower Antonio, has been forced to sell his three daughters.

BISHOP NICHOLAS Sell his daughters!

CLOTHSELLER #1 Yes, signore, to the slave buyer. Antonio owes much money to the duke. If he pays his taxes, he cannot feed his daughters. If he does not pay, he will be imprisoned.

CLOTHSELLER #2 The tax collector comes to his house this very day.

BISHOP NICHOLAS I wonder what can be done to help this man?

CLOTHSELLER #1 Ordinary folk such as we are powerless, signore. But if only Bishop Nicholas would hear of this, he would find a way to save Antonio's daughters from shame.

BISHOP NICHOLAS You think so? *(Rises.)*

CLOTHSELLER #1 I know so! Throughout the entire Christian world, from sunny Palestine to the dark forests of Erin, it is said that Bishop Nicholas of Myra has helped scores of the poor and afflicted by giving away his own fortune.

CLOTHSELLER #2 He is indeed the last refuge of the poor, before God Himself.

BISHOP NICHOLAS Then perhaps a prayer should be offered to God for this Bishop's assistance. I must be on my way. Many thanks for your hospitality. *(Turns and exits left.)*

CLOTHSELLER #1 *(Waves.)* Addio, signore! Farewell!

CLOTHSELLER #2 *(Shakes her head.)* A prayer to Bishop Nicholas. As if he would ever hear!

(LIGHTS OUT RIGHT, LIGHTS UP CENTER AND LEFT on Antonio's house where ANTONIO sits at a table facing the audience with THE SLAVE BUYER seated to his left. Behind the Slave Buyer stands the TAX COLLECTOR. Behind Antonio stand his three daughters—ANDREA, FRANCESCA and LUCRETIA—sobbing softly. On the table are a parchment contract, a quill pen and a pouch of money.)

TAX COLLECTOR Antonio, as tax collector for Duke Adolfo, I take no pleasure in your misfortune. But the laws of our land state that the duke must have his due.

ANTONIO Would my life had any value, I would gladly sell myself into slavery to spare my daughters this humiliation!

(The Slave Buyer pushes contract and quill in front of Antonio.)

SLAVE BUYER Alas, Antonio, the time has come for me to acquire my property. Give me your signature, and I will give you my silver.

(Bishop Nicholas enters from left.)

BISHOP NICHOLAS Stay your hand, Antonio. Yield neither hope nor virtue!

SLAVE BUYER Who is this pazzo? Some mad hermit from the desert?

BISHOP NICHOLAS Taxman, you claim to take no pleasure in this man's misfortune. I ask you, then, as one Christian to another, to wait but one more day for your money.

TAX COLLECTOR I suppose I can. And you, a penniless mendicant, will produce enough money to pay Antonio's taxes? From where? The sky? *(Laughs.)*

ANTONIO That would be a miracle!

BISHOP NICHOLAS When Our Lord, Jesus Christ, walked this earth, he made many miracles. Now that he is at home in heaven, do you doubt his ability to make more?

TAX COLLECTOR *(Pauses, thinks.)* Agreed! We meet tomorrow to settle this account. Addio!

(LIGHTS FADE OUT; Antonio, Andrea, Francesca, Lucretia, Tax Collector and Slave Buyer exit left; St. Nicholas exits right. SOUNDS: WIND WHISTLING, THEN FADING INTO CLUMPING NOISES OFFSTAGE; A LOUD THUMP OF A SMALL BUT HEAVY FALLEN OBJECT; ROOSTER CROWING FOR DAYBREAK. LIGHTS FADE UP CENTER AND LEFT as Andrea enters from left, yawning as she crosses to the table.)

ANDREA *(Sighs.)* My last morning as a free citizen.

(She looks toward the hearth and spots a small bag lying in front of the chimney. She crosses to hearth and picks up the bag, opens it and exclaims.)

ANDREA Father! Sisters! Come quickly!

(Antonio rushes in from left followed by Francesca and Lucretia.)

ANTONIO What is it, my daughter?

ANDREA Gold, Father! Someone has left a bag of gold on the hearth!

ANTONIO Impossible!

(Antonio takes the bag, blows off the soot and looks inside, showing it to Francesca and Lucretia.)

FRANCESCA It is a miracle! The stranger said there would be a miracle, and gold has come to us as if by an angel!

ANTONIO *(Looks up the chimney.)* Or by a very generous bird.

LUCRETIA There is a note in the bottom!

ANDREA *(Takes out note, reads.)* "O thou joyful day, O thou blessed day...holy, peaceful Christmastide...Earth's hopes awaken, Christ life hath taken...praise Him, O praise Him on every side." No bird wrote this!

FRANCESCA What does it mean, Father?

ANTONIO *(Grips bag.)* It means we have enough money to keep one of you girls from the slave buyer.

(Slave Buyer and Tax Collector enter from left, bow.)

SLAVE BUYER *(Chuckles.)* And have you had your miracle yet, signore?

TAX COLLECTOR *(Chuckles.)* Yes, your miracle, Antonio? Did it arrive with breakfast?

ANTONIO *(Holds up the bag of gold.)* Si, signores! It fell from the chimney!

(Tax Collector and Slave Buyer cease laughing and LIGHTS FADE OUT; Antonio, Andrea, Lucretia, Tax Collector and Slave Buyer exit left; Francesca sits at table, sleeps. SOUNDS: WIND WHISTLING, THEN FADING INTO CLUMPING NOISES OFFSTAGE; ROOSTER CROWING FOR DAYBREAK. LIGHTS FADE UP CENTER AND LEFT as Francesca awakes, yawning, as Lucretia enters from left.)

LUCRETIA Francesca! Did you hear anything during the night?

FRANCESCA I heard nothing. *(Looks at hearth.)* There is no bag this morning. We are doomed to slavery, Lucretia!

(She lowers head and sobs as Andrea and Antonio enter from left, Antonio crossing to hearth.)

ANTONIO Do not cry my daughters. It was two nights ago I had a dream. A dream that I was fishing in the sea one dark, dreary night. And that even in the darkness, with my net I was catching waves of gold. Wave upon wave of gold washing upon the shore and into my net.

ANDREA That is a wonderful dream, Father. Were that it could be true.

ANTONIO Were that it could!

(He puts his hand up the chimney, pulls down a cloth net, withdraws a small bag and hands it to Francesca.)

ANTONIO Here, my second daughter. Here is your freedom!

FRANCESCA Father! *(Hugs him.)*

LUCRETIA Another miracle!

ANTONIO Before going to bed last night, I made a net and tied it to the chimney to see if, indeed, a generous bird would visit again. And it has! Take the gold to the tax collector, Francesca.

FRANCESCA *(Digs in the bag, pulls out a note.)* Here is another note: "O thou joyful day, O thou blessed day...holy, peaceful Christmastide...Christ's light is beaming, our souls redeeming...praise Him, O praise Him on every side."

ANDREA These are much like the words from last night. Perhaps they are two verses to a poem.

FRANCESCA Or a song.

ANTONIO That I do not know, daughters. But for the sake of our beloved Lucretia—

(Lucretia kneels in front of him; he puts his hands on her head.)

LUCRETIA Yes, Father?

ANTONIO I pray this song has one verse more.

(LIGHTS FADE OUT; Antonio, Andrea, Francesca and Lucretia exit left. SOUNDS: WIND WHISTLING, THEN FADING INTO SILENCE.)

LUCRETIA *(O.S.)* Altolá! Halt!

(SPOTLIGHT UP CENTER ON BISHOP NICHOLAS STANDING BETWEEN HEARTH AND STONE SLAB. He holds a small bag and is preparing to throw it up in the air toward the chimney; Lucretia approaches him holding a torch.)

LUCRETIA You! *You* are the maker of miracles!

(She takes the bag, empties out the gold and pulls out the note.)

LUCRETIA I knew there was a third verse. *(Reads.)* "O thou joyful day, O thou blessed day...holy, peaceful Christmastide...King of Glory, we bow before thee...praise Him, O praise Him on every side."

(Antonio, Andrea and Francesca enter from left; LIGHTS FADE UP CENTER.)

ANDREA It is the *mendicante!* What is he doing here?

LUCRETIA *(Gives bag to Antonio.)* It is he who has been putting the bags of gold down the chimney. It is he who has saved us from slavery!

ANTONIO A total stranger has given us three bags of gold? But why? We are poor, we can never repay you. Signore, you have taken from our back the burden of one crushing debt and placed upon it another equally as heavy.

BISHOP NICHOLAS No, Antonio. The only debt you have now is in giving thanks to Almighty God, in whose debt you have been from the moment of your birth. I am Bishop Nicholas of Myra in Asia Minor. At a young age I inherited the wealth of a great family fortune. I learned quickly that the lust for money is truly the root of much evil in this life. Since I came to follow the words of Jesus Christ, I have traveled the world dispensing my fortune where it can do good in the battle against greed and temptation.

(Antonio, Andrea, Francesca and Lucretia kneel.)

ANTONIO You are a saint, O Nicholas!

ANDREA, FRANCESCA & LUCRETIA Blessed, blessed be Saint Nicholas!

BISHOP NICHOLAS If generosity to one's fellows is the mark of sainthood, then we can all be saints every day of our lives. Rise, my children, and follow my example, as I have followed the example of the Son of God whose birthday we celebrate this season.

(Antonio, Andrea, Francesca and Lucretia rise.)

BISHOP NICHOLAS I must continue my journey. Please, I beg you, tell no one how you came by the gold. Let it be considered...a miracle.

(Antonio, Andrea, Francesca and Lucretia murmur assent. Bishop Nicholas exits right as Antonio and his daughters bow.)

ANDREA May his kindness be remembered for all time.

FRANCESCA It is a shame we must not speak of his generosity.

LUCRETIA We should honor him in some way.

ANTONIO *(Shakes bag of gold.)* If there is a little money left over, perhaps I will buy a harp. And each Christmas, we can sing the song he left with the bags of gold.

(Antonio and his daughters laugh, then exit left. LIGHTS FADE OUT, THEN UP RIGHT ON TWO CLOTHSELLERS SITTING ON STONE SLAB.)

CLOTHSELLER #1 I heard a curious tale at the market, Befana.

CLOTHSELLER #2 About how the widower Antonio got the money to keep his daughters from slavery?

CLOTHSELLER #1 My cousin the fishmonger told me that *she* heard one of the blacksmith's sons telling *his* friend Pablo something about a man throwing gold down a chimney. And then singing this strange song:

(Clothseller #1 begins singing "O Thou Joyful Day.")

CLOTHSELLER #1 *(Sings.)*
O thou joyful day
O thou blessed day
Holy, peaceful Christmastide

CLOTHSELLERS #1 & #2 *(Sing.)*
Earth's hopes awaken
Christ life hath taken

(Bishop Nicholas enters from right and sings.)

CLOTHSELLERS #1 & #2 & BISHOP NICHOLAS *(Sing.)*
Praise Him, O praise Him on every side

(Antonio, Andrea, Francesa, Lucretia, Slave Buyer and Tax Collector enter from left and sing.)

ALL *(Sing.)*
O thou joyful day
O thou blessed day
Holy, peaceful Christmastide
Christ's light is beaming
Our souls redeeming
Praise Him, O praise Him on every side

ALL *(Sing.)*
O thou joyful day
O thou blessed day
Holy, peaceful Christmastide
King of Glory
We bow before thee
Praise Him, O praise Him on every side

(LIGHTS OUT.)

THE END

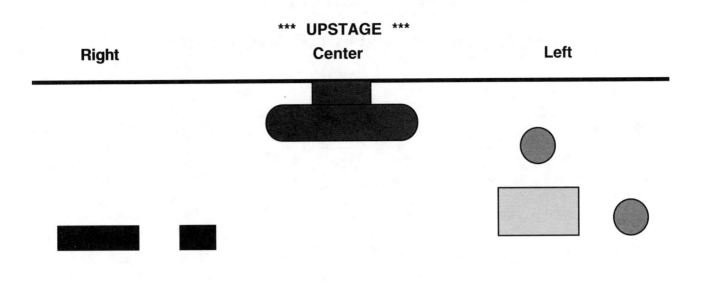

Stage Plan—*O Thou Joyful Day*

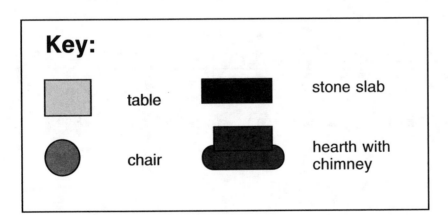

Key:

table

chair

stone slab

hearth with
chimney

O Thou Joyful Day

(traditional, arranged by L.E. McCullough)

O thou joy-ful day____ O thou bles-sed day____

Ho- ly, peace-ful _____ Christ- mas- tide

Earth's ____ hopes a- wa- ____ ken Christ ____ life hath ta- ____ ken

Laud ____ Him, O laud ____ Him on ev- 'ry side

Let Us Go, O Shepherds

Though it was not until the early 1500s that the Spaniards brought Christian Christmas celebrations to the New World, Native Americans in the Southwestern United States had for centuries held large dance festivals to induce the winter sun to return the following spring. One of the most popular Christmas customs in Mexico today is *la posada* ("the inn"), a ceremony that commemorates Mary and Joseph's search for lodging the night Jesus was born in Bethlehem. On December 16 a procession carrying the figures of Mary and Joseph goes throughout the town for nine nights, seeking shelter at various houses whose occupants play the roles of the innkeeper and his family. After much singing and reciting, the "innkeeper" admits the procession into the house, and the figures of Mary and Joseph are set in the manger. On the ninth night, Christmas Eve, the figure of the Christ child is added to the scene.

Let Us Go, O Shepherds

TIME: Christmas Eve, 1701

PLACE: **A windswept desert plain in southern New Mexico**

CAST:

Manuel	Joseph
Señor Porfiado	Mary
Old Man	3 Shepherds
Old Woman	Young Man
2 Young Women	

STAGE SET: large rock; large cactus

PROPS: shepherd staff; guitar with strap; tortilla; swaddling clothes for infant; infant doll; crèche; stuffed or cutout lamb

SPECIAL EFFECTS: sound—wind whistling, coyote howling in distance

COSTUMES: characters dress in early 18th-century Mexican peasant clothes—a simple tunic, pantalones, sash and huarache sandals; Manuel wears a serape over his tunic and has a belt pouch where he keeps his tortilla; Señor Porfiado may wear a sombrero to mark his status as master shepherd

☆ ☆ ☆

(LIGHTS UP RIGHT ON MANUEL, A SHEPHERD BOY, sitting against a rock, strumming his guitar and whistling a tune—the melody to "Let Us Go, O Shepherds." SEÑOR PORFIADO enters from right with THREE SHEPHERDS following and confronts Manuel.)

SEÑOR PORFIADO Manuel!

MANUEL *(Stands.)* Buenas dias, Señor Porfiado! Is this not a beautiful Noche Buena?

SEÑOR PORFIADO Yes, Manuel, this is a very beautiful Christmas Eve. Can you tell me what you have done with my very beautiful sheep?

MANUEL Your sheep? Ah, yes, the sheep. *(Points left.)* They are just over the hill, waiting for the Christ child to come at midnight.

SEÑOR PORFIADO *(To Shepherd #1.)* Pablo! Go find the sheep and count them.

SHEPHERD #1 Si, señor. *(Trots offstage left.)*

SHEPHERD #2 *(To Shepherd #3.)* Poor little boy. He still believes the old fairy tales about Christmas. *(Laughs.)*

SHEPHERD #3 I have heard him talking to angels!

SHEPHERD #2 And he says they talk back!

(Shepherds laugh as Manuel lightly strums his guitar and Señor Porfiado paces impatiently; Señor Porfiado stops and stares at Manuel, who stops playing and puts his guitar down against the rock, momentarily chastened. Shepherd #1 re-enters from left.)

SEÑOR PORFIADO Did you find the flock?

SHEPHERD #1 I found them, señor. But there is one lamb missing.

SEÑOR PORFIADO Missing!

SHEPHERD #2 Maybe it didn't like the sound of Manuel's little guitar. *(Laughs.)*

SEÑOR PORFIADO Silencio! This is no laughing matter. Before your parents died, Manuel, I promised them I would provide an honest livelihood for you. And for two years I have been very patient. But this is too much! You must find that lost lamb and bring it back to the hacienda—or don't come back at all!

MANUEL But, Señor Porfiado—

SEÑOR PORFIADO I don't care if you have to search all of New Mexico! Find that lamb! *(To shepherds.)* Vamanos!

SHEPHERD #3 See if you can sing the lamb to come home, Manuel. *(Laughs.)*

(Señor Porfiado exits right, followed by the Three Shepherds.)

MANUEL *(Sighs.)* I will pray to Santo Nicolo. He is the patron saint of children. Perhaps he can help me.

(He starts to walk left, then turns and picks up the guitar.)

MANUEL Maybe I *will* sing that lamb home.

(LIGHTS OUT. SOUND: WIND WHISTLING, COYOTE HOWLING IN DISTANCE. SPOTLIGHT ON MANUEL STANDING DOWN LEFT.)

MANUEL *(Calls.)* Come here, little lamb! It is so cold in the desert! Even with your fleece, I know you must be cold! Come to Manuelito, and we will enjoy the warm fire at our master's hacienda!

(The weary voice of an OLD MAN comes from offstage left.)

OLD MAN *(O.S.)* Muchacho!

MANUEL *(Whirls left.)* Hola! Who is there?

(SPOTLIGHT WIDENS TO INCLUDE OLD MAN HOBBLING OUT FROM LEFT.)

MANUEL Who are you, señor? Are you a *penitente?* Are you a hermit?

OLD MAN I am an old, old man, my son. And I have wandered the desert many, many years from California to the Rio Grande. *(Falls to his knees, shivering.)* I am so cold...so cold.

(Manuel takes off his serape and puts it over the old man's shoulders.)

OLD MAN Bless you, my son. May you find a reward in heaven.

MANUEL I am not looking for a reward, señor. I am looking for a lamb. And I hope I can find it before I go to sleep tonight. Have you seen a lamb anywhere around here?

(The Old Man points right.)

MANUEL Gracias, señor. Adios.

(LIGHTS OUT. SOUND: WIND WHISTLING, COYOTE HOWLING IN DISTANCE. SPOTLIGHT ON MANUEL STANDING DOWN RIGHT.)

MANUEL *(Strums his guitar, calls.)* Come home, little lamb! Come home to Manuel! Come home before los coyotes make you their Christmas dinner!

(The weary voice of an OLD WOMAN comes from behind Manuel.)

OLD WOMAN Muchacho!

MANUEL *(Whirls around.)* Hola! Who is there?

(SPOTLIGHT WIDENS TO INCLUDE OLD WOMAN SITTING ON ROCK; MANUEL GOES TO HER SIDE.)

OLD WOMAN I am an old, old woman. And I have wandered this desert many, many years. I am so hungry...so very, very hungry. Have you any food?

MANUEL I have one tortilla. It is all I have. I was saving it for the long trip home to Las Cruces.

OLD WOMAN I am so hungry...so very, very hungry.

(Manuel takes tortilla from his pouch, looks at it longingly, then gives it to the Old Woman.)

MANUEL Here, señora. Please take my tortilla.

OLD WOMAN Gracias, gracias.

MANUEL I do not suppose you have seen a little lamb anywhere nearby?

OLD WOMAN I have seen a most beautiful Lamb. The most beautiful Lamb my eyes have ever seen. *(Points left.)*

MANUEL Gracias, señora, gracias.

(LIGHTS OUT. SOUND: WIND WHISTLING, COYOTE HOWLING IN DISTANCE. SPOTLIGHT ON MANUEL STANDING DOWN RIGHT.)

MANUEL *(Calls.)* Little lamb! Little lamb, where are you? I am cold and hungry! And very lost!

(The strong voice of a YOUNG MAN comes from behind Manuel.)

YOUNG MAN Muchacho!

MANUEL *(Whirls around.)* Hola! Who is there?

(SPOTLIGHT WIDENS TO INCLUDE YOUNG MAN STANDING AT MID RIGHT.)

MANUEL Oh, another traveler through the desert. Señor, I have given away my serape and my last morsel of food.

YOUNG MAN Yes, Manuel, you have been very generous.

MANUEL Muy gracias, señor—wait a minute! *(Approaches Young Man.)* How do you know my name? Have I ever met you before?

YOUNG MAN Every night, when you pray to the Holy Spirit.

MANUEL Well, I have nothing more to give, only this old guitar.

YOUNG MAN You need give nothing more, Manuel. It is now *your* turn to receive. *(Points to center stage.)*

(LIGHTS UP CENTER STAGE ON A LARGE CACTUS sheltering a man (JOSEPH) and a woman (MARY); the woman holds a newborn infant. TWO YOUNG WOMEN stand on either side of the cactus.)

MANUEL La Navidad! Joseph, Mary and the Infant Jesus!

YOUNG MAN Si, Manuel—*here* is the Lamb you seek.

(The Young Man leads Manuel to the group; Manuel kneels and bows his head.)

YOUNG WOMAN #1 In the Gate of Bethlehem there is great light; for there has been born the Messiah who is to set us at liberty.

YOUNG WOMAN #2 Blow the whistles and play your guitars, for there has come to earth the King of the Heavens.

YOUNG WOMAN #1 Now the roosters crow, and the devil weeps, because already is born the King of Glory.

YOUNG WOMAN #2 Let us render homage of unequaled affection to the exalted Mary, to Joseph and their Son.

MANUEL Oh, beautiful Mary full of loving and sweetness, the desired night of your glory has arrived. Immaculate star of heaven, I give you my heart so you may have shelter. Blessed Savior, my soul I give you also with the heart. *(Bows head.)*

YOUNG MAN You have received his blessing, Manuel. Now, you must go and tell others that Christ has come to his people once again.

(Manuel rises and runs offstage left. LIGHTS OUT. SOUND: MANUEL'S GUITAR STRUMMING CHORDS TO "LET US GO, O SHEPHERDS." LIGHTS UP RIGHT ON SEÑOR PORFIADO AND THREE SHEPHERDS; Señor Porfiado sits on rock.)

SHEPHERD #2 That Manuel is muy loco! He probably fell asleep under a cactus.

(Shepherds laugh; Manuel enters from left, strumming across stage.)

SEÑOR PORFIADO *(Jumps up.)* Manuel! Where is the lamb?

MANUEL *(Sings.)*
Let us go, O shepherds
Come ye one and all
You will see the Virgin
And her Babe so small

SHEPHERD #1 The poor boy. He has lost his mind.

MANUEL No, Pablo. I have found the Lamb. Come follow and you shall see with your own eyes.

SEÑOR PORFIADO This had better not be some silly joke, Manuel.

(Manuel walks to center, singing chorus as Señor Porfiado and the Shepherds follow cautiously.)

MANUEL *(Sings.)*
For in the humble stable
The Son of God does lay
Bringing peace and comfort
Upon this Christmas day

(LIGHTS UP CENTER ON CACTUS, with Joseph, Mary, Young Man, Two Young Women, Old Man and Old Woman standing around a crèche holding the Infant Jesus. A lamb sits next to the crèche.)

MANUEL Here is the Lamb I found, Señor Porfiado—Jesus, the Lamb of God.

(Señor Porfiado and the Shepherds kneel, cross themselves, bow heads as Manuel begins singing "Let Us Go, O Shepherds.")

MANUEL *(Sings.)*
> Let us go, O shepherds
> Come ye one and all
> You will see the Virgin
> And her Babe so small

ALL *(Sing.)*
> For in the humble stable
> The Son of God does lay
> Bringing peace and comfort
> Upon this Christmas day

ALL *(Sing.)*
> Now this tiny Baby
> Came from yonder sky
> Sing a song to please Him
> Sing a lullaby
> For in the humble stable
> The Son of God does lay
> Bringing peace and comfort
> Upon this Christmas day

> Angels told the shepherds
> "Go to Bethlehem
> Hasten to adore Him
> Jesus, Heaven's gem"

> For in the humble stable
> The Son of God does lay
> Bringing peace and comfort
> Upon this Christmas day

(LIGHTS OUT.)

THE END

Right   **Center**   **Left**

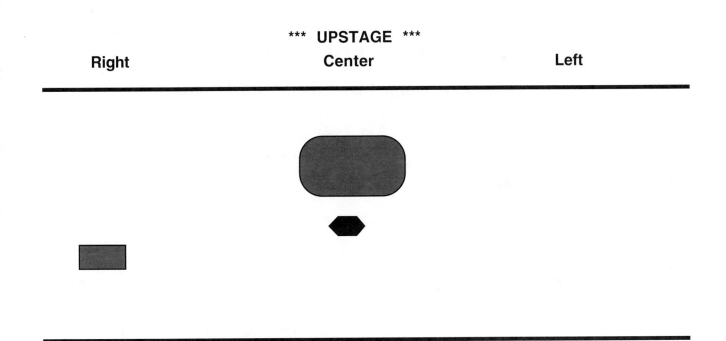

Stage Plan—*Let Us Go, O Shepherds*

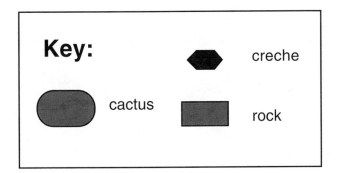

Key:

creche

cactus

rock

Let Us Go, O Shepherds

(traditional, arranged by L.E. McCullough)

Let us go, O shep-herds, come ye one and all

You will see the Vir-gin and her Babe so small For

in the hum-ble sta-ble the Son of God does lay

Bring-ing peace and com-fort u-pon this Christ-mas day

Bring a Torch, Jeannette, Isabella

Bring a Torch, Jeannette, Isabella is a song from Provence in southern France, a region that still maintains many distinctive and ancient Christmas customs. Music and dancing are always a great part of the festivities in Provence, as is the decoration of an elaborate crèche and the celebration of *le réveillon*, the family supper following Midnight Mass that is considered the culinary zenith of the holiday. Another popular Christmas tradition in Provence is the making of *santons* ("little saints"), plaster figures used to decorate the crèche. Originally, the *santons* were basic images of Jesus, Mary, Joseph, the shepherds and angels of the Nativity scene; over the years they have come to include dozens of real characters in the *santon* maker's village.

Bring a Torch, Jeannette, Isabella

TIME: Christmas Eve, 1676

PLACE: A small boarding house in Provence, France

CAST:

Camille, age 11	The Philosopher
Jeannette, age 10	The Composer
Isabella, age 10	6 Dancers

STAGE SET: dining table; two chairs; a hearth and chimney; a large crèche

PROPS: tea pot; 2 tea cups; towel; infant doll; large decorated crèche; a torch and torch holder attached to chimney

SPECIAL EFFECTS: sound—dog barking, cow mooing, chickens cackling

MUSIC: *Bring a Torch, Jeannette, Isabella* performed as a farandole on flute

COSTUMES: Camille, Jeannette, Isabella and Dancers dress in late 17th-century French peasant clothes; The Philosopher and The Composer wear more formal, urban garb—waistjackets with brocade and cuffs (see paintings of Louis XIV era for period detail.)

☆ ☆ ☆

(LIGHTS UP FULL. Two men, THE PHILOSOPHER and THE COMPOSER, sit at a kitchen table drinking tea.)

COMPOSER So you are telling me, monsieur, that though the Bible says the baby Jesus was born in a stable, he may actually have been born in a temple? Or a theatre? A library? A pleasure boat sailing down the Red Sea to Arabia?

PHILOSOPHER What I am saying, monsieur, is that the Bible was written for the whole human race to be read for all time. We should not quibble about details that may change as the story is told through time. They are merely the vehicle for presenting the message of God's love for the human race. The baby Jesus could have been born anywhere at any time. He could be born tonight. Here in Provence in the year 1676.

COMPOSER Bah! You philosophers have no grasp of reality. As a composer, I work with a set number of sounds. With instruments that have certain set properties. With notes that are of a certain set pitch and duration. Physical properties that have defined limits in the real world.

PHILOSOPHER I respect your reality and your limits, monsieur. But you cannot put limits on God.

(CAMILLE enters from stage right, frowning, and begins vigorously wiping the table with a towel, pushing aside the teacups and teapot and interrupting the conversation.)

COMPOSER Ah, it is our landlady's delightful eldest daughter! The always joyous Camille.

(Camille stops wiping, frowns at the Composer, resumes wiping.)

PHILOSOPHER Bonjour, mademoiselle. How are you this fine Christmas Eve?

CAMILLE As well as can be expected listening to you two prattle on! Always jawing about such unimportant matters—history...politics...the universe!

PHILOSOPHER There are more important matters than those?

CAMILLE Mais, oui! For instance, what dress am I to wear tonight for the grand ball in the village? The blue one? Or the white one? And shall I pin my hair up *(Pushes hair above her head.)* or pull it back? *(Pulls hair back.)*

COMPOSER Indeed, mademoiselle, those *are* very important matters. Why, King Louis should devote the entire attention of his court to your dilemma. *(Laughs.)*

CAMILLE *(Calls.)* Jeannette, Isabella! Where are those silly young sisters of mine? Jeannette, Isabella! Come to the kitchen immediately, s'il vous plaît!

(JEANNETTE and ISABELLA, 10-year-old twins, skip onstage from right and curtsey to Philosopher and Composer.)

JEANNETTE *(To Philosopher.)* Bonjour, Monsieur Spinoza.

ISABELLA *(To Composer.)* Bonjour, Monsieur Cambert.

CAMILLE Have you two gadabouts finished dusting the parlor?

JEANNETTE Yes, Camille. And mother said when we were finished, to help you prepare the goose for *le réveillon*.

CAMILLE Prepare the goose? Why is *mother* not preparing the goose?

ISABELLA Because she has gone to Marseille to take care of Madame Moreau, who is very sick. She will be gone till the day after Christmas.

JEANNETTE Did you not see her before she left? She said we must remain here and take charge of the house tonight. All three of us!

CAMILLE *(Wrings towel.)* This I cannot believe! Mother has left me alone with you two simpletons?

ISABELLA It will be fun, Camille! We will cook the supper—

JEANNETTE And clean the dishes—

ISABELLA And make the tea—

JEANNETTE And finish decorating the crèche—

ISABELLA *(Grabs the Philosopher's hands.)* And dance with Monsieur Spinoza!

CAMILLE Dance! Quelle misère! I will miss the dance in the village!

JEANNETTE So? We will have a dance here.

ISABELLA Monsieur Cambert will play the spinet.

JEANNETTE I will play the flute.

ISABELLA It will be so exciting!

CAMILLE *(Throws towel at hearth.)* Hush! You babies! Can you not see that I *must* go to the grand ball? I have been planning for months! Everyone is expecting me. If I do not come, they will think I am a misfit! Une imbécile!

JEANNETTE But you cannot disobey mother.

ISABELLA And the new boarders may need your help. The shed outside is very cold. The woman has lain in bed all day.

CAMILLE Help them yourselves, Jeannette, Isabella! My Christmas is ruined!

(Camille folds her arms across her chest and pouts.)

JEANNETTE *(To Isabella.)* Perhaps we should look in on our guests.

ISABELLA We can bring them some soup. Adieu, monsieurs.

COMPOSER & PHILOSOPHER Adieu, filles.

(Jeannette and Isabella exit right as Camille continues to sulk.)

COMPOSER There, philosopher, stands a classic conflict between duty and desire.

PHILOSOPHER Desire is the very essence of man. We want what we cannot have. What we may have, we do not want.

COMPOSER Then if Mademoiselle Camille cannot go to the grand ball—which is what she wants—what is it that she *may* have?

PHILOSOPHER Why, the highest happiness humanity may ever have: to know the love of God.

CAMILLE *(Walks to crèche, faces audience.)* Listen to these old men jabber on. Sure, I believe in God. But all that business about Jesus coming to Earth happened sixteen centuries ago. What does it have to do with me? God would not waste His time coming to this stupid village, when He could go to Lyons or to Paris—where they have the best parties!

(SOUND: DOG BARKING, COW MOOING, CHICKENS CACKLING OFFSTAGE LEFT.)

CAMILLE Now what? The barnyard is in an uproar! *(Calls.)* Jeannette, Isabella! Hush those animals! This house has been topsy-turvy since those new boarders arrived. Of all the places in the world to have a baby, *she* had to come here to our house! Jeannette, Isabella!

(Camille throws up her hands in exasperation and stalks off left. MUSIC: "Bring a Torch, Jeannette, Isabella" performed as a farandole on flute by Jeannette, who enters from right followed by Isabella leading SIX DANCERS in a merry farandole—a skipping chain dance in 6/8 time. They grab The Philosopher and The Composer and dance around the stage, circling the crèche, two times through the tune, then stop at center stage and cheer.)

ALL Noël! Noël! Joyeux Noël! May blessings come upon all here! And God watch over us another year! Joyeux Noël! *(They applaud, cheer.)*

JEANNETTE Monsieurs! We have brought the ball to Camille!

ISABELLA Where is she?

COMPOSER There was a disturbance in the barnyard. But that was some time ago.

PHILOSOPHER *(Points offstage left.)* Who is that in the yard now?

(All look left.)

JEANNETTE It is our new boarders! And...and some others...strangers...

ISABELLA And the animals! Look, they are kneeling!

ISABELLA It is as if they are praying!

CAMILLE *(O.S. LEFT.)* Bring a torch, Jeannette, Isabella!

(Jeannette runs to hearth, picks up the torch from the torch holder and starts to cross to left exit when Camille enters from left carrying an infant wrapped in white linens. Everyone gasps with amazement as Camille sets the infant in the crèche.)

CAMILLE *Now* we have finished decorating the crèche.

(All cheer.)

ALL Huzzah! Huzzah for the newborn babe!

PHILOSOPHER *(To Composer, pointing to crèche.)* There are your physical properties, monsieur. Are they real enough?

COMPOSER Details, monsieur, details! Let us not quibble about details!

(All join hands and stand around the crèche and sing "Bring a Torch, Jeannette, Isabella.")

ALL *(Sing.)*

Bring a torch, Jeannette, Isabella!
Bring a torch, to the cradle run!
It is Jesus, good folk of the village
Christ is born and Mary's calling
Ah! Ah! Beautiful is the Mother
Ah! Ah! Beautiful is her Son

It is wrong when the Child is sleeping
It is wrong to talk so loud
Silence, all, as you gather around
Lest your noise should waken Jesus
Hush! Hush! See how fast He slumbers
Hush! Hush! See how fast He sleeps

Softly to the little stable
Softly for a moment come
Look and see how charming is Jesus
How He is white, His cheeks are rosy
Hush! Hush! See how the Child is sleeping
Hush! Hush! See how He smiles in dreams

(LIGHTS OUT.)

THE END

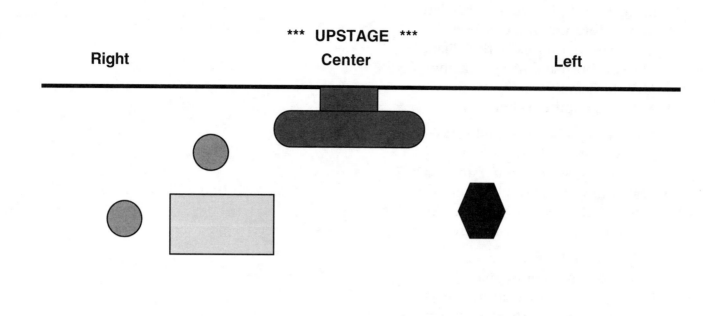

*** UPSTAGE ***

Right   Center   Left

Stage Plan—*Bring a Torch, Jeannette, Isabella*

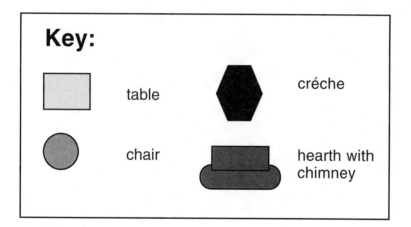

Key:

table

chair

créche

hearth with chimney

Bring a Torch, Jeannette, Isabella

(traditional, arranged by L.E. McCullough)

We Three Kings of Orient Are

Magu is an ancient Persian word meaning a magician or member of a priestly caste, and the appearance of the Magi—the Three Kings or Wise Men—in St. Matthew's account of the first Christmas is an indication that the larger world outside Palestine will soon be greatly affected by the birth of Christ. The gifts brought to the newborn Messiah also have symbolic significance: gold is the purest metal and deserving of a king, frankincense was used in the worship of a god, myrrh was a substance for healing—thus, Jesus is acclaimed as king, god and healer. The modern verses to *We Three Kings of Orient Are* were written in 1857 by Reverend John Henry Hopkins, Jr. of Williamsport, Pennsylvania and were first published in 1862.

We Three Kings of Orient Are

TIME: During the reign of Caesar
                               Augustus

PLACE: Bethlehem, Palestine

CAST:
   Balthasar of Ethiopia   Balthasar's Physician
   Melchior of Arabia   Melchior's Daughter
   Gaspar of Tarsus   Beggar
   Joseph   Roman Centurion
   Mary   Shepherd
   2 Angels

STAGE SET: stool; scrim or curtain; stable lean-to with straw pallet

PROPS: physician's bowl; parchment scroll; box of frankincense; perfume bottle of myrrh; sack of gold; sword; shepherd staff; infant doll

COSTUMES: characters dress in ancient garb; the Three Kings have more colorful fabrics, jewelry, crowns; Roman Centurion wears helmet, armor breastplate and sword

☆ ☆ ☆

(LIGHTS UP STAGE RIGHT. At down right BALTHASAR, King of Ethiopia, sits listlessly on his throne, facing the audience; his PHYSICIAN hovers anxiously to his left, offering a bowl of medicinal herbs to the King.)

PHYSICIAN Please try these herbs, Your Highness. They are a potent medicine from Iberia and are certain to cure the melancholy that has lately seized your heart and weakened your health.

BALTHASAR *(Waves away bowl.)* Earthly roots and flowers will not cure me, Physician. For my malaise is not of earthly cause.

PHYSICIAN Not of earthly cause? Surely mischievous ghosts and spirits do not trouble mighty Balthasar, King of Ethiopia?

BALTHASAR I am troubled, yes. But not by spirits. It is men—men of flesh and blood, men of cruel, pitiless hearts—who bring sorrow to my advancing years with the evil they inflict upon the world each day. Here in the reign of Caesar Augustus, every nation in the world is at war. Men die, women wail, children go hungry and unschooled. What powers can save us from ourselves?

PHYSICIAN Not these Iberian herbs, I imagine.

BALTHASAR No, the answer is in the heavens. *(Stands, points out to audience.)* In the heavens where life began and our lives strive to end. May whatever heavenly hand controls our destiny make itself known—and soon.

(LIGHTS OUT STAGE RIGHT; Balthasar and Physician exit right removing stool. LIGHTS UP STAGE LEFT. At down left MELCHIOR, King of Arabia, stands facing the audience with his DAUGHTER standing at his right holding a parchment scroll.)

DAUGHTER Father, you must undertake this journey!

MELCHIOR My daughter, it is a long and dangerous journey. I might never return. Who would defend the Kingdom of Arabia from its many enemies?

DAUGHTER *(Shows him the scroll.)* But the proof is in this report from Palestine! The Messiah has arrived! You must meet him and seek his aid!

MELCHIOR *(Slowly shakes his head.)* I, Melchior King of Arabia, have lived well nigh three score years...never have I witnessed such strange occurrences in nature. And in the violent behavior of men. The soothsayers declare the end of the world is close at hand...they may be right.

DAUGHTER All the more reason for you to find the Messiah!

MELCHIOR Perhaps. But before I take to the road, I must see a sign...a sign offering proof the Messiah has come to give this world one more chance to redeem itself.

(LIGHTS OUT STAGE LEFT; Melchior's Daughter exits left. LIGHTS UP STAGE RIGHT. Entering from right is GASPAR, King of Tarsus, carrying a box filled with frankincense. He pauses and stares out at the audience as if looking upward at the sky.)

GASPAR It is the most beautiful sight in the world! O, bright star of the east, you fill my heart with such joy!

(LIGHTS UP STAGE LEFT AND CENTER. Gaspar sees Melchior walking toward him from left carrying a sack of gold and walks to meet him at down center.)

GASPAR Hail, stranger! I am Gaspar, King of Tarsus.

MELCHIOR And I am Melchior, King of Arabia. You have traveled far from home.

GASPAR I follow the star. *(Points up and out to audience.)* Have you ever seen the like?

MELCHIOR Never. My astrologers say it is a celestial messenger from another realm of the universe.

GASPAR Aye, and bearing a message for mankind from the One who has made this universe and all others.

(Balthasar enters from right carrying a large bottle of myrrh and crosses to center.)

BALTHASAR I am Balthasar, King of Ethiopia. I seek the Messiah in all his power and glory.

MELCHIOR Join us then; we seek him likewise.

GASPAR For it is written in the Psalms of the Jews that "All kings shall fall down before him."

(BEGGAR enters from left, raving hysterically as he approaches the Three Kings.)

BEGGAR Cured! I am cured!

BALTHASAR Of what are you cured? Your reason?

BEGGAR This morning I was blind! I saw nothing but darkness! And now He has cured me!

MELCHIOR Who has cured you?

BEGGAR And I am not the only one, good sirs! He touched the ear of a deaf woman; she now can hear. He laid his finger upon the crutch of a cripple; now the man can run fast as the wind! Oh, thanks be to Him! Thanks be to the Messiah and His miracles! *(Exits right.)*

GASPAR This Messiah must be a very powerful magician.

(A ROMAN CENTURION enters from left, staggering as if dazed, and approaches the Three Kings.)

MELCHIOR Look, it is a Roman centurion. Perhaps they have given the Messiah a military escort.

(The Centurion stops and regards the sword in his hands with incredulity, then drops it on the ground.)

CENTURION Begone, instrument of Lucifer! You shall cause torment on this earth no more!

BALTHASAR Centurion! Are we far from Bethlehem?

CENTURION Bethlehem? It is a few miles down the road.

GASPAR Where is your legion, Centurion?

CENTURION My legion, sire? My legion has disbanded. Soldiers everywhere are throwing down their weapons and refusing to fight. The rule of mighty Caesar cannot long stand against this new ruler! *(Exits right.)*

BALTHASAR This Messiah is indeed a powerful lord! He cures the sick—

MELCHIOR And defeats Roman legions without striking a single blow!

GASPAR Perhaps our gifts are too modest for a king of such majesty. He may deem our paltry offerings an insult.

(A SHEPHERD enters from left.)

BALTHASAR Shepherd! Do you know where dwells the Messiah?

SHEPHERD There is born today in the City of David a Savior, which is Christ the Lord. Look! See the angels passing overhead!

(All look out at audience and stare in amazement for several seconds.)

MELCHIOR Have you seen this Christ? Is He a fearsome warrior?

GASPAR How large is His palace? He must be the richest noble in the land.

SHEPHERD I have seen Him, O kings of the East. He humbly awaits your presence.

(Scrim or curtain at mid center stage is pulled back revealing a Nativity stable scene with MARY lying on a straw pallet holding an infant, JOSEPH standing over her and TWO ANGELS, one on each side of the Holy Family. The Shepherd and Three Kings gather around.)

BALTHASAR This is the Messiah!

MELCHIOR He is but a babe!

GASPAR The stories of his miracles...and his power...how can this be?

ANGEL #1 True power comes not from the point of a sword—

ANGEL #2 But from purity of heart.

ANGEL #1 Offer your gifts and worship him.

ANGEL #2 Lift your voices on high, for he is the Messiah!

(Melchior, Gaspar and Balthasar begin singing "We Three Kings of Orient Are.")

MELCHIOR, GASPAR & BALTHASAR *(Sing.)*
    We three kings of Orient are
    Bearing gifts we traverse far
    Field and fountain, moor and mountain
    Following yonder star

(Angels, Shepherd, Mary and Joseph join on chorus.)

ALL *(Sing.)*
    O star of wonder, star of light
    Star with royal beauty bright
    Westward leading, still proceeding
    Guide us to thy perfect light

(Melchior lays his sack of gold before Mary and the infant.)

MELCHIOR *(Sings.)*
    Born a King on Bethlehem's plain
    Gold I bring to crown Him again
    King forever, ceasing never
    Over us all to reign

ALL *(Sing.)*

    O star of wonder, star of light
    Star with royal beauty bright
    Westward leading, still proceeding
    Guide us to thy perfect light

(Gaspar lays his box of frankincense before Mary and the infant.)

GASPAR *(Sings.)*

    Frankincense to offer have I
    Incense owns a Deity nigh
    Prayer and praising, all men raising
    Worship Him, God on high

(Balthasar's Physician, Beggar and Centurion enter from right, Melchior's Daughter from left, and sing.)

ALL *(Sing.)*

    O star of wonder, star of light
    Star with royal beauty bright
    Westward leading, still proceeding
    Guide us to thy perfect light

(Balthasar lays his bottle of myrrh before Mary and the infant.)

BALTHASAR *(Sings.)*

    Myrrh is mine; its bitter perfume
    Breathes a life of gathering gloom
    Sorrowing, sighing, bleeding, dying
    Sealed in the stone-cold tomb

ALL *(Sing.)*

    Glorious now behold Him arise
    King and God and Sacrifice
    Heaven sings "Alleluia!"
    "Alleluia!" the earth replies

(LIGHTS OUT.)

THE END

Right   **Center**   **Left**

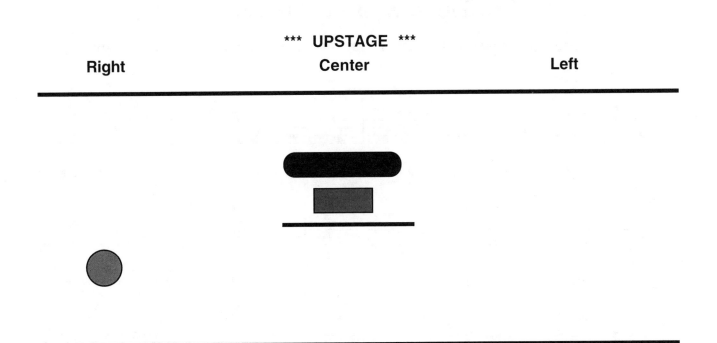

Stage Plan—*We Three Kings of Orient Are*

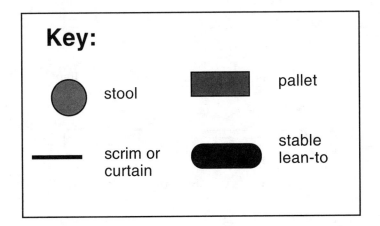

Key:

stool

pallet

scrim or curtain

stable lean-to

We Three Kings of Orient Are

(Words: John Hopkins / Music: Traditional / Arranged: L.E. McCullough)

Go Tell It on the Mountain

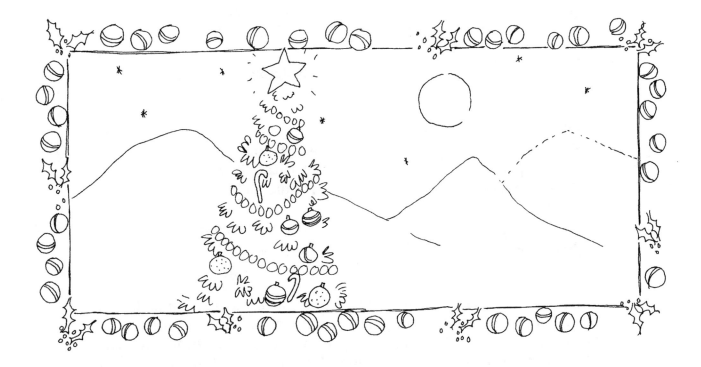

Go Tell It on the Mountain is a song from the tradition of African-American spirituals. The lyrics and melody used here sprang from the anonymous folk tradition and were being sung by the late 1800s in church congregations throughout the South. The tradition of towns and even whole counties divided by feuding families is also a part of 19th-century and early 20th-century Southern folklore; the disputes were not always solved as peacefully in this story. Perhaps the feuders should have listened to music more often?

Go Tell It on the Mountain

TIME: Christmas Eve, 1898

PLACE: Mistletoe, Georgia

CAST:

Pops	The Stranger
Jed Cooper	Martha Calloway
Becky Cooper	Lonnie Calloway
Cindy Cooper	Burton Calloway
Adam Cooper	Willard Calloway
Nancy Cooper	Polly Calloway

STAGE SET: two large Christmas trees, one living with ornaments, the other bare and dead; curtain; sign reading "Mistletoe, Georgia, Pop. 222"; rocking chair (Switching between the living Christmas tree and the dead Christmas tree can be done by using two different trees or cutouts with the one hidden behind a black curtain when not in use.)

PROPS: tree ornaments; Christmas packages; harmonica; sheet of paper

MUSIC: *Go Tell It on the Mountain*, harmonica instrumental

COSTUMES: characters dress in late 19th-century clothes common to the rural Southern Appalachians

☆ ☆ ☆

(MUSIC: Offstage harmonica playing chorus of "Go Tell it on the Mountain" as LIGHTS FADE UP. An old man, POPS, sits in a rocking chair at down right; a younger man, JED COOPER, is hanging ornaments on the left side of the large Christmas tree standing at center stage.)

POPS Yessiree, it's Christmas Eve again! Christmas is my favorite time of the year, especially here in a little town like Mistletoe, Georgia. Everybody just smiles more, and the whole world seems to be a brighter, happier place. Course, it wasn't always that way here in Mistletoe. Nosiree-bob! Why back in my grandfather's time, Christmas was the season that brought out the worst in folks.

(A YOUNG BOY, LONNIE CALLOWAY, and his MOTHER, MARTHA CALLOWAY, enter from right carrying a handful of tree ornaments. They cross to tree and begin hanging ornaments on the right side of the tree. Jed Cooper and Martha Calloway pause and look at each other for a moment, but give no greeting and hang ornaments in silence for several seconds.)

LONNIE CALLOWAY Good morning, Mr. Cooper.

MARTHA CALLOWAY *(To Lonnie, angrily.)* Lonnie Calloway, how many times have I told you not to talk to strangers?

LONNIE CALLOWAY But Mr. Cooper isn't a stranger, mama. He's our neighbor.

MARTHA CALLOWAY He's a Cooper! And you're a Calloway! Don't ever forget it!

(BECKY COOPER, CINDY COOPER, ADAM COOPER and NANCY COOPER enter from left; BURTON CALLOWAY, WILLARD CALLOWAY and POLLY CALLOWAY enter from right. They all carry a tree ornament and hang them on their respective side of the tree, taking a moment to glare across at the opposing family before exiting, Coopers to the left, Calloways to the right. LIGHTS FADE OUT.)

POPS Course, nobody in Mistletoe *ever* forgot whether they were a Cooper or a Calloway. There'd been some kind of feud going between the two families for nobody knew how long. Nobody could remember what had started it. And nobody cared about ending it. In Mistletoe, *everything* was divided down the middle; even the town's official Christmas tree had a Cooper side and a Calloway side. And never the twain would meet—until that fateful Christmas Eve in eighteen and ninety-eight. *(Exits right.)*

(MUSIC: Offstage harmonica playing chorus of "Go Tell it on the Mountain" as LIGHTS SLOWLY FADE UP; the Christmas tree has shed its branches and all ornaments have disappeared. Becky Cooper enters from left, carrying a couple Christmas packages and walking nonchalantly toward center stage; she notices tree and screams.)

BECKY COOPER Aaaaiiiii!

(Adam Cooper runs onstage from left.)

ADAM COOPER Becky, what is it? Did you see another snake crossing the road?

(She points at tree, he gasps.)

ADAM COOPER What in tarnation? *(Calls to offstage left.)* Help! Come quick! The tree's been killed!

(CINDY COOPER, JED COOPER and NANCY COOPER enter from left; BURTON CALLOWAY, WILLARD CALLOWAY, POLLY CALLOWAY, MARTHA CALLOWAY and LONNIE CALLOWAY enter from right; all stand at center on their respective sides of the tree and glower at the other family.)

BURTON CALLOWAY Some no-account skunk has destroyed our town's Christmas tree!

WILLARD CALLOWAY *(Sniffs air.)* A skunk that smells like a Cooper!

JED COOPER *(Rolls up shirt sleeves.)* Why, you lowdown, mealy-mouthed—

(Lonnie Calloway steps between Jed Cooper and Willard Calloway.)

LONNIE CALLOWAY Uncle Willard, maybe the tree just got sick. Maybe there's something in the air around here...something bad that made the tree not able to live anymore.

MARTHA CALLOWAY Lonnie, you say the strangest things. I wonder if you really are a Calloway.

(MUSIC: Offstage harmonica playing chorus of "Go Tell it on the Mountain.")

NANCY COOPER What in the world is that music? I've been hearing it all last night and all today!

POLLY CALLOWAY Where is it coming from?

(A STRANGER enters from behind the Christmas tree; he holds a harmonica, puts it to his lips and blows a glissando as he strolls to center stage between the two factions.)

STRANGER You have heard it said, "Love your neighbor and hate your enemy"? I say to you, love your enemies as you love your neighbors.

MARTHA CALLOWAY Who are you, mister? What are you doing here in Mistletoe?

ADAM COOPER Bet he's one of those fancy lawyers from Atlanta come to stir up trouble.

BURTON CALLOWAY Like there isn't enough trouble already? Look at our Christmas tree!

CINDY COOPER *Your* Christmas tree? It's ours as much as you Calloways'!

WILLARD CALLOWAY Then how come you Coopers wrecked it?

JED COOPER *(Brandishes fists.)* That's the last straw—

STRANGER Judge nothing before the time when the Lord comes, who will bring to light the hidden things of darkness and reveal the true counsel of your hearts.

POLLY CALLOWAY I think he's some crazy actor run off from a minstrel show.

NANCY COOPER Or maybe he's a gunslinger. Maybe somebody—and I'm not saying who—maybe somebody named Calloway hired him to come to town and—

STRANGER If you have anything against anyone, forgive them, that your Father in heaven may also forgive you.

ADAM COOPER Well, mister, we appreciate the friendly advice. But if you really want to be helpful, you might tell us how to make this Christmas tree come alive again.

STRANGER Whoever says to this mountain, "Be removed and cast into the sea," and believes in his heart that this will be done, it will be done.

BURTON CALLOWAY Mountain? What mountain is he talking about?

CINDY COOPER We're talking about a Christmas tree, mister, not no durn mountain!

(The Stranger sits down on the ground in front of the tree and plays "Go Tell It on the Mountain" chorus on the harmonica. The Coopers and Calloways drift offstage, left and right respectively, staring at the Stranger and shaking their heads in doubt.)

LONNIE CALLOWAY But mama, he was talking about the tree. It's our hatred that made the tree sick!

MARTHA CALLOWAY Lonnie, stop that foolish talk!

(She yanks him behind her; he trots offstage, waving at the stranger, and the Stranger holds up his hand in a greeting of farewell and peace. LIGHTS OUT; MUSIC STOPS. Voices speak in the darkness.)

JED COOPER Those Calloways...maybe they *didn't* kill the tree.

(MUSIC: bars 1-2 of "Go Tell It on the Mountain" chorus on harmonica.)

BURTON CALLOWAY That Cindy Cooper is a right pretty girl. If we didn't have this silly feud, I'd like to court her.

(MUSIC: bars 3-4 of "Go Tell It on the Mountain" chorus on harmonica.)

BECKY COOPER If we weren't feuding with the Calloways, we could have decorated that tree even nicer.

(MUSIC: bars 5-6 of "Go Tell It on the Mountain" chorus on harmonica.)

POLLY CALLOWAY That stranger...maybe there is something to what he said...

(MUSIC: bars 7-8 of "Go Tell It on the Mountain" chorus on harmonica.)

(LIGHTS UP SLOWLY. The Stranger is gone, but the Christmas tree is living and decorated again; the Coopers and Calloways drift onstage and marvel.)

WILLARD CALLOWAY The tree is alive!

ADAM COOPER It's a miracle!

BECKY COOPER Something must have cured it during the night.

NANCY COOPER But what? What could have made this miracle?

BURTON CALLOWAY Look! Under the tree!

MARTHA CALLOWAY It's a piece of paper. And that harmonica the Stranger was playing.

(Lonnie Calloway picks up the harmonica and the paper and reads the paper.)

LONNIE CALLOWAY "Whoever says to this mountain, 'Be removed and cast into the sea,' and believes in his heart that this will be done, it will be done."

JED COOPER Those were the last words the Stranger said.

LONNIE CALLOWAY There's more.

POLLY CALLOWAY *(Takes the paper.)* It looks like a poem, or a song. *(Reads.)* "Go tell it on the mountain, over the hills and everywhere. Go tell it on the mountain, Jesus Christ is born."

(Lonnie Calloway begins playing the chorus of "Go Tell It on the Mountain" on the harmonica. The others join in singing.)

CINDY COOPER & BURTON CALLOWAY *(Sing.)*
Go tell it on the mountain
Over the hills and everywhere
Go tell it on the mountain
Jesus Christ is born

ADAM COOPER *(Sings.)*
When I was a sinner
I prayed both night and day

POLLY CALLOWAY *(Sings.)*
I asked the Lord to help me
And he showed me the way

ALL *(Sing.)*
Go tell it on the mountain
Over the hills and everywhere
Go tell it on the mountain
Jesus Christ is born

WILLARD CALLOWAY *(Sings.)*
When I was a seeker
I sought both night and day

NANCY COOPER *(Sings.)*
I asked the Lord to help me
And he taught me to pray

ALL *(Sing.)*
Go tell it on the mountain
Over the hills and everywhere
Go tell it on the mountain
Jesus Christ is born

BECKY COOPER *(Sings.)*
Down in a lonely manger
The humble Christ was born

MARTHA CALLOWAY *(Sings.)*
And God sent out salvation
That blessed Christmas morn

ALL *(Sing.)*

Go tell it on the mountain
Over the hills and everywhere
Go tell it on the mountain
Jesus Christ is born

Go tell it on the mountain
Over the hills and everywhere
Go tell it on the mountain
Jesus Christ is born

(LIGHTS OUT.)

THE END

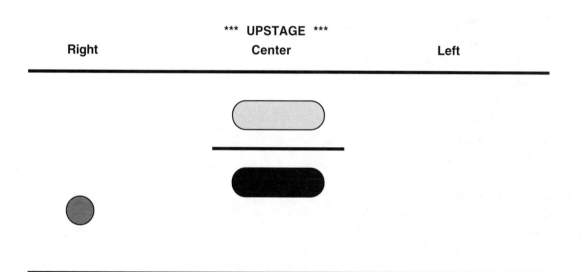

Stage Plan—*Go Tell It on the Mountain*

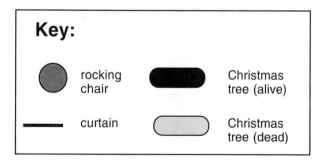

Key:

⬤	rocking chair	▬	Christmas tree (alive)
—	curtain	▭	Christmas tree (dead)

Go Tell It on the Mountain
(traditional, arranged by L.E. McCullough)

When I was a sin- ner I prayed both night and day I

asked the Lord to help me and he showed me the way

Go tell it on the moun- tain o- ver the hills and ev- 'ry- whe-re___

Go tell it on the moun- tain Je- sus Christ is born

About the Author

L.E. McCULLOUGH, PH.D. is a playwright, composer and ethnomusicologist whose studies in music and folklore have spanned cultures throughout the world. Formerly Assistant Director of the Indiana University School of Music at Indianapolis and a touring artist with Young Audiences, Inc., Dr. McCullough has performed for elementary and high schools throughout the U.S. and has recorded with Irish, French, Cajun, Latin, blues, jazz, country, bluegrass and rock ensembles on 31 albums for Angel/EMI, Log Cabin, Kicking Mule, Rounder, Bluezette and other independent labels. Winner of the 1995 Playwrights' Preview Productions Emerging Playwright Award, he is the author of *Blues for Miss Buttercup, Buddy Lee Perriman Reflects on the Persian Gulf Crisis, Day 15* and two Celtic Ballets co-authored with T. H. Gillespie, *Connlaoi's Tale: The Woman Who Danced On Waves* and *The Healing Cup: Guinevere Seeks the Grail.* He is the author of *The Complete Irish Tinwhistle Tutor* and *Favorite Irish Session Tunes,* two highly acclaimed music instruction books, and has composed film scores for three PBS specials—*Alone Together, A Place Just Right* and *John Kane.* Since 1991 Dr. McCullough has received 35 awards in 26 national literary competitions and had 178 poem and short story publications in 90 North American literary journals. Dr. McCullough is a member of The Dramatists Guild, Inc. and the American Conference for Irish Studies.